# Surviv

## GLOBAL POLITICS AND STRATEGY

Volume 65 Number 2 | April–May 2023

G000017286

'Western assistance has brought Ukraine to an impressive point, but it's not clear that it can yield a fires advantage for Ukraine sufficient to ensure further operational breakthroughs or strategic gains … Even with more effective wide-scale combined-arms training and precision strikes … it is unlikely that the Ukrainian armed forces will be able to escape attrition.'

**Franz-Stefan Gady and Michael Kofman**, Ukraine's Strategy of Attrition, pp. 17–18.

'There is a yawning gap between freezing and seizing [Russian assets], and between political aspirations and legal pitfalls.'

**Maria Shagina**, Enforcing Russia's Debt to Ukraine: Constraints and Creativity, p. 27.

'Because the United States can never convince a sceptical ally that it will use nuclear weapons on its behalf, efforts to raise the salience of nuclear weapons only increase such an ally's anxieties. The goal should be the opposite: to assure Seoul that the alliance is sufficiently capable that its security does not depend on US nuclear use.'

**Adam Mount**, The US and South Korea: The Trouble with Nuclear Assurance, p. 125.

# Survival

## GLOBAL POLITICS AND STRATEGY

Volume 65 Number 2 | April–May 2023

# Contents

# Survival
## GLOBAL POLITICS AND STRATEGY

## The International Institute for Strategic Studies

2121 K Street, NW | Suite 600 | Washington DC 20037 | USA
Tel +1 202 659 1490   Fax +1 202 659 1499   E-mail survival@iiss.org   Web www.iiss.org

Arundel House | 6 Temple Place | London | WC2R 2PG | UK
Tel +44 (0)20 7379 7676   Fax +44 (0)20 7836 3108   E-mail iiss@iiss.org

14th Floor, GBCorp Tower | Bahrain Financial Harbour | Manama | Kingdom of Bahrain
Tel +973 1718 1155   Fax +973 1710 0155   E-mail iiss-middleeast@iiss.org

9 Raffles Place | #49-01 Republic Plaza | Singapore 048619
Tel +65 6499 0055   Fax +65 6499 0059   E-mail iiss-asia@iiss.org

Pariser Platz 6A | 10117 Berlin | Germany
Tel +49 30 311 99 300   E-mail iiss-europe@iiss.org

**Survival Online** www.tandfonline.com/survival and www.iiss.org/publications/survival

**Aims and Scope** *Survival* is one of the world's leading forums for analysis and debate of international and strategic affairs. Shaped by its editors to be both timely and forward thinking, the journal encourages writers to challenge conventional wisdom and bring fresh, often controversial, perspectives to bear on the strategic issues of the moment. With a diverse range of authors, *Survival* aims to be scholarly in depth while vivid, well written and policy-relevant in approach. Through commentary, analytical articles, case studies, forums, review essays, reviews and letters to the editor, the journal promotes lively, critical debate on issues of international politics and strategy.

Editor **Dana Allin**
Managing Editor **Jonathan Stevenson**
Associate Editor **Carolyn West**
Editorial Assistant **Charlie Zawadzki**
Production and Cartography **Alessandra Beluffi, Ravi Gopar, Jade Panganiban, James Parker, Kelly Verity**

Contributing Editors

| | | | | |
|---|---|---|---|---|
| **William Alberque** | **Chester A. Crocker** | **Melissa K. Griffith** | **Irene Mia** | **Karen Smith** |
| **Målfrid Braut-Hegghammer** | **Bill Emmott** | **Emile Hokayem** | **Meia Nouwens** | **Angela Stent** |
| | **Franz-Stefan Gady** | **Nigel Inkster** | **Benjamin Rhode** | **Robert Ward** |
| **Aaron Connelly** | **Bastian Giegerich** | **Jeffrey Mazo** | **Ben Schreer** | **Marcus Willett** |
| **James Crabtree** | **Nigel Gould-Davies** | **Fenella McGerty** | **Maria Shagina** | **Lanxin Xiang** |

**Published for the IISS** by
Routledge Journals, an imprint of Taylor & Francis, an Informa business.

**About the IISS** The IISS, a registered charity with offices in Washington, London, Manama, Singapore and Berlin, is the world's leading authority on political–military conflict. It is the primary independent source of accurate, objective information on international strategic issues. Publications include *The Military Balance*, an annual reference work on each nation's defence capabilities; *Survival*, a bimonthly journal on international affairs; *Strategic Comments*, an online analysis of topical issues in international affairs; and the *Adelphi* series of books on issues of international security.

## SUBMISSIONS

To submit an article, authors are advised to follow these guidelines:

- *Survival* articles are around 4,000–10,000 words long including endnotes. A word count should be included with a draft.
- All text, including endnotes, should be double-spaced with wide margins.
- Any tables or artwork should be supplied in separate files, ideally not embedded in the document or linked to text around it.
- All *Survival* articles are expected to include endnote references. These should be complete and include first and last names of authors, titles of articles (even from newspapers), place of publication, publisher, exact publication dates, volume and issue number (if from a journal) and page numbers. Web sources should include complete URLs and DOIs if available.
- A summary of up to 150 words should be included with the article. The summary should state the main argument clearly and concisely, not simply say what the article is about.
- A short author's biography of one or two lines should also be included. This information will appear at the foot of the first page of the article.

Please note that *Survival* has a strict policy of listing multiple authors in alphabetical order.

Submissions should be made by email, in Microsoft Word format, to survival@iiss.org. Alternatively, hard copies may be sent to *Survival*, IISS–US, 2121 K Street NW, Suite 801, Washington, DC 20037, USA.

The editorial review process can take up to three months. *Survival's* acceptance rate for unsolicited manuscripts is less than 20%. *Survival* does not normally provide referees' comments in the event of rejection. Authors are permitted to submit simultaneously elsewhere so long as this is consistent with the policy of the other publication and the Editors of *Survival* are informed of the dual submission.

Readers are encouraged to comment on articles from the previous issue. Letters should be concise, no longer than 750 words and relate directly to the argument or points made in the original article.

*Survival: Global Politics and Strategy* (Print ISSN 0039-6338, Online ISSN 1468-2699) is published bimonthly for a total of 6 issues per year by Taylor & Francis Group, 4 Park Square, Milton Park, Abingdon, Oxon, OX14 4RN, UK. Periodicals postage paid (Permit no. 13095) at Brooklyn, NY 11256.

Airfreight and mailing in the USA by agent named World Container Inc., c/o BBT 150-15, 183rd Street, Jamaica, NY 11413, USA.

**US Postmaster:** Send address changes to Survival, World Container Inc., c/o BBT 150-15, 183rd Street, Jamaica, NY 11413, USA.

Subscription records are maintained at Taylor & Francis Group, 4 Park Square, Milton Park, Abingdon, OX14 4RN, UK.

**Subscription information:** For more information and subscription rates, please see tandfonline.com/pricing/journal/TSUR. Taylor & Francis journals are available in a range of different packages, designed to suit every library's needs and budget. This journal is available for institutional subscriptions with online-only or print & online options. This journal may also be available as part of our libraries, subject collections or archives. For more information on our sales packages, please visit librarianresources.taylorandfrancis.com.

For support with any institutional subscription, please visit help.tandfonline.com or email our dedicated team at subscriptions@tandf.co.uk.

Subscriptions purchased at the personal rate are strictly for personal, non-commercial use only. The reselling of personal subscriptions is prohibited. Personal subscriptions must be purchased with a personal cheque, credit card or BAC/wire transfer. Proof of personal status may be requested.

**Back issues:** Taylor & Francis Group retains a current and one-year back-issue stock of journals. Older volumes are held by our official stockists to whom all orders and enquiries should be addressed: Periodicals Service Company, 351 Fairview Avenue, Suite 300, Hudson, NY 12534, USA. Tel: +1 518 537 4700; email psc@periodicals.com.

**Ordering information:** To subscribe to the journal, please contact T&F Customer Services, Informa UK Ltd, Sheepen Place, Colchester, Essex, CO3 3LP, UK. Tel: +44 (0) 20 8052 2030; email subscriptions@tandf.co.uk.

Taylor & Francis journals are priced in USD, GBP and EUR (as well as AUD and CAD for a limited number of journals). All subscriptions are charged depending on where the end customer is based. If you are unsure which rate applies to you, please contact Customer Services. All subscriptions are payable in advance and all rates include postage. We are required to charge applicable VAT/GST on all print and online combination subscriptions, in addition to our online-only journals. Subscriptions are entered on an annual basis, i.e., January to December. Payment may be made by sterling cheque, dollar cheque, euro cheque, international money order, National Giro or credit cards (Amex, Visa and Mastercard).

**Disclaimer:** The International Institute for Strategic Studies (IISS) and our publisher Informa UK Limited, trading as Taylor & Francis Group ('T&F'), make every effort to ensure the accuracy of all the information (the 'Content') contained in our publications. However, IISS and our publisher T&F, our agents and our licensors make no representations or warranties whatsoever as to the accuracy, completeness or suitability for any purpose of the Content. Any opinions and views expressed in this publication are the opinions and views of the authors, and are not the views of or endorsed by IISS or our publisher T&F. The accuracy of the Content should not be relied upon and should be independently verified with primary sources of information, and any reliance on the Content is at your own risk. IISS and our publisher T&F make no representations, warranties or guarantees, whether express or implied, that the Content is accurate, complete or up to date. IISS and our publisher T&F shall not be liable for any losses, actions, claims, proceedings, demands, costs, expenses, damages and other liabilities whatsoever or howsoever caused arising directly or indirectly in connection with, in relation to or arising out of the use of the Content. Full Terms & Conditions of access and use can be found at http://www.tandfonline.com/page/terms-and-conditions.

Informa UK Limited, trading as Taylor & Francis Group, grants authorisation for individuals to photocopy copyright material for private research use, on the sole basis that requests for such use are referred directly to the requestor's local Reproduction Rights Organization (RRO). The copyright fee is exclusive of any charge or fee levied. In order to contact your local RRO, please contact International Federation of Reproduction Rights Organizations (IFRRO), rue du Prince Royal, 87, B-1050 Brussels, Belgium; email ifrro@skynet.be; Copyright Clearance Center Inc., 222 Rosewood Drive, Danvers, MA 01923, USA; email info@copyright.com; or Copyright Licensing Agency, 90 Tottenham Court Road, London, W1P 0LP, UK; email cla@cla.co.uk. This authorisation does not extend to any other kind of copying, by any means, in any form, for any purpose other than private research use.

**Submission information:** See https://www.tandfonline.com/journals/tsur20

**Advertising:** See https://taylorandfrancis.com/contact/advertising/

**Permissions:** See help.tandfonline.com/Librarian/s/article/Permissions

All Taylor & Francis Group journals are printed on paper from renewable sources by accredited partners.

**April–May 2023**

# Ukraine's Strategy of Attrition

**Franz-Stefan Gady and Michael Kofman**

The war of Russian aggression in Ukraine has continued for roughly a year. With no clear end in sight, there is a need for an enhanced understanding of the Armed Forces of Ukraine's war-fighting strategy, which we seek to provide here. Such an understanding would help clarify for Western policy-makers and defence planners the kinds of military support required going forward. Greater detail about this strategy and the character of war fighting in Ukraine would also facilitate realistic assessments of the duration of the military conflict and its likely cost in terms of both personnel and materiel. Finally, a more nuanced account of Kyiv's strategy would illuminate a plausible end to the conflict.

## The salience of attrition

Success in war involves a combination of attrition – that is, the slow but sustained process of wearing down an opponent and eventually breaking its will by inflicting much higher losses in personnel and materiel than one's own side is suffering – and manoeuvre. An attritional approach typically privileges firepower over mobility, and direct attack over flanking action or otherwise seeking to attain advantage by position. Ukraine's war-fighting strategy was initially based on defence-in-depth, or in some cases mobile

**Franz-Stefan Gady** is IISS Senior Fellow for Cyber Power and Future Conflict. **Michael Kofman** is the Research Program Director of the Russia Studies Program at the Center for Naval Analyses and an Adjunct Senior Fellow at the Center for a New American Security.

**Survival** | vol. 65 no. 2 | April–May 2023 | pp. 7–22          https://doi.org/10.1080/00396338.2023.2193092

defence, which it then transitioned to offence. Its offensive effort proved successful in autumn 2022 because the conditions had been set by Russian forces' structural personnel deficit and extensive attrition. The attrition had multiple causes, including combat losses, soldiers who refused to fight and depleted morale due to exhaustion.[1]

Attrition has been both sides' primary approach at the tactical level of war; manoeuvre warfare yielded operational results because extensive attrition made it possible. This is not unexpected, as most major conventional wars feature attrition, manoeuvre and reconstitution. Advanced Western weapons, such as the US-supplied High Mobility Artillery Rocket System (HIMARS), augmented by intelligence, surveillance and reconnaissance (ISR) assistance, have not allowed Ukraine to escape the grind of sustained attritional combat. HIMARS did provide Ukrainian forces with a capability they did not have – long-range precision strike – enabled by sustained US intelligence support. Its main effect was to diminish Russia's artillery advantage, which indirectly enabled Ukrainian offensive operations.

Broadly in line with the theory of manoeuvre warfare, the Ukrainian armed forces did seek to degrade the Russian forces' physical, mental and moral cohesion by targeting critical support systems such as command-and-control nodes and supply depots. In practice, though, this was primarily accomplished by attrition and mass fires rather than by manoeuvre and precision strike. Ukrainian artillery has often operated on its own, and offensive manoeuvre has yielded mixed results against a prepared defence with a high density of forces. It is the combination of traditional fires and repeated ground assaults that set the stage for offensive Ukrainian operations. Long-range precision strikes on Russian command and control, ammunition and ground lines of communication did not appear to significantly enhance Ukraine's ability to conduct manoeuvre warfare. Manoeuvre warfare proved successful when prolonged attrition made it easy. Ukraine has not been able to make military gains on short timelines without major increases in available personnel, materiel and ammunition.[2] The Ukrainian armed forces' offensives in Kharkiv and Kherson illustrated their limitations as well as their prowess.

### The Kharkiv offensive

Ukraine's lightning counter-offensive in early September in Kharkiv *oblast* in northeastern Ukraine was a spectacular tactical victory. In less than ten days, beginning on 6 September, the Ukrainian armed forces liberated more than 6,000 square kilometres of territory following a rapid breakthrough into Russian-controlled territory north of Izyum near Kupiansk.[3] On the Russian side, an incohesive mixture of forces held that sector of the front. The Russian forces initially encountered at Balaklia consisted of Rosgvardia (national guard) units and Russian Special Rapid Response Units (known by the Russian acronym SOBR and similar to Western SWAT, or special weapons and tactics, outfits), backed by mobilised units from the Luhansk People's Republic. The bulk of the Russian forces in and around Izyum were remnants of the Western Group of Forces, in some places at 25% strength, exhausted and suffering low morale, and further depleted due to desertions and refusals to deploy.[4]

Russia's redeployment of regular army units and substantial equipment to the Kherson and Zaporizhia *oblast*s in July and August 2022 in anticipation of largely feinted Ukrainian onslaughts there proved essential to Ukraine's success in the Kharkiv offensive.[5] Ukrainian units quickly bypassed Russian irregulars, and parts of the Russian line south of Izyum buckled as elements of the 11th Corps from Kaliningrad abandoned their positions. Once the front line was broken, Russian forces were unable to reinforce it in time to contain the offensive or launch a successful counter-attack. Ukrainian forces were able to achieve manoeuvre depth largely unopposed due to the dearth of Russian reserves in the area. This quickly led to a collapse of the Russian position, a complete rout of Russia's Western Group of Forces, and the seizure of a significant amount of equipment, including hundreds of armoured vehicles, some damaged or inoperable.[6]

Russian forces attempted to stop the Ukrainian offensive at Lyman, a strategically important town, but were too depleted and disorganised to mount a substantial defence. Nevertheless, they delayed Ukraine's advance by more than a week, giving some Russian forces time to begin establishing a defensive line between Svatove and Kreminna farther east. At that point, Russian forces depended on reserve units, known by the acronym BARS, and what was left of the Western Group of Forces. The Ukrainian counter-offensive culminated in the capture of Lyman on 1 October.

On the Ukrainian side, at least six manoeuvre brigades, including the 92nd mechanised and 3rd tank brigades, were involved in the attack.[7] It was preceded by a three-month-long campaign of precision strikes by 16 US-supplied HIMARS units, which, aided by targeting data supplied by Western intelligence services, reportedly hit more than 400 targets in the rear of the Russian front including ammunition dumps, command centres, logistical hubs, railroad junctions and bridges.[8]

Various analysts have touted HIMARS as a critical element of Ukraine's successful Kharkiv counter-offensive.[9] But there is little evidence that HIMARS strikes on the Russian supply system in Kharkiv *oblast* in August were decisive with respect to the repositioning of Russian forces to other parts of Ukraine. Media reports indicated that Russian forces had advance warning of the deployment of HIMARS to the Kharkiv front line even though at least three Russian command posts were hit.[10] Russian forces appeared to adapt by repositioning logistical hubs, hardening command centres and using decoys, gradually decreasing the effectiveness of HIMARS strikes. It does not appear that Ukraine conducted a decisive deep-battle campaign, which would have aimed to delay, disrupt or divert enemy reserves and sever supply lines. The Russian military's chief problem was not damage to rear areas, but rather insufficient aggregate personnel on the front lines, scarcity of infantry, no reserves to speak of, and lack of capacity to rotate out exhausted units. It is arguable that attrition, along with the Ukrainian feint, forced the Russian forces to choose between reinforcing Kharkiv and defending Kherson.

*There is little evidence that HIMARS strikes were decisive*

Ukraine's artillery requirement remains at approximately 90,000 shells per month. This figure has stayed relatively stable since the summer, implying a strong dependence on field-artillery firepower. There was a notable decline in Russian fire rates over the winter, but this was likely due to a combination of reduced fighting intensity, diminished front lines to defend and the need to ration artillery use.[11] HIMARS did make the Russians' logistics less efficient, forcing them to move ammo dumps out of range and reorganise in ways that reduced the overall fire rate. But these changes took place within a few months of HIMARS's appearance on the battlefield, over the course of the summer. The more significant constraint on the Russian side was, and likely remains, stockpile availability and the ammunition-production rate.

The main element was attrition, as months of heavy-artillery duels, reportedly costing both sides significant casualties, set the conditions for the counter-offensive.[12] Fighting over the summer in the Donbas depleted both Russian and Ukrainian forces, and forced the former to redeploy troops and assets out of Kharkiv *oblast* to defend elsewhere.[13] Hence the offensive took advantage of six months of attrition, prior localised attacks in Izyum and Russia's structural deficit of manpower across a broad front.[14]

From this perspective, Ukraine's Kharkiv operations did not illustrate the effectiveness of precision-guided munitions so much as they high-lighted the consequences of a low force-to-space ratio on the Russian side combined with steady attrition that enabled Ukrainian forces to manoeu-vre. While Russian forces could observe the build-up of Ukrainian forces in Kharkiv in July and August, Russia still elected to relocate some of its best ground forces of existing formations deployed to Ukraine as part of the Eastern Group of Forces to southern Ukraine. Other units were engaged in fighting at Bakhmut, and much of the Central Group of Forces was unable to provide reinforcement. This left Kharkiv a thinly covered area with badly depleted, incohesive units that could not effectively mount a defence.[15]

Finally, while the initial phase of the Kharkiv offensive saw a break-down of Russian command and control, and reportedly hundreds of Russian soldiers captured and a large inventory of Russian military kit seized, Russia's military leadership did not suffer general paralysis and breakdown. Following the initial defeat, the commander of the Western Group of Forces was quickly replaced by the former head of the Central Group of Forces, who 'aimed to restore' firm control over Russian forces.[16] The new commander established temporary new defensive lines, first along the Oskil River then along the Krasna River, and Russian forces fought several delaying actions. A Russian counter-attack across the Oskil failed. Establishing new defensive lines and coordinating a counter-attack, however, would not have been possible had there been a general break-down of command and control in that sector of the Russian front.

## The Kherson offensive

Likewise, attrition set the stage for Ukraine's successful Kherson offensive. But Kherson, unlike Kharkiv, proved a slog. Ukrainian forces enjoyed a favourable position, as the Russian front was separated from its logistical support by the Dnipro River. The right riverbank was connected via two roads and two rail bridges to Russian supply lines running from Crimea. Russian positions in Kherson were further bisected by the Inhulets River, meaning the front could be even further isolated by offensive action. Months of HIMARS strikes had limited the Russian logistical pipeline to one bridge at the Kakhovka dam and a network of ferries. In Kherson itself, Ukraine arrayed a sizeable force of brigades, backed by artillery, HIMARS, drones and fixed-wing aircraft. With Russian forces in no position to mount a counter-attack, the Ukrainians could prosecute their assault at will. Unlike in Kharkiv, however, Russian forces deployed in high density and included regular units from the Southern and Eastern groups of forces and elite airborne forces, later supplemented by reservists and newly mobilised per-sonnel. The Ukrainian attacks thus encountered layered Russian defences, and both sides launched prolonged artillery, rocket and drone strikes in what became an arduous attritional fight.

Ukraine attempted to move along three axes – north, central and south – in hopes of severing Russian units along the right side of the riverbank, enveloping them in several spots and eventually pushing depleted forces back across the river.[17] As in Kharkiv, Ukraine had been conducting localised attacks to gain better positions since the spring. This had led to a highly fluid situation, with towns changing hands. Ukrainian artillery and most importantly HIMARS systems had been striking Russian logistical hubs, bridges and critical infrastructure for two months in advance of the Ukrainian offensive. Its initial thrust, which started in late August, quickly stalled, with significant casualties taken.[18] After replacing the commander, a renewed Ukrainian offensive at the beginning of October made headway along the river, establishing a salient.[19] Yet Russian forces were able to contain the breakthrough and maintain defensive artillery fire despite Ukrainian interdiction and long-range precision strikes.

Fighting at a disadvantage, the Russian commander sought to withdraw to pursue a defensive strategy and preserve the force, and was allowed to do so given that an attritional battle favoured Ukraine and a forced Russian retreat appeared inevitable.[20] Over several weeks, the Russians withdrew in an organised manner, taking their serviceable equipment with them. Western analysts had expected heavy Russian casualties from long-range precision strikes. But those strikes were unable to impede the withdrawal of 30,000 to 40,000 Russian troops from Kherson, and Ukraine could not force the collapse of the Russian lines.[21] Russian forces left relatively unscathed.

## Taking stock

Ukraine mobilised at the outset of the war. It was able to attain a significant personnel advantage and, with the benefit of Western military assistance, outlast the Russians in the Donbas by compelling them to expend soldiers they couldn't afford and lose their fires advantage, which left them vulnerable to Ukrainian counter-offensives. Attrition proved a double-edged sword: it weakened Russian forces, but also took a toll on Ukrainian forces. Both Ukrainian counter-offensives did involve direct attacks on Russian positions. In Kharkiv, however, attrition made defence infeasible for the Russian military, which chose to prioritise Kherson. For that reason, the Kherson counter-offensive was the more operationally significant operation. It was successful but costly, and allowed the Russian military to preserve its forces for redeployment elsewhere.

The Russian armed forces' qualified ability to adapt to HIMARS attacks has been underappreciated.[22] Evidence suggests that HIMARS was not decisive, and that Russian difficulties had several causes. More broadly, attrition is a key element of Ukraine's strategy. This finding should not be surprising, as Ukraine's army features large artillery units, resembling the Russian army in force structure. It has struggled in combined-arms manoeuvre, and casualties have further degraded the quality of the force.

Neither army looks like it did at the beginning of the war, each having become a variegated force composed of mobilised personnel, auxiliaries, foreign fighters and, in Russia's case, mercenaries – including ex-prison inmates – in the Wagner Group.

Over the winter, Ukraine has sought to generate additional combat power and defend against localised Russian offensives. Despite making incremental gains outside Kreminna, Ukraine ceded the initiative to Russia between November and February owing to the need to recover from losses in the fight for Kherson, unfavourable weather and Russian pressure at Bakhmut. Ukraine has also had to divert resources to counter Russia's ongoing attacks on critical infrastructure, which threatened to deplete Ukraine's longer-term capacity to sustain the war. Shortfalls in materiel – above all, heavy artillery and air-defence ammunition – have also compromised Ukraine's war effort, and they are likely to persist through 2023.[23] Ukraine's approach depends heavily on ammunition, and uncertainties remain about its availability and production. The Ukrainian armed forces have been expending 2,000 to 4,000 artillery shells a day, outpacing foreign production rates and depleting Western stockpiles.[24] In addition, wear and tear on all platforms and weapons systems – especially tank and artillery barrels – amplified by high fire rates will increasingly become an issue; about a third of the Ukrainian forces' 350 Western-supplied guns are out of action at any given time. Western countries have sought to significantly increase production, but in the medium term shortfalls will have to be made up from strained US stockpiles.

Owing to its general mobilisation, Ukraine has no wholesale military-personnel shortage and can draw on a large pool of reserves. However, there remains a dearth of trained and experienced personnel, made more acute by high rates of attrition in some of the most elite units and formations of the Ukrainian armed forces. Ukraine is currently believed to field around 40 manoeuvre brigades, including activated reserve formations, but excluding the Territorial Defence Force.[25] Considering US casualty estimates and known Ukrainian equipment, a high percentage of these manoeuvre formations must have been depleted and replenished during the war.[26] General Valeriy Zaluzhnyi, their commander-in-chief, and a fellow general wrote in September: 'The only way to radically change the strategic situation is undoubtedly for the Ukrainian Army to launch several consecutive, and ideally, simultaneous counterstrikes throughout 2023.' According to Zaluzhnyi, a large-scale offensive would require 'one or more operational (operational–strategic) groupings of forces consisting of 10 to 20 combined-arms brigades, depending on the intent and ambitions of the Ukrainian Command'.[27]

The effects of attrition have been pronounced on both sides, as neither Ukraine's nor Russia's military appears capable of executing large-scale combined-arms manoeuvres that would mitigate them. A key question is therefore how quickly the Ukrainian armed forces can regenerate their offensive potential to conduct a sustained ground offensive against Russian forces in Ukraine. One indication of the difficulty of regaining combat effectiveness in existing manoeuvre

*The effects of attrition have been pronounced*

brigades is the fact that in the past several months, the primary tactical unit on both sides has been not the battalion or brigade but rather the company. One Western analyst, using information from a Russian source, reported that a Ukrainian company tactical group as of June 2022 consisted of 20–25 tracked infantry fighting vehicles, 10–12 tanks, 6–12 self-propelled guns, up to six multiple-launch rocket systems, and 250–450 personnel.[28] Based on estimated casualty rates and equipment losses, current Ukrainian company tactical groups are likely much smaller.

The United States and its NATO allies are making focused efforts to address this challenge and related ones. The US is providing Ukraine with a qualitative advantage in precision fires and with others is equipping it with armoured fighting vehicles, including tanks, in quantity. Furthermore, the US Army has established in Germany a combined-arms training programme geared to battalion-sized units. In February, the programme's first five-week training course, involving approximately 635 Ukrainian soldiers and focusing on the M2 *Bradley* fighting vehicle, was completed. Two further courses – one centred again on the *Bradley* and another on M109 *Paladin* field artillery – were under way, with courses for a second *Paladin* rotation and an M1126

*Stryker* battalion to follow.[29] The British-led, multinational *Operation Interflex* has provided immersive platoon-level training for thousands of Ukrainian troops, as well as leadership instruction for dozens of select Ukrainian officers in the United Kingdom.[30] In October 2022, the European Union set up the EU Military Assistance Mission Ukraine – EUMAM Ukraine – in part to provide training for an initial tranche of 15,000 Ukrainian soldiers, which is under way in Germany and Poland under Polish operational command and led by Dutch, French, German and Polish military officers.[31] Salutary as these separate efforts are, there remains a need for coordination and standardisation among them, purposefully focused on combined-arms operations.[32]

Ukraine still faces a daunting task. It no longer enjoys a personnel advantage, and faces an entrenched Russian military with a much higher density of forces relative to terrain. The introduction of additional land-based precision-fire capabilities, such as the American ground-launched small-diameter bomb, into Ukraine's arsenal is unlikely to fundamentally alter the military balance between the Ukrainian and Russian forces because the latter have been effectively adjusting to precision attacks.[33] These considerations suggest that future Ukrainian gains are likely to be more incremental and to come at higher cost, unless the Russian military significantly misspends combat power in its own offensive operations. Ukraine's preferred way of war centres on the use of artillery fire to facilitate decisive attritional effects on the opposing force, which it then exploits with manoeuvre. Accordingly, the war has produced high expenditures of ammunition and rates of casualties on both sides.[34] Land warfare still favours the defender and, between adversaries of comparable strength, breaking out of attrition and overcoming the defensive advantage is still far from easy. Future military operations in Ukraine will likely have more in common with the attrition phase in the run-up to the Russian withdrawal from Kherson city and *oblast* west of the Dnipro than the Kharkiv offensive.

\*     \*     \*

During spring and summer 2022, the Russian armed forces were short on personnel and capable leadership, for which they compensated with concentrated fires, expending millions of shells. Being essentially an artillery army, they burned through a resource that was central to how they fought.[35] The Russian military now has more soldiers due to mobilisation, but it lacks the ammunition needed to sustain the rates of artillery fire it achieved earlier in the war. Hence it has gone from inferiority in mass and superiority in fires, to relative parity in mass and at best parity, if not inferiority, in fires. It also lacks experienced and well-trained soldiers, having lost much of its junior leadership and its best troops over more than a year of fighting. On balance, the Russian military may be unable to restore the offensive capacity it had earlier in the war.

Nevertheless, in January 2023, the Russians undertook a series of offensive operations focused on seizing the Donbas, counter-attacking Ukrainian positions outside Kreminna and launching offensives at Vuhledar and Mariinka. As of early March, these appeared unlikely to generate major breakthroughs, as the Russian military has continued to suffer from poor force quality and dwindling artillery ammunition. Moscow appeared intent on extending the war in the hope of making it materially unsustainable for Ukraine and its Western partners.

It remained unclear whether Ukraine could capitalise on these deficits over the course of the spring. It sought to maintain pressure on Russian forces while generating additional units to set up another major offensive. Unpacked, its war-fighting strategy has three components: symmetrical attrition of Russian forces selectively along a 1,000 km front line; extending Russian forces with simultaneous pressure along disparate segments of the front line; and, once those forces have been sufficiently weakened, offensive operations with manoeuvre characteristics, ideally in combined-arms mode.

Western assistance has brought Ukraine to an impressive point, but it's not clear that it can yield a fires advantage for Ukraine sufficient to ensure further operational breakthroughs or strategic gains. Seasoned analysts are anticipating a drawn-out conflict.[36] In this light, it is sensible for the Pentagon and allied defence ministries to try to scale up combined-arms training and provide additional types and greater numbers of precision-guided weapons. Higher combined-arms proficiency could offer Ukraine a qualitative advantage on the battlefield by enabling its forces to more effectively coordinate the joint use of weapons systems such as armoured infantry fighting vehicles, main battle tanks, self-propelled artillery and air-defence systems, among other assets. Even with more effective wide-scale combined-arms training and precision strikes, however, it is unlikely that the Ukrainian armed forces will be able to escape attrition.

## Notes

[1] See Robert Dalsjö, Michael Jonsson and Johan Norberg, 'A Brutal Examination: Russian Military Capability in Light of the Ukraine War', *Survival*, vol. 64, no. 3, June–July 2022, pp. 7–28.

[2] See 'General Hodges Makes Forecast for Liberation of Mariupol, Melitopol, Crimea', Ukrinform, 12 November 2022, https://www.ukrinform.net/rubric-ato/3613120-general-hodges-makes-forecast-for-liberation-of-mariupol-melitopol-crimea.html.

[3] See Henry Foy et al., 'The 90km Journey that Changed the Course of the War in Ukraine', *Financial Times*, 27 September 2022, https://ig.ft.com/ukraine-counteroffensive/.

[4] See Mari Saito, Maria Tsvetkova and Anton Zverev, 'Abandoned Russian Base Holds Secrets of Retreat in Ukraine', Reuters, 26 October 2022, https://www.reuters.com/investigates/special-report/ukraine-crisis-russia-base/.

[5] See Isobel Koshiw, Lorenzo Tondo and Artem Mazhulin, 'Ukraine's Southern Offensive "Was Designed to Trick Russia"', *Guardian*, 10 September 2022, https://www.theguardian.com/world/2022/sep/10/ukraines-publicised-southern-offensive-was-disinformation-campaign.

[6] See Igor Kossov, 'Hundreds of Russian Vehicles, Weapons Systems Seized During Kharkiv Counterattack', *Kyiv Independent*, 26 September 2022, https://kyivindependent.com/national/hundreds-of-russian-vehicles-weapon-systems-seized-during-kharkiv-counterattack.

[7] See Konrad Muzyka, 'The Kharkiv Offensive and Its Consequences', *Riddle*, 19 September 2022, https://ridl.io/the-kharkiv-offensive-and-its-consequences/.

[8] See Foy et al., 'The 90km Journey that Changed the Course of the War in Ukraine'; and Simon Shuster and Vera Bergengruen, 'Inside the Ukrainian Counterstrike that Turned the Tide of the War', *Time*, 26 September 2022, https://time.com/6216213/ukraine-military-valeriy-zaluzhny/?utm_source=twitter&utm_medium=social&utm_campaign=editorial&utm_term=world_ukraine&linkId=183047256.

[9] See, for example, Steve Maguire, 'Yes, Manoeuvre Is Alive. Ukraine Proves It', *Wavell Room*, 4 November 2022, https://wavellroom.com/2022/11/04/yes-manoeuvre-is-alive-ukraine-proves-it/.

10 See, for example, Saito, Tsvetkova and Zverev, 'Abandoned Russian Base Holds Secrets of Retreat in Ukraine'.

11 See Natasha Bertrand, Oren Liebermann and Alex Marquardt, 'Russian Artillery Fire Down Nearly 75%, US Officials Say, in Latest Sign of Struggles for Moscow', CNN, 10 January 2023, https://www.cnn.com/2023/01/10/politics/russian-artillery-fire-down-75-percent-ukraine/index.html.

12 See Marc Santora, 'Hard-hit Kharkiv Is Rocked by More Blasts', *New York Times*, 17 August 2022, https://www.nytimes.com/live/2022/08/17/world/ukraine-russia-news-war#a-missile-strike-on-a-residential-building-in-kharkiv-kills-at-least-6-people.

13 See Yana Dlugy, 'Ukraine's Heavy Losses', *New York Times*, 1 June 2022, https://www.nytimes.com/2022/06/01/briefing/russia-ukraine-war-military-morale-east-nuclear.html.

14 See Jason Beaubien, 'Ukraine's Offensive in Kharkiv Was Hard and Bitter, Say Soldiers Who Did the Fighting', NPR, 29 September 2022, https://www.npr.org/2022/09/29/1125278321/ukraine-offensive-russia-borshchova-kharkiv-oblast. Regarding heavy losses in Lyman, see 'James', 'The Bloodiest Battle of the War: An Encirclement of the Russians at Lyman Could Upset the Entire Front', *Postedia*, 30 September 2022, https://thepostedia.com/world/90093.html.

15 It is in any case unlikely that Russian military commanders would have been able to react in time without exposing other parts of the front due to the low Russian force density in Ukraine and apparent friction in the Russian intelligence-collection process and the Russian chain of command. In this war, neither side has been able to establish defence-in-depth along the entire 850 km front line. See 'Active Front Line Is 850 Kilometers Long – General Staff of Ukraine's Armed Forces', Ukrinform, 29 September 2022, https://www.ukrinform.net/rubric-ato/3582273-active-front-line-is-850-kilometers-long-general-staff-of-ukraines-armed-forces.html.

16 'Russian Western Army Group Commanders Fired Following Major Defeat, Ukrainian Intelligence Says', *New Voice of Ukraine*, 12 September 2022, https://english.nv.ua/nation/russia-fires-senior-commanders-responsible-for-kharkiv-front-ukraine-war-50269418.html.

17 See Isabelle Khurshudyan et al., 'Inside the Ukrainian Counteroffensive that Shocked Putin and Reshaped the War', *Washington Post*, 29 December 2022, https://www.washingtonpost.com/world/2022/12/29/ukraine-offensive-kharkiv-kherson-donetsk/.

18 See John Hudson, 'Wounded Ukrainian Soldiers Reveal Steep Toll of Kherson Offensive', *Washington Post*, 7 September 2022, https://www.washingtonpost.com/world/2022/09/07/ukraine-kherson-offensive-casualties-ammunition/.

19 See Khurshudyan et al., 'Inside the Ukrainian Counteroffensive that Shocked Putin and Reshaped the War'.

20 See Sam Mednick, 'Russia Announces Withdrawal from Key Ukrainian City of Kherson in Another Setback for Invasion', PBS News

Hour, 9 November 2022, https://
www.pbs.org/newshour/world/
russia-announces-withdrawal-from-
key-ukrainian-city-of-kherson-in-
another-setback-for-invasion.

21  See Max Hunder and Tom Balmforth,
'Exclusive: Russia Needs Time to
Pull Back from Kherson, Fighting to
Slow in Winter – Kyiv', Reuters, 11
November 2022, https://www.reuters.
com/world/europe/exclusive-russian-
withdrawal-kherson-take-least-week-
kyiv-2022-11-10/.

22  See, for example, Morgan Douro,
'MLRS and the Totality of the
Battlefield', RUSI, 21 February 2023,
https://rusi.org/explore-our-research/
publications/commentary/mlrs-and-
totality-battlefield; and 'Russians
Have Adapted to HIMARS. What Are
Ukraine's Alternatives?', Euromaidan
Press, 9 January 2023, https://
euromaidanpress.com/2023/01/09/
russians-have-adapted-to-himars-
what-are-ukraines-alternatives/.

23  See Roman Olearchyk and
Ben Hall, 'Military Briefing:
Escalating Air War Depletes
Ukraine's Weapons Stockpile',
Financial Times, 13 December
2022, https://www.ft.com/content/
fbd6dc6e-4a41-4bfa-977b-8c3ef4482dcc.

24  See Joe Gould, 'Army Plans
"Dramatic" Ammo Production Boost
as Ukraine Drains Stock', Defense
News, 5 December 2022, https://www.
defensenews.com/pentagon/2022/12/05/
army-plans-dramatic-ammo-
production-boost-as-ukraine-drains-
stocks/; John Ismay and Thomas
Gibbons-Neff, 'Artillery Is Breaking
in Ukraine. It's Becoming a Problem
for the Pentagon', New York Times,

25 November 2022, https://www.
nytimes.com/2022/11/25/us/ukraine-
artillery-breakdown.html; and Bojan
Pancevski and Alistair McDonald,
'Many of Ukraine's Western Weapons
Await Repairs Far from the Front
Line', Wall Street Journal, 10 December
2022, https://www.wsj.com/articles/
many-of-ukraines-western-weapons-
await-repairs-far-from-the-front-
line-11670667085?reflink=share_
mobilewebshare.

25  This total comprised five reconnaissance
battalions, four tank brigades, nine
mechanised brigades, two mountain
brigades, four motorised infantry brigades, one light infantry brigade, two
tank brigades in reserve, and two mechanised brigades in reserve. International
Institute for Strategic Studies, The
Military Balance 2021 (Abingdon:
Routledge for the IISS, 2021), p. 209.

26  See Stijn Mitzer and Jakub Janovsky,
'Attack on Europe: Documenting
Ukrainian Equipment Losses During
the 2022 Invasion of Ukraine', Oryx,
13 December 2022, https://www.
oryxspioenkop.com/2022/02/attack-
on-europe-documenting-ukrainian.
html; and 'Ukraine War: US Estimates
200,000 Military Casualties on All
Sides', BBC News, 10 November
2022, https://www.bbc.com/news/
world-europe-63580372.

27  Valeriy Zaluzhnyi and Mykhailo
Zabrodskyi, 'Prospects for Running a
Military Campaign in 2023: Ukraine's
Perspective', Ukrinform, 7 September
2022, https://www.ukrinform.net/
rubric-ato/3566404-prospects-for-
running-a-military-campaign-
in-2023-ukraines-perspective.
html?fbclid=IwAR31RCvVxcCRDR_

Ci8-CrKsrDS__enSlBp8-lFoklOWFgjNkTyivcLkM7zk.

28  Henry Schlottman, 'Company Tactical Groups', Military and OSINT Analysis, Substack, 10 December 2022, https://henryschlottman.substack.com/p/company-tactical-groups?utm_campaign=auto_share&fbclid=IwAR3ALKXmIAI11HphRNqEIXsyr_2QnBUwRImgjK1Zvsgpm2eqA-g6UDXtR0.

29  See Meghann Myers, 'Ukrainian Battalion Completes First Combined-arms Training in Germany', *Defense News*, 17 February 2023, https://www.defensenews.com/news/your-army/2023/02/17/ukrainian-battalion-completes-first-combined-arms-training-in-germany/.

30  See Richard Thomas, 'Operation Interflex: Ukrainian Recruits Prepare for War', *Army Technology*, 11 November 2022, https://www.army-technology.com/features/operation-interflex-ukrainian-recruits-prepare-for-war/.

31  See 'France to Train Ukrainian Soldiers in Poland', First News, 2 February 2023, https://www.thefirstnews.com/article/france-to-train-ukrainian-soldiers-in-poland-36213.

32  See, for example, Jahara Matisek, Will Reno and Sam Rosenberg, 'The Good, the Bad and the Ugly: Assessing a Year of Military Aid to Ukraine', RUSI, 22 February 2023, https://rusi.org/explore-our-research/publications/commentary/good-bad-and-ugly-assessing-year-military-aid-ukraine; and Richard Thomas, 'Promise of Armour and Combined-arms Training to Ukraine Point to New Phase in Russia War', *Army Technology*, 6 January 2023,

https://www.army-technology.com/features/promise-of-armour-and-combined-arms-training-to-ukraine-point-to-new-phase-in-russia-war/.

33  See Mike Stone, 'Exclusive: US Weighs Sending 100-mile Strike Weapon to Ukraine', Reuters, 28 November 2022, https://www.reuters.com/business/aerospace-defense/100-mile-strike-weapon-weighed-ukraine-arms-makers-wrestle-with-demand-sources-2022-11-28/. On Russia adapting to HIMARS strikes, see Zoe Strozewski, 'Russia Developing "New Tactics" to Counter US HIMARS: Ukraine Official', *Newsweek*, 11 August 2022, https://www.newsweek.com/russia-new-himars-tactic-ukraine-war-oleksiy-danilov-1733047.

34  See Dan Lamothe, Liz Sly and Annabelle Timsit, '"Well Over" 100,000 Russian Troops Killed or Wounded in Ukraine, US Says', 10 November 2022, https://www.washingtonpost.com/world/2022/11/10/number-russian-troops-killed-injured-ukraine/.

35  See, for example, Lester W. Grau and Charles K. Bartles, 'The Russian Way of War: Force Structure, Tactics and Modernization of the Russian Ground Forces', Foreign Military Studies Office, US Training and Doctrine Command, 2016, p. 232, https://www.armyupress.army.mil/portals/7/hot%20spots/documents/russia/2017-07-the-russian-way-of-war-grau-bartles.pdf.

36  See, for instance, Michael Jonsson and Johan Norberg, 'Russia's War Against Ukraine: Military Scenarios and Outcomes', *Survival*, vol. 64, no. 6, December 2022–January 2023, pp. 91–122.

# How the War Has Changed Russia

**Nigel Gould-Davies**

When Russian President Vladimir Putin invaded Ukraine, he expected a quick victory. His failure transformed the Kremlin's main task from managing his re-election in 2024 to mobilising Russia's human and material resources to win a major war of aggression. This fundamental policy shift has broken long-standing bargains with society and elites. It is also straining the resources needed to fight the war and maintain domestic control.

## The bargain with society

Before the war, the regime had a clear authoritarian bargain with the population: stay out of politics and the state will leave you alone. Despite a decade-long decline in real incomes, this remained a compelling proposition for most Russians, especially as repression grew more severe.

The war has driven even greater repression. Opposition politics and independent media are outlawed. New laws criminalise even the mention of 'war', with up to 15 years in prison. Internet censorship and surveillance, including software to detect authors of anonymous posts, have intensified.[1] But the biggest change is one not of degree but of kind: the regime now seeks not to demobilise the population from politics but to mobilise it behind the war. This demand for active support, not merely acquiescence, marks a fundamental shift from authoritarian towards totalitarian rule. State media and the Orthodox Church now serve up a vitriolic and

**Nigel Gould-Davies** is IISS Senior Fellow for Russia and Eurasia. A version of this article appeared on the IISS Analysis blog in February 2023 at https://www.iiss.org/blogs/analysis/2023/02/how-the-war-has-changed-russia.

**Survival** | vol. 65 no. 2 | April–May 2023 | pp. 23–26          https://doi.org/10.1080/00396338.2023.2193093

hysterical diet of wartime propaganda. Education and training instil these messages into schools, universities and administrations.[2] The militarisation of Russian society is under way.

But despite public (and sometimes shrilly performative[3]) expressions of support, there are few signs of genuine mass enthusiasm for the war. Escalating repression suggests the Kremlin lacks confidence that the war is, or will remain, popular. The fact that the regime began the September 2022 'partial mobilisation' of over 300,000 conscripts so late, kept it so short and recruited from prisons shows the state's sensitivity to the public anxiety fuelled by demanding the ultimate sacrifice.[4] Even in this repressive environment, the Kremlin's internal polling suggests that a majority of the population now favours peace talks.[5]

## The bargain with elites

Elite opinion matters more than popular views in Russia. The regime needs elites to fulfil essential functions, and they are also better placed to protect their interests. Their pre-war bargain was obedience in return for relative wealth and security, including the ability to travel and send their money and families to the West.

By decisively subordinating stability and prosperity to geopolitical obsession, the war is breaking this bargain too. State control over the economy is growing as the economy moves towards a war footing and businesses are pressured to produce for, and make financial contributions to, the war effort. Sanctions are harming economic growth, disrupting supply chains and cutting off elites from the West. The domestic business environment is becoming more unpredictable and violent. Armed crime has risen by 30%.[6] Some elites, notably the *siloviki* (security personnel), have internalised Putin's justification for invasion. Politicians express performative support, such as with visits to the front lines, to advance their careers. But a large part of the elite has been unhappy with the war from the start yet continues to work for the system that launched it. More informed and less susceptible to propaganda than the general public, but also subjected to growing surveillance,[7] they do so out of fear and, in some cases, a conviction that they are serving the people, rather than the regime.[8]

## Strains on resources

The war has strained Russia's resources. Real incomes are falling; Russia has recorded its second-highest budget deficit since the break-up of the Soviet Union; and nearly a million citizens, many highly educated, have fled the country. At the same time, war-fuelled federal spending rose by 58.7% over the past year. Nearly one-third of federal-government spending will be devoted to defence and domestic security.[9] Reflecting these difficulties, much economic data has been classified.

Since the regime is more concerned about defeat in Ukraine than domestic instability, it will continue the war by demanding even more of its people while offering steadily less. But to avoid provoking a dangerous adverse reaction it will, where possible, calibrate resource mobilisation – habituating the population to the war and preparing the ground for further escalation.

## Russia's system now and tomorrow

The war has made Russia more repressive, intrusive, secretive and isolated from the West, as well as poorer. In all these ways, it increasingly resembles the Soviet Union. But three differences suggest that Russia will find it harder to manage the stresses that war imposes.

Firstly, for all its repression, the state is still less controlling than in Soviet times. There is no ruling party to penetrate and monitor every institution (though the Federal Security Service is a functional equivalent) and no coherent ideology to legitimate the regime. And while the state's role has deepened, private ownership remains the basis of the economy.

Secondly, for all its isolation, Russia is still more open to the outside world. Russians can access the internet – including, with a VPN, blocked websites – and can leave the country without difficulty. Curtailing these freedoms are obvious next steps. The war has also stoked unprecedented public infighting, albeit within limits defined by Putin, among *silovik* structures. Even state-television propaganda shows occasionally carry critical views about the war.

Thirdly, Russia is much weaker in relation to the West than the Soviet Union was during the Cold War. As former finance minister Mikhail Zadornov recently noted, the West's resources are 'incomparable'.[10] If the

West commits to giving Ukraine the means to win the war, the contest will be very unequal.

In short, Russia's capacity to mobilise and indoctrinate its citizens is weaker, and the resources it needs are greater, than those of the Soviet Union during the Cold War. Against this background, Putin has launched the country's most costly aggression since the 1939–40 Winter War against Finland. There are no signs yet that the breaking of key stabilising bargains is bringing the system close to crisis. But the strains it faces will deepen.

## Notes

[1] See Valentin Châtelet, 'Data Leak Suggests Crackdown on Anti-war Social Media Posts by Russia's Telecom Regulator', DFRLab, 9 February 2023, https://medium.com/dfrlab/data-leak-suggests-crackdown-on-anti-war-social-media-posts-by-russias-telecom-regulator-f2a3d09d6b2f; and Marina Tiuniaeva, 'Roskomnadzor gotovitsia zapustit' sistemu obezvrezhivaniia infobomb v internete', *Vedomosti*, 20 February 2023, https://www.vedomosti.ru/technology/articles/2023/02/20/963570-roskomnadzor-gotovitsya-zapustit-sistemu-obezvrezhivaniya-infobomb.

[2] See Anna Smolchenko, '"Existential War": Putin Steels Russia for Long Conflict', *Moscow Times*, 19 February 2023.

[3] See Emma Burrows, 'Russians Told to Attend Pro-war Vladimir Putin Rally in Moscow or "Resign" from Jobs', ITV News, 18 March 2022.

[4] See Lev Gudkov and Christina Hebel, '"Russians Have Little Compassion for the Ukrainians"', Spiegel International, 5 January 2023.

[5] Andrey Pertsev, trans. Anna Rasumnaya, 'Make Peace, Not War', Meduza, 30 November 2022, https://meduza.io/en/feature/2022/11/30/make-peace-not-war.

[6] Dmitrii Serkov and Anastasia Antipova, 'V Rossii pochti na 30% vyroslo chislo prestuplenii s ispol'zovaniiem oruzhiia', rbc.ru, 23 November 2022, https://www.rbc.ru/society/23/11/2022/637ccfa59a79478ef249f44d.

[7] Andrei Vinokurov and Elena Rozhkova, 'Oruzhiie massovogo raz''iasneniie', *Kommersant*, 22 April 2022, https://=/www.kommersant.ru/doc/5326305.

[8] See Max Seddon and Polina Ivanova, 'How Putin's Technocrats Saved the Economy to Fight a War They Opposed', *Financial Times*, 16 December 2022.

[9] Darya Korsunskaya, 'Analysis: Surge in Russia's Defence and Security Spending Means Cuts for Schools and Hospitals in 2023', Reuters, 22 November 2022.

[10] 'Eks-glava dvukh krupnykh gos-bankov predrek krakh ekonomike Putina', Moscow Times Russian Service, 14 February 2023.

# Enforcing Russia's Debt to Ukraine: Constraints and Creativity

**Maria Shagina**

As Russia continues to wage war against Ukraine, Western policymakers have begun to contemplate the country's post-war reconstruction. The longer the war continues, the greater the bill for damages will be. As of early 2023, direct damages to infrastructure came to $138 billion.[1] It could eventually cost up to $1 trillion to rebuild the country – a truly immense sum measured against Ukraine's GDP of about $200bn.[2] The value of Russia's assets immobilised by the West through multilateral efforts, however, totals only about $300bn in foreign reserves and $58bn in Russian private assets.[3]

Marking one year of war in Ukraine, G7 leaders affirmed a commitment to find 'an international mechanism to register the damages Russia has inflicted'.[4] Western nations agree that holding Russia accountable for the physical damage as well as the atrocities and crimes it has committed in Ukraine is imperative. The moral case for using Russian assets has a political dimension for many external funders, who are loath to divert Western resources originally intended for deserving recipients in the Global South to remedy Russian-inflicted destruction. Yet sanctions on Russian individuals, companies and foreign reserves, though unprecedented, do not provide a legal basis for confiscation. There is a yawning gap between freezing and seizing, and between political aspirations and legal pitfalls. Countries differ in their preferred approaches; current legal frameworks are not suitable for Ukraine's situation; and international law is by its nature a somewhat

**Maria Shagina** is the Diamond-Brown Senior Fellow for Economic Sanctions, Standards and Strategy at the IISS.

**Survival** | vol. 65 no. 2 | April–May 2023 | pp. 27–36          https://doi.org/10.1080/00396338.2023.2193094

amorphous work in progress. Even if a legal mechanism is found or created, the process of confiscation will be slow and fraught.

## Baseline considerations

Private and sovereign assets require different asset-recovery mechanisms, each of which faces a specific legal challenge: the fundamental right to property and the principle of state immunity. Regarding Russia's sovereign assets, based on the principle of sovereign equality embedded in the United Nations Charter, no state is entitled to pass judgement on another state, and central-bank assets enjoy special protection. The fact that Russia has violated the UN Charter, however, arguably compromises its legal capacity to invoke that protection. Furthermore, there are explicit exceptions to state immunity for cases involving genocide, crimes against humanity, war crimes and crimes of aggression, and Russian conduct falls into at least three of these categories. Under customary international law, however, central-bank foreign reserves are strictly off limits, and are not subject even to these exceptions.

Confiscation of private assets would usually require a criminal conviction or a judgment of forfeiture. Money laundering, corruption, organised crime, illegal-drug dealing, arms trafficking and terrorism can serve as bases for confiscation. Civil-asset forfeiture involves a lower standard of proof – the 'balance of probabilities' – than the criminal standard of 'beyond reasonable doubt'.

Identifying the exact amount and location of Russian assets is also difficult.[5] Most reporting refers to 'more than $300 billion' of Russian foreign reserves instead of citing an exact figure. The approximate figures are based on a Bank of Russia report issued in January 2022.[6] But there is little information on what happened to the reserves between January and March of that year, when they were blocked, due to weak reporting requirements with respect to central-bank sanctions. To ensure a uniform application of the asset-freeze provisions, the European Union's tenth sanctions package, issued in February 2023, obligates European operators to report to member states and the European Commission on immobilised – though not frozen – assets and reserves. Until this requirement was imposed, there was no country-by-country breakdown of immobilised assets, as it remained within the purview of member states whether to publish such information. France has been the only EU country to have publicly announced the value of Russian central-bank assets ($22bn) it has blocked.

## Differing national approaches and constraints

The US government was the first to float the idea of confiscation, but most proposals there have stalled or focused on narrowly linking seizure to organised crime and corruption. The Fourth Amendment of the US Constitution is construed as barring the federal government from seizing assets based on sanctions designations, but it has considerable latitude to do so for alleged crimes. In October 2022, US senators proposed targeting the assets of Russian oligarchs and channelling the proceeds towards Ukraine's reconstruction.[7] Last year, the United States seized a superyacht owned by Viktor Vekselberg, a close political ally of Russian President Vladimir Putin, and more recently the US Department of Justice seized an aircraft owned by the Russian oil company Rosneft. The department is planning to proceed apace with more seizures of private Russian assets.[8]

Public discussion in the US about seizing Russian sovereign assets has been guarded. US Treasury Secretary Janet Yellen has noted that under the current legal framework it is not permissible to seize Russian sovereign assets. One of her long-term priorities is to avoid diminishing the role of the US dollar as the world's dominant reserve currency. While such concerns are warranted, the process of de-dollarisation in central-bank reserves had already been under way in Russia, triggered by financial sanctions before major fears of confiscation materialised. As a result, US institutions hold only 6% of Russia's foreign reserves, significantly less than Germany (16%), France (10%) or even Japan (9%). But Yellen is also likely concerned about legal issues.

In the United Kingdom, confiscating assets is authorised exclusively by the Proceeds of Crime Act 2002. The UK sought to follow Canada's lead on amending the laws to allow confiscation, but concerns over property rights and due process seem to have slowed progress. Nevertheless, the government is 'considering all options on the seizure of Russian-linked assets in the UK'.[9] In February 2023, Labour MP Chris Bryant introduced a bill in the

House of Commons to provide a framework for the seizure of both Russian private and public assets. The bill was rejected, but it will be given a second hearing. Having frozen more than £18bn in assets last year, London, like Washington, is accelerating the seizure and forfeiture of Russian oligarchs' assets. As part of the deal between one such oligarch, Roman Abramovich, and the UK's Office of Financial Sanctions Implementation, Chelsea Football Club, which Abramovich owned, was sold for £2.5bn in May 2022.[10] The proceeds of the sale will be deposited in a frozen bank account and later redirected to victims of the war in Ukraine. Furthermore, the expedited passage of the Economic Crime and Corporate Transparency Bill in March 2022 introduced significant reforms to Unexplained Wealth Orders, an investigative tool that can speed up asset recovery of private funds.

At the EU level, discussions on confiscation have revolved more around private assets than public ones. In May 2022, the European Commission proposed amending its directive on asset recovery and confiscation, with a focus on organised crime and racketeering.[11] The proposal highlights the need for effective asset tracing and identification. The EU has also expanded the list of criteria for conduct that would constitute crime, adding the violation or evasion of sanctions.[12] It emphasises sanctions evasion as the main justification for asset seizure. As of November 2022, EU countries had frozen around €18.9bn-worth of Russian private assets.

Like the US, the EU is wary of pursuing Russian sovereign assets. While its concerns about the role of the euro as a reserve currency are minor, EU officials are keen to maintain the moral high ground and avoid distorting international law to fit their foreign-policy objectives the way authoritarian states do. Their bottom line is to ensure that any EU legal framework for seizure is able to withstand a legal challenge by the Russian state. Germany also wants to avoid setting a precedent for state immunity whereby the Greek, Italian or Polish governments might seek reparations for Second World War forfeitures.

Despite the limited legal room for manoeuvre, however, there seems to be considerable enthusiasm within the EU to explore all feasible options. Under the Swedish presidency, a new working group has been set up at the Council of the European Union to 'carry out a legal, financial, economic and political analysis of the possibilities of using frozen

Russian assets'.[13] The European Commission has suggested creating a trust fund through which to invest Russian foreign reserves for rebuilding Ukraine.[14] In the short term, the ownership of the assets would not change, thus bypassing the issue of state immunity. It is unclear whether the fund would be centralised at the EU, decentralised at the member-state level or placed in a third country like Switzerland, and how seized sovereign assets would be channelled to Ukraine. In the longer term, Russian central-bank reserves would be returned upon negotiated settlement and Russia's payment in full of agreed compensation to Ukraine.

While the trust fund is inventive, it remains unclear what would happen if the trust investments generated losses, potentially putting the EU in the awkward position of having to guarantee Russian sovereign assets with EU public money. The long-term solution also seems to exaggerate the leverage that immobilised Russian central-bank assets would afford

*The European Commission has suggested a trust fund*

the West in compelling Russia to reach a peace agreement. Due to record-high energy prices last year, Russia accumulated about $250bn from the export of hydrocarbons – almost the equivalent of its immobilised assets. In addition, the EU mechanism would rely strongly on Russia abiding by the rules and paying reparations to Ukraine against the backdrop of a raft of flagrant Russian violations of international law.

Canada is the only G7 country to have amended its legislation to allow for the seizure of assets.[15] Under the amendments, the proceeds of the forfeited property can be used for the reconstruction of a foreign state to the extent that it is adversely affected by a grave breach of international peace and security, and the proceeds are needed to restore pre-conflict conditions and compensate victims. Thus, Canada's new powers allow it to go after Russia's central-bank assets, which amount to almost C$20bn.[16]

Overall, G7 leaders have been keen to advance their initiatives in a coordinated manner and avoid unilateral confiscation. Yet differences in legal cultures and varying degrees of political willingness to push boundaries have produced an uneven, poorly coordinated process, with Canada at the forefront and the US lagging behind. Between these two poles there has been relative inertia. While other G7 countries have shown theoretical interest in Canada's initiative, none have taken corresponding action. And none demurred when Switzerland and Japan ruled out the confiscation of Russian assets.

## Bolder action?

There are several precedents for freezing another country's foreign reserves. Somewhat ironically, all are from the United States – a laggard on Ukraine. In the past, Washington has used such measures against Afghanistan, Iran, Iraq and Venezuela.

The most relevant case is the United States' confiscation of the Iraqi government's assets over its invasion of Kuwait in 1990. In February 2022, the United Nations Compensation Commission processed the final compensation to Kuwait, amounting to $52.4bn. Similarly, the US blocked $1.75bn of Iranian central-bank assets for Iran's involvement in the suicide bombing of the US Marine barracks in Beirut in 1983. A 2012 US law required Citibank to hand over the assets to the families of the victims of the Beirut bombing.[17]

Other cases are less directly applicable but still relevant. The US blocked $7bn of Afghanistan's central-bank reserves, holding half for prospective damages in ongoing litigation by victims of the 9/11 terrorist attacks.[18] In February 2023, a federal court rejected the victims' claims on the assets, citing the United States' lack of legal authority to seize the funds.[19] While the decision frustrated the United States' bid to compensate the families of victims, it is arguably inapposite to the Ukraine case insofar as the Taliban and not the Afghan state had been held liable for the attacks.[20]

\*      \*      \*

Unprecedented times call for unprecedented solutions. The current legal framework is unsuited to the Russia–Ukraine war, as the rules were written for peacetime. There is an urgent moral as well as political need to push the legal boundaries to holding Russia accountable.

Some legal experts argue that the expropriation of Russian public assets can be justified as a third-party countermeasure.[21] The idea is that Russia has lost its right to immunity by way of its blatant disregard for international law, and that by transferring the funds to Ukraine the West would be helping Kyiv to exercise its inherent right of self-defence.[22] This theory is admittedly untested in international law, which has not authoritatively examined whether third-party states not directly affected by a wrongful act can impose countermeasures on behalf of one that is directly affected. Another potential obstacle is that the application of third-party counter-measures is customarily recognised as legitimate only to induce a country to comply with legal obligations, as opposed to effectuating outright punishment.[23] Sustaining countermeasures' non-punitive nature by making confiscation reversible would be problematic, as would a lack of clarity as to what laws or rules Western states would be asking Russia to obey.

International law is, however, apprehended as a work in progress that of necessity must evolve. Acting in concert with like-minded allies is crucial to allay concerns that the fabric of international law will be ruptured. Accordingly, states are justified in urging innovations in international legal norms to accommodate unanticipated circumstances that fall outside the boundaries of existing international jurisprudence. Russia's unprovoked attack on Ukraine, egregiously illegal under firmly accepted principles of international law, is surely one. In the words of British barrister Amal Clooney, 'peace – like war – must be waged. And justice, too, is something we must fight for.'[24]

## Notes

1  Kyiv School of Economics, 'The Total Amount of Damage Caused to Ukraine's Infrastructure Due to the War Has Increased to Almost $138 Billion', 24 January 2023, https://kse.ua/about-the-school/news/the-total-amount-of-damage-caused-to-ukraine-s-infrastructure-due-to-the-war-has-increased-to-almost-138-billion/.

2  President of Ukraine, 'Ukraine Will Become a Role Model of Reconstruction – President Addressed the General Assembly of the International Bureau of Expositions Regarding the Holding of Expo 2030 in Odesa', 29 November 2022, https://www.president.gov.ua/en/news/ukrayina-stane-vzircem-vidbudovi-prezident-zvernuvsya-do-gen-79513.

3  US Department of the Treasury, 'Joint Statement from the REPO Task Force', 9 March 2023, https://home.treasury.gov/news/press-releases/jy1329.

4   White House, 'G7 Leaders' Statement',
    24 February 2023, https://www.
    whitehouse.gov/briefing-room/
    statements-releases/2023/02/24/
    g7-leaders-statement-5/.

5   See Martin Sandbu, 'There Is Too
    Much We Don't Know About Russia's
    Central Bank Reserves', *Financial Times*,
    28 February 2023, https://www-ft-com.
    ezp.lib.cam.ac.uk/content/37a4143b-
    ce25-4491-a946-3423cce5598b.

6   See Bank of Russia, 'Bank of Russia
    Foreign Exchange and Gold Asset
    Management Report', January
    2022, https://d1e00ek4ebabms.
    cloudfront.net/production/uploaded-
    files/2022-01_res_en-a3dd71b9-7484-
    4668-8deb-a4a72306f506.pdf.

7   See US Senate Foreign Relations
    Committee, 'Senators Offer Russian
    Asset Seizure Legislation', 4 October
    2022, https://www.foreign.senate.
    gov/press/rep/release/senators-offer-
    russian-asset-seizure-legislation.

8   See Dylan Tokar and Ian Talley,
    'Justice Department Hiring Dozens of
    New Prosecutors to Enforce Russian
    Sanctions', *Wall Street Journal*, 2 March
    2023, https://www.wsj.com/articles/
    justice-department-hiring-dozens-of-
    new-prosecutors-to-enforce-russian-
    sanctions-4e9b9047.

9   UK Parliament, 'Post-conflict
    Reconstruction Assistance to Ukraine',
    Research Briefing, 16 February 2023,
    https://commonslibrary.parliament.
    uk/research-briefings/cbp-9728/.

10  See Tariq Panja and Rory Smith,
    'Inside the Chelsea Sale: Deep Pockets,
    Private Promises and Side Deals', *New
    York Times*, 24 May 2022, https://www.
    nytimes.com/2022/05/24/sports/soccer/
    chelsea-sale-abramovich-boehly.html.

11  See European Commission, 'Proposal
    for a Directive of the European
    Parliament and of the Council on Asset
    Recovery and Confiscation', COM(2022)
    245 final, 25 May 2022, https://eur-lex.
    europa.eu/legal-content/EN/TXT/PDF/?
    uri=CELEX:52022PC0245&from=EN.

12  See Council of the European Union,
    'Council Decision (EU) 2022/2332 of
    28 November 2022 on Identifying the
    Violation of Union Restrictive Measures
    as an Area of Crime that Meets the
    Criteria Specified in Article 83(1) of
    the Treaty on the Functioning of the
    European Union', *Official Journal of the
    European Union*, 29 November 2022,
    https://eur-lex.europa.eu/legal-content/
    EN/TXT/HTML/?uri=CELEX:32022D23
    32&qid=1675161606172&from=en.

13  Government Offices of Sweden,
    'EU Working Group to Look at
    Using Frozen Russian Assets for
    Reconstruction of Ukraine', 14 February
    2023, https://www.government.se/
    articles/2023/02/eu-working-group-to-
    look-at-using-frozen-russian-assets-for-
    reconstruction-of-ukraine/.

14  See European Commission, 'Ukraine:
    Commission Presents Options to
    Make Sure that Russia Pays for Its
    Crimes', 30 November 2022, https://
    ec.europa.eu/commission/presscorner/
    detail/en/ip_22_7311.

15  See Janyce McGregor, 'Canada Can
    Now Seize, Sell Off Russian Assets.
    What's Next?', CBC News, 27 June
    2022, https://www.cbc.ca/news/
    politics/c19-russia-sanctions-asset-
    seizures-test-case-1.6496047.

16  The Kremlin called a plan discussed
    by the G7 in May 2022 to use frozen
    Russian foreign reserves to finance
    Ukraine's reconstruction 'theft'. See

Amy Cheng, 'Russia Calls West's Idea to Use Frozen Funds to Rebuild Ukraine "Theft"', *Washington Post*, 18 May 2022, https://www.washingtonpost.com/world/2022/05/18/russia-reserves-sanctions-g7-ukraine-rebuild/.

17  See Molly Quell, 'Iran Faces US in International Court Over Asset Seizure', AP News, 19 September 2022, https://apnews.com/article/middle-east-iran-lebanon-636c555049c8666855c8dcc5d54f9bef.

18  White House, 'FACT SHEET: Executive Order to Preserve Certain Afghanistan Central Bank Assets for the People of Afghanistan', 11 February 2022, https://www.whitehouse.gov/briefing-room/statements-releases/2022/02/11/fact-sheet-executive-order-to-preserve-certain-afghanistan-central-bank-assets-for-the-people-of-afghanistan/.

19  See Charlie Savage, 'Judge Rejects Bid by Sept. 11 Families to Seize Frozen Afghan Central Bank Funds', *New York Times*, 21 February 2023, https://www.nytimes.com/2023/02/21/us/politics/judge-sept-11-afghan-central-bank.html.

20  In the Venezuelan case, no confiscation actually occurred; rather, the US conferred control over the country's central-bank assets to the disputed interim president, Juan Guiadó.

21  See Philippa Webb, 'Ukraine Symposium – Building Momentum: Next Steps Towards Justice for Ukraine', Lieber Institute, West Point, 2 May 2022, https://lieber.westpoint.edu/building-momentum-next-steps-justice-ukraine/.

22  See, for example, Janyce McGregor, 'RCMP Says $123M in Russian Assets Frozen, $289M in Transactions Blocked Since Ukraine Invasion', CBC News, 9 June 2022, https://www.cbc.ca/news/politics/rcmp-russia-sanctions-totals-ukraine-war-1.6483952.

23  See Ingrid (Wuerth) Brunk, 'Central Bank Immunity, Afghanistan, and Judgments Against the Taliban', 1 February 2023, https://www.lawfareblog.com/central-bank-immunity-afghanistan-and-judgments-against-taliban.

24  Clooney Foundation for Justice, 'CFJ Co-founder Amal Clooney Addresses the UN on Accountability for War Crimes in Ukraine', 28 April 2022, https://cfj.org/news_posts/cfj-co-founder-amal-clooney-addresses-the-un-on-accountability-for-war-crimes-in-ukraine/.

# *Zeitenwende* One Year On

**Bastian Giegerich and Ben Schreer**

On 27 February 2022, three days after Russia's invasion of Ukraine, German Chancellor Olaf Scholz announced a *Zeitenwende*, or historical turning point, for German foreign and defence policy. Expectations of profound German geopolitical, geostrategic and geo-economic transformation were raised both in Germany and among Berlin's allies. Geopolitically, Scholz promised a radical rethink of Germany's relations with Russia. Geostrategically, he announced a major boost for the German armed forces, proposing a €100 billion off-budget fund (*Sondervermögen*). And geo-economically, he pledged to drastically reduce the country's dependence on Russian energy. One year on, commentators seem to agree the move was bold but remains incomplete.[1]

Germany's greatest success has appeared to come, perhaps unexpectedly, in the geo-economic arena. While the declared objective of Foreign Minister Annalena Baerbock to reduce Germany's energy imports from Russia to zero has not yet been achieved, major progress has been made. By the end of 2022, the share of Russian natural-gas imports had dropped to 22% from 52% a year earlier.[2] Norway overtook Russia as the main supplier, accounting for 33% of the total volume. Moreover, the crude-oil import volume from Russia dropped by approximately 51% between November 2021 and November 2022. In addition, the Scholz government closed a deal with Qatar for the delivery of liquefied natural gas to new terminals in

**Bastian Giegerich** is Director of Defence and Military Analysis at the IISS. **Ben Schreer** is the Executive Director of IISS–Europe and the Head of the IISS European Security and Defence Programme. A version of this article appeared on the IISS Analysis blog in February 2023 at https://www.iiss.org/blogs/analysis/2023/02/zeitenwende-one-year-on.

**Survival** | vol. 65 no. 2 | April–May 2023 | pp. 37–42       https://doi.org/10.1080/00396338.2023.2193095

Germany from 2026, and explored opportunities with Iraq for the delivery of crude oil and gas.[3] Germany is creating a new energy infrastructure and is working on new partnerships that will structurally remove dependence on Russian energy.

Geopolitically, the picture is less convincing. While Scholz has committed to the defence of NATO territory against potential Russian aggression, it is not obvious whether the German government really perceives Russia as a direct threat to the country. Indeed, most of the discussion in Germany following the start of Russia's war of aggression was focused on the need to reassure Eastern European allies, rather than identifying Russia as a threat to Germany itself. Moreover, allies could not fail to notice that while Scholz repeatedly stated that Russia must not succeed, he (unlike Baerbock and recently appointed Defence Minister Boris Pistorius[4]) also refused to state that victory was necessary for Ukraine or to spell out the desired outcome for Kyiv. In Berlin, the conviction remains strong that there can be no military solution – such as a complete Russian defeat in Ukraine – to the conflict and that a return to a post-war relationship with Moscow is essential.

Such thinking not only defies historical lessons that some conflicts are decided on the battlefield, it also underestimates the loss of trust in Germany among Berlin's allies because of its previous blindness to the threat from Russia. Moreover, it overlooks the fact that the war in Ukraine and the impending NATO memberships of Sweden and Finland have shifted the geopolitical centre of gravity in Europe towards the east and north. Ultimately, this ambivalence stands in the way of Germany taking a convincing view on security guarantees for Ukraine and the idea that Ukraine's long-term security and defence, including through eventual NATO membership, is essential for Germany's own security. It remains to be seen if Germany's first-ever National Security Strategy – delayed because of disagreements between the Chancellery and the Federal Foreign Office – will formulate stronger geopolitical foundations. Germany could position itself as the major continental power organising Europe's security and defence against Russia, but to do so it first needs to rebuild trust among its closest friends. Currently, the list of countries that wish to be led by Germany is short.

## Need for strategic reform

This leads to the geostrategic element of the *Zeitenwende*, arguably the area that has seen the least progress thus far. At the leadership level, Christine Lambrecht, defence minister until 16 January 2023, failed to give shape to much-needed Bundeswehr reform or to create a sense of urgency around readiness and procurement challenges. For instance, the Federal Ministry of Defence does not yet seem to have fully incorporated the lessons learned from Ukraine in a systematic way to guide future military strategy, operational planning or procurement. Moreover, the cumbersome defence-procurement process has remained largely unchanged, leading to major backlogs, limited orders for the defence industry and a general sense of drift. A recent dialogue between senior bureaucrats and defence-industry representatives organised by the chancellor's office ended without concrete solutions to break this impasse. There is no concerted push to develop a German 'war economy', and therefore no mechanism to rapidly turn fresh funding into new contracts.

It is already evident that the additional €100bn for defence, which is partially being eaten up by inflation, rising interest rates and VAT, will not be sufficient to fund a comprehensive reform of the Bundeswehr. The *Sondervermögen* will need to be used until the next election in 2025 to come close to reaching NATO's minimum target for allied defence spending of 2% of GDP, because the core defence budget is likely to decline in real terms based on current budget-planning documents. Whereas most NATO allies have come to view the 2% target as a floor, Scholz at least seems to still consider it a ceiling.[5] This would be problematic also because to meet Germany's own climate and sustainability goals by 2030, the Bundeswehr would require projected additional funding of over €40bn – funds which have not been reflected in defence-budget planning thus far.[6]

Finally, it can be difficult to change the strategic culture of a nation. Germany's reluctance to use military force is deeply ingrained in the national psyche. Tellingly, an opinion poll in February 2023 showed that only 11% of Germans would volunteer to take up arms to defend the country in case of an attack.[7] In contrast, in a May 2022 poll, a record 83% of Finnish citizens were ready to militarily defend their nation.[8]

The *Zeitenwende* will be meaningful only if its effects stretch across economics, strategy and military matters. Nothing less than a full rethink of Germany's fundamental positions – its addiction to cheap energy to fuel the economy, belief in dialogue as a way of resolving deep-seated disagreements among nations and conviction that military force is a nasty hangover of a bygone time – is required to reconcile Germany with the security environment in which it finds itself. Scholz's decisions since his 27 February 2022 speech illustrate this. For instance, Germany's provision of lethal military assistance and general defence support to Ukraine at levels higher than any other continental European power is a powerful case in point.[9] Pistorius seems to be embracing, rather than deflecting as did his predecessor, the challenge of making the Bundeswehr fit for purpose. Significant geopolitical and geostrategic change in Germany's foreign and defence policy can happen, but it will depend on external pressure from partners and allies, and will require leaders in Berlin who are ready to break the mould.

## Notes

[1] See 'Germany's Bold Policy Shift Remains a Work in Progress', *Financial Times*, 17 February 2023, https://www.ft.com/content/d1ab1c9e-746f-4122-b86f-0ea95f5c05bc.

[2] 'German 2022 Gas Imports Dropped 12.3%, Norway Helped Replace Russia – Regulator', Reuters, 6 January 2023, https://www.reuters.com/business/energy/german-2022-gas-imports-dropped-123-norway-helped-replace-russia-regulator-2023-01-06/.

[3] On the opening of Germany's second terminal for the import of liquefied natural gas in January 2023, see Nikolaus J. Kurmayer, 'Germany's Second LNG Terminal Open for Business', EURACTIV, 16 January 2023, https://www.euractiv.com/section/energy/news/germanys-second-lng-terminal-open-for-business/.

[4] 'Die Ukraine muss diesen Krieg gewinnen', *Die Zeit*, 18 February 2023, https://www.zeit.de/politik/deutschland/2023-02/boris-pistorius-verteidigungsminister-muenchner-sicherheitskonferenz.

[5] Hans Von Der Burchard, 'German Chancellor Vows "Leadership" with Call to Further Arm Ukraine', *Politico*, 17 February 2023, https://www.politico.eu/article/olaf-scholz-germany-ukraine-arms-tanks/.

[6] Markus Decker, 'Klimaschutz: Bundeswehr rechnet mit Milliardeninvestitionen', Redaktions Netzwerk Deutschland, 9 February 2023, https://www.rnd.de/politik/klimaschutz-bundeswehr-rechnet-mit-

milliarden-investitionen-6FJSU2TZ-
6VHIZDSLQG5XX24FXM.html.

7    'Umfrage: Fünf Prozent der Deutschen
würden im Kriegsfall freiwillig zur
Waffe greifen', Redaktions Netzwerk
Deutschland, 10 February 2023,
https://www.rnd.de/politik/umfrage-
jeder-zehnte-deutsche-im-angriffsfall-
bereit-fuer-kriegsdienst-56W4FHF-
DUCDDDCBWUFTIVY2MVM.html.

8    'Poll: Citizens' Willingness to Defend
Finland, Support for Nato Hit All
Time High', YLE News, 3 December
2022, https://yle.fi/a/74-20006876.

9    Christoph Trebesch et al., 'The Ukraine
Support Tracker: Which Countries
Help Ukraine and How?', Kiel
Working Papers 2218, February 2023,
https://www.ifw-kiel.de/publications/
kiel-working-papers/2022/the-ukraine-
support-tracker-which-countries-help-
ukraine-and-how-17204/.

# Asia's Ukraine Problem

**Lynn Kuok**

Many Asian governments regard Russia's war with Ukraine as a distant event with limited impact on the region beyond raising food and energy prices. To the extent that they have considered the geopolitical implications of the war, they have largely focused on whether it increases the risk of China attacking Taiwan. But the war has strained the rule of law and is entrenching divisions along ideological lines, introducing unnecessary complexity into alliances and partnerships. It has also raised questions about the extent to which Europe will be able to play a meaningful role in the Indo-Pacific. Asian governments should be alert to these developments and their negative implications for regional peace and security. For them to condemn Russia's invasion of Ukraine and defend the rule of law would not be blindly supporting the West, and would be entirely consistent with their national interests. The West must also do its part to avoid worsening geopolitical fault lines. In particular, framing great-power competition as a battle between autocracies and democracies is unhelpful.

## Asia's complacency

In April 2022, Shivshankar Menon, who served as national security adviser to former Indian prime minister Manmohan Singh, argued that while the Russia–Ukraine war was a 'seismic event', it would 'neither reshape the global order nor presage an ideological showdown' because 'many of the world's

---

**Lynn Kuok** is IISS Shangri-La Dialogue Senior Fellow for Asia-Pacific Security and co-editor of the IISS's *Asia-Pacific Regional Security Assessment*.

**Survival** | vol. 65 no. 2 | April–May 2023 | pp. 43–51      https://doi.org/10.1080/00396338.2023.2193097

biggest democracies, including India, have so far not joined the US-led economic campaign against Russia or even explicitly condemned the invasion'.[1] Sentiments that the war's impact would be limited have resonated widely in the region. They are, to say the least, too sanguine.

In recent years, China's coercive behaviour has undermined international law. In the South China Sea, China has militarised disputed land features and low-tide features within the jurisdiction of coastal states, encroached on coastal states' exclusive economic zones, and objected to lawful assertions of innocent passage and freedom of the seas by the US and other navies.[2] Should Russia succeed in further seizing and holding sovereign Ukrainian territory, international law would be severely compromised, which could in turn encourage revisionist behaviour by China and other countries.

The war in Ukraine has deepened geopolitical divisions. On 4 February 2022, less than three weeks before Russia's assault on Ukraine, China issued a joint statement with Russia declaring a 'no limits' friendship with no 'forbidden' areas of cooperation.[3] Beijing has since refused to condemn Moscow's actions, even if it has so far stopped short of providing military assistance, and continues to expand its trade with Russia, which hit a record 1.28 trillion yuan ($190 billion) last year.[4] American strategist Hal Brands has assessed that the 'Sino-Russian convergence … raises the prospect that America's two great-power rivalries could merge into a single contest against an autocratic axis'.[5]

Other analysts suggest that fears of Sino-Russian cooperation are overblown, pointing to constraints on the Sino-Russian partnership, which include great-power rivalry, ongoing territorial disputes and Russia's resentment of junior status. China's ambassador to the US has highlighted that while there are no forbidden areas of cooperation, China's 'bottom line' is 'the tenets and principles of the United Nations Charter, the recognised basic norms of international law and international relations'.[6] Nevertheless, the position China has taken has reinforced the presumption of a strong ideological bond.

## America's shortsightedness
American rhetoric and policy have bolstered that presumption. US President Joe Biden declared in a speech in Warsaw a month after the Russian invasion

that the battle over Ukraine was one 'between democracy and autocracy, between liberty and repression'.[7] This buttressed a strongly ideological message that his administration – and before that the Trump administration – had already been pushing. The US-hosted Summit for Democracy in December 2021 included only three of the ten Association of Southeast Asian Nations member states and excluded Singapore and Vietnam – countries that the US Indo-Pacific strategy issued in February 2022 described as 'leading regional partners' with which the US sought to strengthen relations.[8]

In general, Asian assessments of the challenges facing their countries and the region have little to do with threats posed by authoritarian governments. At the International Institute for Strategic Studies' (IISS) 2022 Shangri-La Dialogue, the Malaysian defence minister cited instead an increase in transboundary crime from border reopenings; an upsurge in online disinformation arising from terror groups and extremists; the continued threat of biological warfare; and food security.[9] The Indonesian defence minister registered faith that 'the leaders of China will stand up to their responsibility with wisdom and benevolence because it is their philosophical teaching' while reminding the West that what remained in Indonesia's 'subconscious' was its 'experience of being colonised'.[10] The Philippines' defence minister suggested that 'geopolitical competition among major powers' was concerning.[11] His Vietnamese counterpart highlighted the dangers of an arms race that could crowd out socio-economic development.[12] But neither singled out China for criticism or mentioned its system of government. Singapore's defence minister observed that 'Asian countries are too diverse and pluralistic and there would be few takers for a battle royale to ensue on [an ideological] basis'.[13]

The democracies-versus-autocracies framing also sits uneasily with the position India, the world's largest democracy, has taken on Ukraine. New Delhi has refrained from condemning Russia's invasion of Ukraine, and abstained from two UN General Assembly resolutions deploring Russia's aggression against Ukraine and demanding the immediate cessation of its use of force against its neighbour. India's stance is particularly notable given that it is the 'pacing partner' of the Quadrilateral Security Dialogue, the linchpin of the United States' and other Western nations' Indo-Pacific strategy.[14] US regional allies have also avoided taking sharply ideological positions. The Japanese National Security Strategy issued in December 2022 does not frame geopolitical competition as being between democracies and autocracies, though it does emphasise the importance of upholding 'universal values such as freedom, democracy, respect for fundamental human rights, and the rule of law'.[15] South Korea's Indo-Pacific Strategy unveiled in January 2023 explicitly states that South Korea supports 'an Indo-Pacific where nations that represent diverse political systems can move forward together peacefully through competition and cooperation based on rules'.[16]

The United States' tendency to paint China and Russia with the same broad ideological brush is counterproductive. Moscow's actions are not Beijing's, and China's official reaction to Russia's invasion of Ukraine suggested a government in an awkward position trying to calibrate its response.[17] Although it did not condemn Russia's actions, China repeatedly called for the exercise of restraint and care. On 24 February 2023 – the one-year anniversary of Russia's invasion of Ukraine – Beijing issued a position paper that sought to re-establish the appearance of restraint by calling for respect for the sovereignty of all countries, ceasing hostilities, resuming peace talks, resolving the humanitarian crisis, non-use of nuclear weapons and an end to 'bloc confrontation'.[18]

## The Taiwan question

How and to what extent the Russia–Ukraine war will affect Chinese calculations on Taiwan is unclear. One fear, implicit in Japanese Prime Minister Kishida Fumio's declaration that 'Ukraine today may be East Asia tomorrow', is that if the West acquiesced in Russia's use of force to change the status quo, China could be emboldened to invade and seize Taiwan as Russia had Ukraine. Such worries appear overwrought.

Some Taiwanese officials and American analysts believe China would simply attack Taiwan if it had the capability to take it by force. Others assess that China would refrain from attacking unless a red line were crossed. A Taiwanese declaration of independence would clearly be a red line, but it is not China's only one. China's 2005 Anti-Secession Law, for instance, provides that the state shall employ non-peaceful means where 'possibilities for a peaceful reunification [are] completely exhausted'.[19] The latter clearly affords China considerable latitude short of a Taiwanese declaration of independence. But the Russia–Ukraine war could well induce greater caution on Beijing's part given the immense costs that Russia has incurred in terms of combat losses and international sanctions, even if sanctions would be harder to impose on China given its importance to the global economy.[20]

Moreover, any Chinese decision to try to take Taiwan by force would in large part depend on its assessment of whether the US was likely to come to Taiwan's defence. The White House has taken pains to reassure Taiwan of its 'robust' support for it, including by sending a delegation of former senior defence and security officials there soon after Russia's invasion of Ukraine. Through September 2022, Biden had stated four times during his presidency that the United States would defend the island against a Chinese attack.[21] This is a deterrent. China's decision would also depend on its judgement about Taiwan's ability to 'hold the fort' until the US intervened, and the extent to which Chinese missiles could keep US carrier strike groups at bay.[22]

Against this backdrop, China's standing approach to bolstering its security – namely, operating in the grey zone to forge incremental political and territorial gains – is likely to continue.

### Europe in Asia

A secondary area of concern is the possible diminishment of Europe's engagement in the Indo-Pacific, which had intensified over the four years preceding the war, with various European countries and the European Union issuing Indo-Pacific policy statements.[23] While sustained US regional engagement – facilitated by its own strategic priorities and concomitant discipline in avoiding escalation in Ukraine – is paramount, Europe's involvement with the region remains important for supporting the rule of law and softening US–China competition.

It is too early to assess conclusively how the war in Ukraine will affect European commitments to the Indo-Pacific. The financial demands of the war will no doubt exert some pull on European resources. But given the transatlantic solidarity that the war has generated behind preserving the rule of law, European countries will probably seek to at least maintain planned levels of commitment. France sees itself as an Indo-Pacific power, with overseas territories, 1.65 million citizens in the region, and 93% of its exclusive economic zone in the Indian and Pacific oceans, while the United Kingdom, at least under the current Conservative government, appears similarly devoted to maintaining a strong security presence in the region.

*    *    *

The West has important economic and political interests in the Indo-Pacific. Preserving those interests will require it to limit the negative impacts of the Russia–Ukraine war on Asia. The United States, in particular, may need to relax its characterisation of great-power competition as an ideological battle. Otherwise, Washington would further roil already troubled relations with China, alienate some regional partners and cede strategic space to China.

There are plenty of valid reasons for calling out Beijing. It has, for example, breached international law in the South China Sea, disregarded human rights in its treatment of minorities in Xinjiang, reneged on agreements regarding the governance of Hong Kong, sought to economically coerce Australia and South Korea, and employed unfair trade practices. Western criticism of China should focus on its questionable conduct.

Biden still appears unduly attached to the autocracies-versus-democracies concept, reiterating it in his State of the Union address on 8 February 2023 and his speech in Warsaw on 21 February.[24] Yet there is room in the United States' existing policy framework for a recalibrated approach. The US National Security Strategy released in October 2022 is nuanced and flexible in its framing of the United States' strategic challenge, identifying the real threat as stemming from 'powers that layer authoritarian governance with a revisionist foreign policy' and leaving the door open to working with 'non-democracies [that] join the world's democracies in forswearing [revisionist] behaviors'.[25]

German Chancellor Olaf Scholz described Russia's invasion of Ukraine as a 'historic turning point' (*Zeitenwende*). It is pivotal not just for Europe, but for Asia as well. The window of opportunity in which Asian states must decide whether they want a bifurcated world in which power can prevail over the rule of law, or one in which countries, despite differences, can find common cause on the basis of key shared principles, has become smaller. India's External Affairs Minister S. Jaishankar was correct when he declared that not all of Europe's problems were the world's problems, and justly criticised Europe for being insufficiently attentive to troubles outside its neighbourhood.[26] Conversely, however, Asia has a Ukraine problem it may not fully appreciate.

## Notes

1. Shivshankar Menon, 'The Fantasy of the Free World: Are Democracies Really United Against Russia?', *Foreign Affairs*, 4 April 2022, https://www.foreignaffairs.com/articles/united-states/2022-04-04/fantasy-free-world. For a deeper understanding of India's position, see Sharinee L. Jagtiani and Sophia Wellek, 'In the Shadow of Ukraine: India's Choices and Challenges', *Survival*, vol. 64, no. 3, June–July 2022, pp. 29–48.

2. See Lynn Kuok, 'How China's Actions in the South China Sea Undermine the Rule of Law', in Tarun Chhabra et al. (eds), *Global China: Assessing China's Growing Role in the World* (Washington DC: Brookings Institution Press, 2021).

3. President of Russia, 'Joint Statement of the Russian Federation and the People's Republic of China on the International Relations Entering a New Era and the Global Sustainable Development', 4 February 2022, http://en.kremlin.ru/supplement/5770.

4. See C.K. Tan, 'China Trade Suffers from COVID Hangover, Weaker External Demand; Import, Export Declines Partly Offset by Record Trade Growth with Russia', NikkeiAsia, 13 January 2023, https://asia.nikkei.com/Economy/Trade/China-trade-suffers-from-COVID-hangover-weaker-external-demand.

5. Hal Brands, 'The Eurasian Nightmare: Chinese–Russian Convergence and the Future of American Order', *Foreign Affairs*, 25 February 2022, https://www.foreignaffairs.com/articles/china/2022-02-25/eurasian-nightmare.

6. Quoted in 'China Envoy Says Xi–Putin Friendship Actually Does Have a Limit', Bloomberg News, 24 March 2022, https://www.bloomberg.com/news/articles/2022-03-24/china-envoy-says-xi-putin-friendship-actually-does-have-a-limit?sref=zJo4jZBU.

7. White House, 'Remarks by President Biden on the United Efforts of the Free World to Support the People of Ukraine', 26 March 2022, https://www.whitehouse.gov/briefing-room/speeches-remarks/2022/03/26/remarks-by-president-biden-on-the-united-efforts-of-the-free-world-to-support-the-people-of-ukraine/#:~:text=But%20we%20emerged%20anew%20in,in%20days%20or%20months%20either.

8. White House, 'Indo-Pacific Strategy of the United States', February 2022, p. 9, https://www.whitehouse.gov/wp-content/uploads/2022/02/U.S.-Indo-Pacific-Strategy.pdf.

9   See Dato' Seri Hishammuddin Tun Hussein, 'Developing New Forms of Security Cooperation', IISS Shangri-La Dialogue, Singapore, 11 June 2022, https://www.iiss.org/-/media/files/shangri-la-dialogue/2022/transcripts/p3/as-delivered/dato-seri-hishammuddin-tun-hussein-senior-minister-of-defence-malaysia-as-delivered.pdf.

10   General (Retd) Prabowo Subianto, 'Managing Geopolitical Competition in a Multipolar Region', IISS Shangri-La Dialogue, Singapore, 11 June 2022, https://www.iiss.org/-/media/files/shangri-la-dialogue/2022/transcripts/p2/as-delivered_/general-retd-prabowo-subianto-minister-of-defense-indonesia-as-delivered.pdf.

11   Delfin Lorenzana, 'Military Modernisation and New Defence Capabilities', IISS Shangri-La Dialogue, Singapore, 11 June 2022, https://www.iiss.org/-/media/files/shangri-la-dialogue/2022/transcripts/p4/new/delfin-lorenzana-secretary-of-national-defense-philippines-as-delivered.pdf.

12   See General Phan Văn Giang, 'Military Modernisation and New Defence Capabilities', IISS Shangri-La Dialogue, Singapore, 11 June 2022, https://www.iiss.org/-/media/files/shangri-la-dialogue/2022/transcripts/p4/general-phan-vn-giang-minister-of-national-defence-vietnam-provisional-transcript.pdf.

13   MINDEF Singapore, 'Speech by Minister for Defence Dr Ng Eng Hen at the 7th Plenary on "New Ideas for Securing Regional Stability" at the Shangri-La Dialogue', 12 June 2022, https://www.mindef.gov.sg/web/portal/mindef/news-and-events/latest-releases/article-detail/2022/june/12jun22_speech/.

14   See Tanvi Madan, 'India and the Quad', in IISS, *Asia-Pacific Regional Security Assessment 2022* (Abingdon: Routledge, 2022), https://www.iiss.org/publications/strategic-dossiers/asia-pacific-regional-security-assessment-2022/aprsa-chapter-9.

15   Ministry of Foreign Affairs of Japan, 'National Security Strategy of Japan', December 2022, p. 1, https://www.cas.go.jp/jp/siryou/221216anzenhoshou/nss-e.pdf.

16   Ministry of Foreign Affairs, Republic of Korea, 'Strategy for a Free, Peaceful, and Prosperous Indo-Pacific Region', December 2022, p. 7, https://www.mofa.go.kr/viewer/skin/doc.html?fn=20230106093833927.pdf&rs=/viewer/result/202303.

17   For a summary of key events and statements from 21 February 2022 through 1 March 2023, see US–China Economic and Security Review Commission, 'China's Position on Russia's Invasion of Ukraine', 3 March 2023, https://www.uscc.gov/research/chinas-position-russias-invasion-ukraine.

18   See Ministry of Foreign Affairs of the People's Republic of China, 'China's Position on the Political Settlement of the Ukraine Crisis', 24 February 2023, https://www.mfa.gov.cn/eng/zxxx_662805/202302/t20230224_11030713.html.

19   'Full Text of Anti-Secession Law', adopted at the Third Session of the Tenth National People's Congress on 14 March 2005, https://www.europarl.europa.eu/meetdocs/2004_2009/

documents/fd/d-cn2005042601/d-cn2005042601en.pdf.

20  See Mick Ryan, 'How China Is Using Ukraine to Wargame Taiwan', *Sydney Morning Herald*, 8 February 2023, https://www.smh.com.au/world/europe/how-china-is-using-ukraine-to-wargame-taiwan-20230206-p5ciao.html.

21  See, for example, Phelim Kine, 'Biden Leaves No Doubt: "Strategic Ambiguity" Toward Taiwan Is Dead', *Politico*, 19 September 2022, https://www.politico.com/news/2022/09/19/biden-leaves-no-doubt-strategic-ambiguity-toward-taiwan-is-dead-00057658.

22  I am grateful to Tim Huxley, Senior Adviser to IISS–Asia, for his thoughts on this subject.

23  See Lynn Kuok, 'Making Room for Middle Powers: ASEAN's Growing Embrace of Europe', in James Bowen (ed.), *Europe's Indo-Pacific Embrace: Global Partnerships for Regional Resilience* (Crawley and Canberra: Perth USAsia Centre and Konrad Adenauer Stiftung, September 2021), https://t.co/9fKS64GtPA.

24  See White House, 'Remarks of President Joe Biden – State of the Union Address as Prepared for Delivery', 7 February 2023, https://www.whitehouse.gov/briefing-room/speeches-remarks/2023/02/07/remarks-of-president-joe-biden-state-of-the-union-address-as-prepared-for-delivery/; and White House, 'Remarks by President Biden Ahead of the One-year Anniversary of Russia's Brutal and Unprovoked Invasion of Ukraine', 21 February 2023, https://www.whitehouse.gov/briefing-room/speeches-remarks/2023/02/21/remarks-by-president-biden-ahead-of-the-one-year-anniversary-of-russias-brutal-and-unprovoked-invasion-of-ukraine/.

25  White House, 'National Security Strategy', October 2022, p. 8, https://www.whitehouse.gov/wp-content/uploads/2022/10/Biden-Harris-Administrations-National-Security-Strategy-10.2022.pdf.

26  S. Jaishankar, 'Reaching New Heights: Allies in the Indo-Pacific Region', speech at the GLOBSEC Bratislava Forum, Slovakia, 3 June 2022.

# Noteworthy

## A furious year

'I apologise to the entire Ukrainian nation for coming to their home as an uninvited guest with a weapon in my hands. Thank God I didn't hurt anyone. I didn't kill anyone. Thank God I wasn't killed. I don't even have the moral right to ask for forgiveness from the Ukrainians. I can't forgive myself, so I can't expect them to forgive me.'

*Konstantin Yefremov, who served as an officer in the Russian army, talks to the BBC on 2 February 2023 about his time in Ukraine.*[1]

'Now we are seeing that unfortunately, the ideology of Nazism – this time in its modern guise – is again creating direct threats to our national security, and we are, time and again, forced to resist the aggression of the collective West.'

*Russian President Vladimir Putin speaks at a gala concert on 2 February marking the 80th anniversary of the defeat of German forces by the Red Army in the Battle of Stalingrad.*[2]

'Your courage has inspired us. You have given us a new sense of purpose. Europe is with you for as long as it takes – until the day when the Ukrainian flag will be raised where it belongs: in Brussels at the heart of the European Union.'

*Ursula von der Leyen, president of the European Commission, addresses the Ukrainian people during a meeting of EU commissioners and members of the Ukrainian government in Kyiv on 2 February.*[3]

'As the world prepares to mark the one-year anniversary of Russia's brutal invasion of Ukraine, I am in Kyiv today to meet with President Zelenskyy and reaffirm our unwavering and unflagging commitment to Ukraine's democracy, sovereignty, and territorial integrity.

When Putin launched his invasion nearly one year ago, he thought Ukraine was weak and the West was divided. He thought he could outlast us. But he was dead wrong.'

*US President Joe Biden speaks in Kyiv during a surprise visit to Ukraine on 20 February.*[4]

'A year ago, on this day, from this very place, at about seven in the morning, I addressed you with a short statement. It lasted only 67 seconds. It contained the two most important things, then and now. That Russia started a full-scale war against us. And that we are strong. We are ready for anything. We will defeat everyone. Because we are Ukraine!

[ … ]

We will never rest until the Russian murderers face deserved punishment. The punishment of the International Tribunal. The judgement of God. Of our warriors. Or all of them together.

The verdict is obvious. Nine years ago, the neighbour became an aggressor. A year ago, the aggressor became an executioner, looter and terrorist. We have no doubt that they will be held accountable. We have no doubt that we will win.

[ … ]

It was a year of resilience. A year of care. A year of bravery. A year of pain. A year of hope. A year of endurance. A year of unity. The year of invincibility. The furious year of invincibility.'

*Ukrainian President Volodymyr Zelenskyy speaks on 24 February, the one-year anniversary of the Russian invasion of Ukraine.*[5]

**Survival** | vol. 65 no. 2 | April–May 2023 | pp. 52–54    https://doi.org/10.1080/00396338.2023.2193099

## Netanyahu's fist

'The Ministry of Foreign Affairs in Gaza condemns, in strongest terms, the barbaric "Israeli" aggression on Jenin camp, which left nine people dead, including a 60-year-old woman, and dozens wounded until the writing of this statement.

[…]

As we condemn this criminal aggression, we warn against the attempts of the extremist government, led by [Benjamin] Netanyahu, to export its internal crises at the expense of Palestinian blood. We, also, call upon the international community to immediately interfere in order to stop this dangerous escalation that threatens the peace and stability in the region.'

*The Palestinian Ministry of Foreign Affairs condemns a raid by Israeli forces on the West Bank city of Jenin on 26 January 2023.[6]*

'Whoever tries to harm us – we will harm them and everyone who assists them. Our answer to terrorism is an iron fist and a powerful, swift and precise response.'

*Israeli Prime Minister Benjamin Netanyahu responds to the shooting of Israelis in Jerusalem on 27–28 January.[7]*

'Members of the coalition – history will judge you for this night. For the damage to democracy, for the damage to the economy, for the damage to security, for the fact that you are tearing the people of Israel apart and you simply do not care.'

*Yair Lapid, who leads the opposition in the Israeli parliament, criticises the government on 20 February for supporting a controversial judicial-reform package.[8]*

'In a democracy, the people vote in elections and the representatives of the people vote here in the Parliament. That is called democracy. Unfortunately, the protest leaders are trampling democracy. They do not accept the results of the election, they do not accept the decision of the majority.'

*Netanyahu criticises protesters opposing the reform package.[9]*

'We are following with deep concern the processes taking place in the State of Israel and in the Air Force these days. From a deep familiarity with the central and special weight of the [Air] Force in national security, which you are well aware of, we are fearful over the consequences of these processes and the serious and tangible danger posed to the national security of the State of Israel.'

*All surviving former chiefs of the Israeli Air Force send a joint letter to Netanyahu opposing the package on 6 March.[10]*

## *Force majeure?*

'The airship is from China. It is a civilian airship used for research, mainly meteorological, purposes. Affected by the Westerlies and with limited self-steering capability, the airship deviated far from its planned course. The Chinese side regrets the unintended entry of the airship into US airspace due to *force majeure*. The Chinese side will continue communicating with the US side and properly handle this unexpected situation caused by *force majeure*.'

*The Chinese Ministry of Foreign Affairs comments on 3 February 2023 on the discovery of what the United States called a 'surveillance balloon' in the airspace over the northwestern US.[11]*

'On Wednesday, when I was briefed on the balloon, I ordered the Pentagon to shoot it down … as soon as possible, without doing damage to anyone on the ground. They decided that the best time to do that was over water within our 12-mile limit. They successfully took it down and I want to compliment our aviators who did it.'

*US President Joe Biden comments on the destruction of the balloon by US forces near the coast of South Carolina on 4 February.*[12]

'We solemnly protest the U.S. action, and retain the right to use the necessary means to deal with similar circumstances.'

*China's Ministry of Defence reacts to the destruction of the balloon.*[13]

'Taking it down over the Atlantic is sort of like tackling the quarterback after the game is over. The satellite had completed its mission. It should never have been allowed to enter the US.'

*Mike Turner, head of the intelligence committee of the US House of Representatives, criticises the Biden administration for allowing the balloon to traverse US airspace.*[14]

**Sources**

1   Steve Rosenberg, 'Russian Army Officer Admits: "Our Troops Tortured Ukrainians"', BBC, 2 February 2023, https://www.bbc.co.uk/news/world-europe-64470092.

2   President of Russia, 'Gala Concert for 80th Anniversary of Defeating German Nazi Forces in Battle of Stalingrad', 2 February 2023, http://en.kremlin.ru/events/president/transcripts/70434.

3   European Commission, 'Opening Remarks by President von der Leyen on the Occasion of the Meeting Between the College and the Government of Ukraine', 2 February 2023, https://euromaidanpress.com/2023/02/02/ukraine-will-be-an-eu-member-one-year-ago-no-one-could-have-imagined-your-speed-ursula-von-der-leyen/.

4   White House, 'Statement from President Joe Biden on Travel to Kyiv, Ukraine', 20 February 2023, https://www.whitehouse.gov/briefing-room/statements-releases/2023/02/20/statement-from-president-joe-biden-on-travel-to-kyiv-ukraine/.

5   President of Ukraine, 'Address by President of Ukraine Volodymyr Zelenskyy "February. The Year of Invincibility", 24 February 2023, https://www.president.gov.ua/en/news/zvernennya-prezidenta-ukrayini-volodimira-zelenskogo-lyutij-81213.

6   State of Palestine Ministry of Foreign Affairs, 'MOFA Condemns Barbaric "Israeli" Aggression on Jenin', 26 January 2023, https://www.mofa.ps/en/press-release/2369/.

7   James Shotter, 'Israel to Loosen Gun Laws After Jerusalem Attacks', *Financial Times*, 29 January 2023, https://www.ft.com/content/00d190c8-f054-4794-8096-3c75d9e11b77.

8   Yair Lapid (@yairlapid), tweet, 20 February 2023, https://twitter.com/yairlapid/status/1627799988620099584.

9   Avishag Shaar-Yashuv, 'Israeli Lawmakers Move to Rein In Judges as Protests Rock Jerusalem', *New York Times*, 20 February 2023, https://www.nytimes.com/2023/02/20/world/middleeast/protest-jerusalem-judicial-overhaul.html.

10  Emanuel Fabian, '10 Ex-IAF Chiefs Pen Letter to PM Amid Reservist Protest: "Stop, Find a Solution"', *Times of Israel*, 6 March 2023, https://www.timesofisrael.com/ex-iaf-chiefs-pen-letter-to-pm-amid-reservist-protest-stop-find-a-solution/.

11  Ministry of Foreign Affairs of the People's Republic of China, 'Foreign Ministry Spokesperson's Remarks on the Unintended Entry of a Chinese Unmanned Airship into US Airspace Due to Force Majeure', 3 February 2023, https://www.mfa.gov.cn/eng/xwfw_665399/s2510_665401/202302/t20230203_11019484.html.

12  Julian Borger, 'US Shoots Down Suspected Chinese Spy Balloon Over East Coast', *Guardian*, 4 February 2023, https://www.theguardian.com/us-news/2023/feb/04/chinese-spy-balloon-shot-down-us.

13  Chris Buckley, 'China Finds Itself with Limited Options After U.S. Shoots Down Balloon', *New York Times*, 5 February 2023, https://www.nytimes.com/2023/02/05/world/asia/china-balloon-united-states.html.

14  Ramsey Touchberry, 'House Intel Chair: Downing Balloon Over Ocean Is "Tackling the Quarterback After the Game Is Over"', *Washington Times*, 5 February 2023, https://www.washingtontimes.com/news/2023/feb/5/mike-turner-downing-spy-balloon-over-ocean-tacklin/.

# About European Sovereignty

**Pierre Buhler**

A few months after his election in 2017, French President Emmanuel Macron declared at the Sorbonne that 'only Europe can guarantee genuine sovereignty, namely our ability to exist in today's world to defend our values and interests. There is a European sovereignty to be built, and it needs to be built.'[1] A year later, European Commission president Jean-Claude Juncker, in his State of the Union speech, noted that 'the geopolitical situation makes this Europe's hour', exhorting the continent to take 'destiny into its own hands' and 'play a role, as a Union, in shaping global affairs', while also cautioning that 'European sovereignty is born of member states' national sovereignty and does not replace it'.[2] The Franco-German Treaty of Aachen, signed in January 2019, calls for a 'united, efficient, sovereign and strong European Union'. But what does 'European sovereignty' really mean?

The notion of sovereignty as an intangible prerogative of the nation-state is rooted in centuries of European statecraft. Since 'sovereign equality' was adopted as a core foundation of the post-Second World War international order under the United Nations Charter, however, the process of European unification has deconstructed the concept in seeking a balance between the sovereignty of member states and supranational federalism. The shocks and crises the European polity has endured – the main ones stemming from

**Pierre Buhler**, a former French diplomat, has served as France's ambassador to Singapore and Poland. He teaches international affairs at Sciences Po (Paris), Hertie School (Berlin) and the College of Europe (Natolin).

**Survival** | vol. 65 no. 2 | April–May 2023 | pp. 55–74          https://doi.org/10.1080/00396338.2023.2193100

the demise of the Soviet Union – have both increased that tension and buttressed the federalist project. While the EU has succeeded in developing tools and policies that have helped it leverage access to its immense internal market, its ability to be a significant actor of world politics remains questionable, especially in the field of hard security.

The reasons lie in the diversity of historical experiences and national interests of its constituent nations, as well as in their unpredictability. They also relate to the status of the United States as a European power – the guarantor of last resort of security on the continent – and to intricate governance mechanisms in which command, a core component of power, is conspicuously absent. This landscape is unlikely to change any time soon. In a time when the rules-based international order is fraying, Europeans should not obfuscate their aims with confusing if grand notions of sovereignty, but instead clarify those aims and precisely identify the tools needed to reach them.

## The concept of sovereignty

The sixteenth-century French philosopher Jean Bodin defined sovereignty as 'the absolute and perpetual power in a commonwealth'.[3] Endowing the sovereign with command authority of last resort, this concept of sovereignty provided the legal framework for the nation-state, equating it with its independence from any foreign entity. It became the cornerstone of the Westphalian order.

Thomas Hobbes considered sovereignty indivisible, but saw the consent of the subjects as its basis. A century later, Jean-Jacques Rousseau went further and cast sovereignty as the expression of the people through the 'general will', which yielded the founding principles of modern democracy. His reading posited freedom, guaranteed by law, as a limit on the arbitrary exercise of power. But it was Montesquieu who conceptualised the division of sovereignty by splitting the powers of the state and balancing them through a legal framework.

His writings inspired the American federalists, who applied that concept with an eye to uniting the 13 colonies into a federation. To win the battle against the anti-federalists, who favoured a treaty-based confederation, Alexander Hamilton and his federalist allies argued that sovereignty belonged to the people, who delegate some of its prerogatives, such as security and commerce, to the federal authority, while leaving the residual ones to the states. Some 75 years later, the American Civil War brought that elegant solution to the brink of collapse. Other countries, notably France, went through painful processes to find a workable balance between the people and the authority entitled to act on their behalf.

## Post-war Europe: federalism vs intergovernmentalism

After the Second World War, the broad aspiration to an order based on the rule of law spurred some Europeans to imagine, building on a UN Charter that the upcoming Cold War would soon weaken, a united Europe. In his 1946 Zurich speech, Winston Churchill famously called for a 'sovereign remedy' to the tragedy that had engulfed the continent – 'a kind of United States of Europe'.[4] In 1948 at The Hague, the 'Congress of Europe' provided a matrix for further developments, at the same time revealing the rift between federalist aspirations and a 'unionist' approach based on intergovernmentalism. It also fostered the rejection of absolute sovereignty and the power associated with it, perceived as responsible for the excesses and horrors of war.

European statesmen thus strived to harness both sovereignty and power. In 1951, six founding countries' two main raw materials of war were pooled under the European Coal and Steel Community, which was intended to become the crucible of the European project. But in 1954, the French National Assembly refused to ratify a treaty to Europeanise the armies of those six countries. From then on, European integration proceeded on a strictly economic track – a common market, a customs union, an agricultural policy and the mutualisation of civilian atomic energy.

Sovereignty remained a source of friction between European institutions and their member states. In 1964, the European Court of Justice asserted the primacy of European treaties and related laws over national law.[5] In 1965, however, with the 'empty chair crisis', French president Charles de Gaulle rejected a new level of integration and supranational rule by switching from unanimity to majority voting on important issues, as proposed by the Commission of the European Communities. After a six-month stalemate, the 'Luxembourg compromise' restored the de facto veto power of any member state deeming one of its 'vital interests' threatened by the majority vote of other member states. This compromise flattened the trajectory of supranationalism, essentially freezing the balance of power between the European institutions and the states.

Reflecting the early polarisation between European federalists and unionists, scholarly debate has pitched functionalism – later 'neo-functionalism' – against intergovernmentalism. The former school of thought, led by Ernst Haas, supported movement towards supranational governance.[6] The latter, influenced by Stanley Hoffmann and David Calleo, was premised on the resilience of nation-states and their capacity to remain the crucial actors and orchestrators of European integration.[7] While developments like the Single European Act of 1986, which allowed for the mobility of goods, services, people and capital, were broadly consistent with the neo-functionalist approach, the reservation of 'regalian' prerogatives such as border control, defence, diplomacy, policing, justice and taxation by national governments reflected the strength of intergovernmentalism. Though Europeanised under the Schengen Agreement in 1985 and the Maastricht Treaty in 1992, these mechanisms were prudentially characterised as intergovernmental cooperation schemes.[8]

## Sovereignty, democracy and the elusive European *demos*

The main debate about sovereignty continued to revolve around its internal dimension – that is, the tug of war between supranational authority and the nation-state. However, an increasingly organised and sometimes populist citizenry is now challenging elite-driven schemes. Domestic politics has framed the handling of the several significant EU crises during the past decade, including the eurozone rescue, the 2015 migration crisis, Brexit and the war in Ukraine.[9] What has emerged is not a European *demos*, but rather national constituencies and eurosceptical parties skilled at engineering discontent and, under the banner of sovereignty, wresting authority from Brussels.

For their part, scholars of international law have observed that 'the EU cannot make a convincing claim to sovereignty under international law, [which] does not vest non-state actors with sovereignty'.[10] Others point to the indivisible nature of sovereignty, not to be shared, divided or even transferred, and member states' monopoly on the use of force on their territory, the right to control their borders and their recognition as states by other states, none of which the EU enjoys. The state, they emphasise, is the polity of last resort, and therefore retains the right to withdraw from those treaties, as illustrated by Brexit. One commentator has asked, sardonically, 'where is the sovereign in this call for European sovereignty?'[11] Another has noted that 'foreign-policy elites' are pushing the concept of European sovereignty with 'little discussion of whether it expresses the will of the people of Europe'.[12] Furthermore, the coexistence of sovereignties points to 'the limits of this European voluntarism [which] are also to be found in its internal contradictions'.[13] The discourse of 'European sovereignty' will sooner or later collide with the wall of state sovereignty, starting with France's. Beyond the fragility of an order susceptible to challenge by member states and their constitutional courts regarding the boundaries of national sovereignty, critics of the idea of European sovereignty point to the lack of clarity about whether it entails greater unity or further integration.[14]

Yet other scholars, drawing on the work of Jürgen Habermas and Neil MacCormick, have stressed the obsolete nature of traditional sovereignty, which they say is 'no longer capable of explaining the contemporary globalized world consisting of overlapping legal orders'.[15] They argue that this fragmentation requires a reinterpretation of the traditional conception of sovereignty towards a post-traditional one, 'severing the allegedly inherent link between State and sovereignty, as well as, consequently, that between sovereignty and territory. As a result, not only States as territorial entities are sovereign, but other functional entities, which exercise certain functions over designated fields, can be sovereign too.'[16]

This movement 'from singular to pluralist sovereignty' allows for the interpretation of the EU as a polity perfectly adapted to a post-sovereign world. And in fact, an accumulation of 'exclusive competences' – customs union, competition policy, trade policy, monetary policy for the euro-area states, fisheries – exercised under the Union's own legal order does seem to define 'a core of European sovereignty' whereby the 'Union takes on, at least for the competences entrusted to it, the shape of a federal state'.[17] Furthermore, these policies are financed by a 'significant budget' amounting to 1% of European GNP, to be doubled under the recovery plan agreed in July 2020 and financed by substantial European public debt.[18]

## A coming of age for the EU?

A prime objective of the post-war European project is peace based on the rejection of raw power. The failure of the European Defence Community in 1954 reinforced the point in effectively exempting Europe from providing for its external security, which during the Cold War was handed over to NATO. That development left the European Economic Community, set up in 1957, ample room to lay the foundations of peace among its six members. As former EU commissioner Pascal Lamy observed, 'the building of peace was the beating heart of the European project, designed to neutralize geopoliti-cal rivalries … to immunize its members against a relapse into a devastating will to power … and to live up to the legacy of the Enlightenment and its quest for perpetual peace'.[19]

The success of the European project fostered the belief that its model – based on taming national sovereignties, managing disputes through the rule of law, and economic and, increasingly, political integration – would be a road map for peace. A robust and efficient Atlantic Alliance supported by well-armed nation-states could contain the existential threat from the Soviet Union. Heralded as a triumph of the West, the end of the Cold War deepened the view that liberal values would prevail. Drawing on Alexandre Kojève's interpretation of G.W.F. Hegel, Francis Fukuyama explored the possibility of the convergence towards an order based on these values, boosted by free trade and globalisation, and guided by the rule of law. Strengthened by the Single European Act and the Maastricht Treaty, the EU seemed to be the appropriate vehicle, endowed with the capacity to shape the world order as a 'normative power' by leveraging access to its huge market and its regulatory clout.[20]

This outlook held up well into the first decade of the new century, as the countries freed by the collapse of the Soviet bloc joined the EU. But the expanding polity also came to be tested by a succession of mostly exog-enous crises, starting with the Balkan conflicts of the 1990s. Russia launched an offensive against Georgia in 2008. In 2014, Moscow failed to prevent Ukraine from establishing a closer relationship with the EU, met with a popular uprising, and in response annexed Crimea and covertly occupied parts of eastern Ukraine. To address the 2015 refugee crisis, the EU effectively outsourced the protection of some of the EU's external borders to a third country, Turkiye.

These successive shocks rocked the EU to its core, prompting a reappraisal of its fundamentals and postulates. As Daniel Fiott observed, the EU came to realise that it 'is more a product than a shaper of its strategic environment'.[21] Since the European project had been predicated from its beginning on a gradual erasing of borders among its members, its champions were inclined to consider them taboo. Outer boundaries too tended to 'blur in the limbo between civilization and barbarity, a never static line constantly extending eastward without a clear delineation'.[22] Many Europeans assumed Europeanisation to be 'the transposition by our neighbours of the European values into their political and legal norms, a force radiating outwards'.[23] This mindset has underpinned the EU's policy on enlargement and neighbourhood. But the European polity has now reached what historian John Pocock has called the 'Machiavellian moment' in which it must confront its 'temporary finitude' and attempt 'to remain morally and politically stable in a stream of irrational events'.[24] Thus, Hans Kribbe notes that Europeans are bidding farewell to the 'idea that the world will eventually become "as us"' in the realisation 'that it is not unipolar anymore, and organized around the West or its ideas, but around divergence, a deep divergence since there is no mechanism, no principle, no rules all parties can agree on'.[25]

The election of Donald Trump and his shambolic presidency further challenged Europe. After the 2017 NATO and G7 summits, Angela Merkel, then chancellor of Germany, stated that 'we Europeans truly have to take our fate into our own hands' and 'fight for our own future and destiny'.[26] China's growing assertiveness prompted the EU to assess it, in March 2019, as a 'systemic rival promoting alternative models of governance'.[27] One international-law scholar observed that the power of the notion of sovereignty 'comes from its capacity to express an important (although less-than-glorious) reality: the EU is in crisis and its very existence as a polity is at risk. The assumption that the European construction is in danger is omnipresent in the EU sovereignty discourse.'[28]

## A semantic and political conundrum

Before Macron ushered in the concept of European sovereignty in his Sorbonne speech, a more modest notion had appeared in the European discourse: strategic autonomy. Coined in 2013 to describe a goal for the European defence industry, it was used in the EU's 'global strategy' of 2016 to encompass security more broadly. A qualifying term – 'appropriate level' – left room for different interpretations.[29] Macron mentioned six fields in which the EU should tilt towards sovereignty: security and defence; borders and migration; Africa and the Mediterranean; sustainable development; digital technologies; and industrial, economic and monetary policy.

The idea of 'strategic sovereignty' has also arisen, initially in think tanks and later in official commentary.[30] The expression has figured prominently in the programme of the German 'traffic light' coalition. In a keynote speech at Charles University in Prague, German Chancellor Olaf Scholz gave it a casual, pragmatic cast: 'I am not interested in semantics here. European sovereignty essentially means that we become more autonomous in all areas.'[31] Christoph Heusgen, a long-time diplomatic adviser of Merkel's, disparaged the idea as 'presumptuous'.[32]

The proliferation of expressions reflects both aspiration and frustration. Many tools, procedures and institutions have been set up and concept papers written to allow the EU to become a more potent and capable actor in the international arena. Since the inception of the European Security and Defence Policy – triggered by the 1998 Franco-British Saint-Malo Declaration calling for the Union to acquire 'the capacity for autonomous action, backed up by credible military forces, the means to decide to use them, and a readiness to do so, in order to respond to international crises' – the EU has established the European Defence Agency (2004), the EU Battlegroups (2005), the European Defence Fund (2017), Permanent Structured Cooperation (2017), the European Intervention Initiative (2018), the Coordinated Annual Review on Defence (2019), the European Peace Facility (2021) and the Strategic Compass (2022).

Yet little of substance has been achieved. This is in part because the United States has been clever at clipping the Europeans' wings. But EU initiatives must also be assessed against the backdrop of shrinking defence budgets in Europe. The European defence effort is dwarfed by those of the world's major military powers – the US, China and Russia. In the assessment of Mark Leonard and Jeremy Shapiro, it is not only 'inadequate relative to Europe's security vulnerabilities' but also 'underfunded relative even to their original, fairly modest, ambitions'.[33] Duplication and fragmentation of the European defence efforts have left yawning gaps, presumptively filled by the United States, and sanctions have been the EU's hard-power instrument of choice. More crucially, 'processes are proposed, principles are articulated, instruments are updated, but the whole leaves an impression of floating in a political and strategic vacuum, from which power relations, antagonisms or fault lines between nations have been evacuated'.[34] Thus, notes Richard Youngs,

> in most instances, it is not an absence of capabilities that has held the EU back from acting autonomously in recent years. Rather, it is political choice … In this sense, the plea for strategic autonomy rests on a faulty core diagnosis. Most frequently, the geostrategic concern arises not from the EU lacking the capacity to act but from the way that the union chooses to use the capacities it does possess.[35]

In this context, 'strategic autonomy' has become suspicious code for an emancipation project of Europe from the US in the field of defence, or has been portrayed as a way for France to seize leadership within the EU after Brexit. 'Strategic sovereignty' might be perceived as more neutral, as it pertains to 'managing interdependencies in trade and critical supplies, of reframing strategic partnerships and sustaining the multilateral order that is under significant pressure'.[36]

Perhaps owing to the political baggage burdening both terms, the simpler notion of power seems to have discreetly crept into the discourse of the EU leadership. 'We must relearn the language of power and conceive of Europe as a top-tier geostrategic actor', opined EU High Representative for Foreign Affairs and Security Policy Josep Borrell. He was quite aware of Europe's ingrained weaknesses: 'we have plenty of levers of influence. Europe's problem is not a lack of power. The problem is the lack of political will for the aggregation of its powers to ensure their coherence and maximize their impact.'[37] Charles Michel, president of the European Council, has called for the EU to be 'a power working for a world that is more respectful, more ethical, and more just. Sovereignty, independence, empowerment … whichever word you use, it's the substance that counts. Less dependence, more influence.'[38]

Power, though hard to measure, has been clearly defined.[39] Raymond Aron called 'power on the international stage the ability of a polity to impose its will on other polities. Power is not an absolute, but a human relationship.' While security may be the primary rationale for power, Aron added, referring to Hobbes, other motivations also enter into play: 'polities crave strength not only to deter aggression … but also to be feared, respected, admired'.[40] More recently, Bart Szewczyk elucidated the difference between sovereignty, 'the independence and supremacy of decision', and power, 'a decision-maker's practical ability to control a particular outcome'.[41] From this angle, power is premised on sovereignty, and sovereignty without it is a hollow theoretical concept.

As the EU was shaped by the Second World War, and evolved through successive enlargements, the collapse of the Soviet bloc and the reunification of Germany, the Union is dense with pre-existing patterns of power. It includes states with different historical experiences, political cultures, demographic and economic weights, and therefore different national interests. It comprises one nuclear power that is also a permanent member of the Security Council, three economic powers that are members of the G7, 23 (soon 24) members of NATO, formerly neutral states that are suspicious of power, committed Atlanticists, smaller states with no particular strategic ambitions, and nations haunted by decades of Soviet occupation that apprehend Russia as an existential threat.

At the same time, the United States, though not part of the EU, is a major European power. This is not only on account of the Cold War, when its military presence formed the backbone of the continent's security, but also because it is an integral part of the current security balance. It took US intervention to extinguish the Balkan wars, and many NATO allies see the United States as the main bulwark against Russian aggression, as illustrated by Finland's and Sweden's rush to join the Alliance after Russia's invasion of Ukraine in 2022.

For decades, the constructive ambiguity ingrained in the European project enabled the EU to steer around intramural power competition and America's security pre-eminence. Still, other European states are reluctant to accept anything that might resemble *directoires* from Germany and France.[42] One of the most outspoken voices in this regard has been Polish Prime Minister Mateusz Morawiecki, who lashed out at France and Germany in an opinion piece:

> The equality of individual countries is of a declarative nature. Political practice has shown that the voice of Germany and France counts above all. Thus, we are dealing with a formal democracy and a de facto oligarchy, where power is held by the strongest. In addition, the strong ones make mistakes and are incapable of accepting criticism from outside.[43]

When 'European' and 'Atlantic' interests conflict, many European states are inclined to support the latter. The power differential between the United States and major European states is so overwhelming that there is no *directoire* from the former, simply leadership. NATO's decision-making procedures take care to maintain the appearance of sovereign equality, such that the control of the Alliance by a single political authority appears to guarantee reliability. For many Europeans, America is a 'power equaliser' that puts Europeans as a whole in a separate category, much more undifferentiated than would be the case in a genuinely independent Europe.[44]

This quasi-organic relationship with the United States cannot, of course, be explained solely in terms of internal balance among Europeans. Any substantial European political assertiveness also necessarily impacts the transatlantic distribution of power. Despite some semblance of flexibility, Washington has stifled European attempts to assert strategic or military autonomy whenever it has perceived any material risk to transatlantic ties. While European states profess a principled attachment to these ties, their strength varies from country to country; they do not all share the same assessment of the risk of damaging them. Over a decade after the end of the Iraq War, the scars of the transatlantic and intra-European rifts are still visible. The fact remains that, however perversely, the United States is a full-fledged European power while the EU is not. Any move by the EU towards developing significant independent power would mean a substantial alteration of its relationship with the US – an undertaking which few European nations, with the possible exception of France, are ready to initiate.

## Shared decision

Another limit to such an undertaking is the EU's decision-making process, whose complexity opens it to all sorts of influences. The system mixes elements of federalism and supranationalism, interweaves European and national levels, and maintains ongoing negotiation mechanisms in parallel. It also involves, alongside representatives of the member states, not only the European Parliament but also myriad lobbyists and pressure groups. While this pattern is typical of advanced democratic systems, decision-making is, in the EU cluster, extraordinarily fragmented. It is less diffuse in matters involving intergovernmental cooperation. In this realm, the member states, through the European Council and the Council of Ministers, remain the primary decision-makers at high political levels. But the large number of decision-makers, the premium placed on consensus, the links among different issues and the practical need to form coalitions make unity of decision and the political command over its execution – essential ingredients of power – elusive.

Further, the openness of the system to outside influence allows the United States, without any formal participation in deliberations, to weigh in heavily on decisions of interest to it. There is no shortage of EU member states willing, for their own reasons, to lend an ear, or even a voice, to American concerns. Such practices are not dishonourable per se, insofar as there is no coherent consensus on what constitutes a specifically 'European interest'. As Gabriel Robin observed two decades ago, 'it is a delusion to imagine that there is an obvious and unique European solution for every political issue'.[45] National interests do not smoothly resolve into European ones. Rather, each country strives to persuade others that its own political preferences best express that elusive interest.

This difficulty, inherent in the European project, is bound to worsen considerably with expanding membership. Since Russia invaded Ukraine, Ukraine and Moldova have become EU candidates, and the stalled candidacies of the Western Balkan countries have been restored to the EU's agenda. But the EU's decision-making mechanisms have not been radically rethought to offset the fragmentation effects of successive enlargements. And the idea of extending qualified majority voting in areas hitherto subject to unanimity, such as foreign affairs and defence,[46] would prompt some member states to raise issues of democratic legitimacy.[47]

In addition, there is no broad consensus on such fundamentals as the distribution of power between national and EU institutions. This area is replete with differing views, powered by the resurgence of populist nationalism especially during crises, such as the 2015 migration surge and the COVID-19 pandemic. While no EU member states have followed the United Kingdom's precedent of withdrawing from the Union, some, like Hungary and Poland, have challenged European institutions by violating their treaty obligations. 'Electoral accidents' have become commonplace, enabling once-outlying political parties to act against the shared European future and 'ever closer Union' the Lisbon Treaty calls for. These parties advocate a loose 'European alliance of nations' that is incompatible with the objective of European sovereignty. The September 2022 elections in Italy reinforced this trend and could galvanise extreme-right parties elsewhere. Such contingencies and uncertainties undermine the credibility of the EU as a power in world politics.

To counter these centrifugal forces, Macron has called for the creation of a 'common political culture', and major changes in decision-making processes are under discussion. The shock of Russia's invasion of Ukraine served to accelerate the maturation process and infused Europeans with a sense of threat unprecedented since the height of the Cold War. The need to act was felt so acutely as to prompt a remarkable mobilisation in a matter of days, with successive packages of sanctions against Russia and decisions to grant military and political support to Ukraine. Germany announced a 'historical turning point' (*Zeitenwende*) in its defence policy, while Sweden and Finland promptly applied for membership in NATO. After a referendum,

Denmark shed its opt-out status regarding the EU's Common Security and Defence Policy.

Another spectacular result, though not widely acknowledged as such, was the heightened role that European Commission President Ursula von der Leyen has assumed. She has made good on her commitment to deliver European leadership. In early April 2022, she was among the first Western leaders to visit the Ukrainian capital. Overriding German, French and Danish reservations, she succeeded in getting the EU to grant Ukraine and Moldova the EU-candidate status they coveted and to reboot the stalled application processes of the Western Balkan states. In her artful and savvy diplomacy, she seems to have understood better than any other European leader the imperative of Pocock's Machiavellian moment.[48] Even so, the jury is still out on whether perceived encroachments on the prerogatives of the member states will swing the pendulum back towards tension and discord.

*     *     *

The broader question is whether the EU can develop and retain authority of the same basic nature as the sovereignty a state exercises. The answer is almost certainly no. French political philosopher Julien Freund observed that 'sovereignty is an attribute of command, and therefore it is not a power of the state but a power that makes the state. It is inherent in the exercise of command.'[49] Vesting state-like power, in the sense of command, in Europe can have no other meaning than to entrust its exercise to a single political authority. That requisite transfer of sovereignty – even if each member state were to retain a residual right of secession – would change the nature of the Union too radically for virtually any contemporary European state to accept. Thus, European sovereignty is, fundamentally, a misnomer.

The EU, then, will remain unable to match the major powers, namely the US, China and Russia. But there may still be room for a more cohesive European polity with a more active role to play in international affairs. Establishing it, however, will not be easy. EU officials should, per Borrell's exhortation, 'speak the language of power' not only to outside interlocutors but also to the domestic constituencies within the Union. Oblique and tortuous semantic fiddling is confusing and unhelpful. They should make it clear that power, not autonomy or sovereignty, is the issue.

Europeans must also appreciate that the EU derives its greatest strength from its unwavering use of the prerogatives entrusted to its 'federal' institutions: the European Commission and the European Central Bank. But those prerogatives cover only part of an increasingly multifaceted power spectrum, falling short of hard power, which remains largely consigned to member states. Notwithstanding the cohesion they have displayed during the Russian war on Ukraine, their lack of unity and constancy weakens the EU's credibility as an autonomous actor for its own security in an ever more anarchic world arena. The Trump presidency was a serious wake-up call that cast doubt on the once-sacrosanct protection offered by the United States. Meanwhile, nativist populism has shaken American democracy to the core. The European polity cannot leave its fate to the contingencies of the US electoral cycle – or even to the Russian threat, which may divide it. Although the EU's 2009 Lisbon Treaty introduced a mutual-defence clause, the common defence it heralds remains a remote prospect, overshadowed by the powerful machinery of NATO. While theoretically possible, a federal leap in that respect appears, under normal circumstances and for all the reasons stated here, highly implausible in the foreseeable future.

Lastly, the very existence of the EU is premised on its fidelity to the values on which it was built: freedom, democracy and the rule of law. They provide its internal cohesion and undergird its capacity to act in support of peace, lawfulness and multilateralism. Straying from core values, as some states are inclined to do, jeopardises these features. To fulfil its mission, the EU must hold them accountable and require them to comply with their treaty commitments. Only then can it remain a viable alternative to lawlessness, arbitrariness and the rule of the strongest, and the beacon of hope it was meant to be.

## Acknowledgements

For their inspiring feedback on an earlier draft of this article, I would like to express my gratitude to Gérard Errera, Jean-Marie Guéhenno, Dick Howard, Maxime Lefebvre, Jean Picq and Pierre Vimont.

## Notes

1  Emmanuel Macron, 'A New
Initiative for Europe', speech at the
Sorbonne University, 26 September
2017, https://www.elysee.fr/en/
emmanuel-macron/2017/09/26/
president-macron-gives-speech-on-
new-initiative-for-europe.

2  Jean-Claude Juncker, 'The Hour
of European Sovereignty', State
of the Union 2018, 12 September
2018, https://ec.europa.eu/info/
priorities/state-union-speeches/
state-union-2018_en.

3  Jean Bodin, *Les six livres de la République*
(Paris: Fayard, 1986), pp. 217–18.

4  Winston Churchill, speech delivered at the University of Zurich,
19 September 1946, https://rm.coe.
int/16806981f3#:~:text=What%20is%20
this%20sovereign%20remedy,of%20
United%20States%20of%20Europe.

5  See European Court of Justice,
'Flaminio Costa v. E.N.E.L', Case
6-64, 15 July 1964, https://eur-lex.
europa.eu/legal-content/EN/
TXT/?uri=CELEX%3A61964CJ0006.
This primacy applied only to law, not
to national constitutions.

6  See Ernst Haas, *The Uniting of Europe:
Political, Social, and Economic Forces,
1950–1957* (Stanford, CA: Stanford
University Press, 1958).

7  See David P. Calleo, *Rethinking
Europe's Future* (Princeton, NJ:
Princeton University Press, 2003);
and Stanley Hoffmann, 'Obstinate or
Obsolete? The Fate of the Nation-state
and the Case of Western Europe',
*Daedalus*, vol. 93, no. 3, Summer
1966, pp. 862–915. In 1999, historian
Alan Milward delivered a compelling description of how the initial
aspiration to a post-national polity
shaped by functionalism yielded to
the pressure of the nation-state. See
Alan Milward, *The European Rescue
of the Nation State*, 2nd ed. (London:
Routledge, 1999).

8  Even the adoption of a single currency
under the Maastricht Treaty, through
which member states delegated monetary policy to a central bank, was a
transfer of competencies rather than
an abandonment of the national power
to mint money, which, like budgetary
and fiscal policy, formally remains in
the hands of national central banks.

9  In light of that transformation, 'neo-
functionalism' has been renamed
'post-functionalism'. See Liesbet
Hooghe and Gary Marks, 'A
Postfunctionalist Theory of European
Integration: From Permissive
Consensus to Constraining', *British
Journal of Political Science*, vol. 39, no. 1,
January 2009, pp. 1–23.

10  Christina Eckes, 'EU Autonomy:
Jurisdictional Sovereignty by a
Different Name?', *European Papers*,
vol. 5, no. 1, 2020, p. 320.

11  Ségolène Barbou des Places,
'Taking the Language of "European
Sovereignty" Seriously', *European
Papers*, vol. 5, no. 1, 2020, p. 290.

12  Hans Kundnani, 'Europe's
Sovereignty Conundrum', *Berlin
Policy Journal*, 13 May 2020,
https://berlinpolicyjournal.com/
europes-sovereignty-conundrum/.

13  Nicolas Leron, 'Les faux-semblants de
la souveraineté européenne', *Esprit*,
May 2019, p. 112.

14   It is also unclear whether European sovereignty requires amending the treaties, an issue on which Juncker was more cautious than Macron.

15   Thomas Verellen, 'European Sovereignty Now? A Reflection on What It Means to Speak of "European Sovereignty"', *European Papers*, vol. 5, no. 1, 2020, p. 309. For background, see Jürgen Habermas, *Zur Verfassung Europas: Ein Essay* (Frankfurt: Suhrkamp Verlag, 2011), published in translation as *The Crisis of the European Union* (Berlin: Wiley, 2012); and Neil MacCormick, *Questioning Sovereignty: Law, State and Practical Reason* (Oxford: Oxford University Press, 1999).

16   Matej Avbelj, 'A Sovereign Europe as a Future of Sovereignty', *European Papers*, vol. 5, no. 1, 2020, p. 300.

17   Maxime Lefebvre, 'Europe as a Power, European Sovereignty, Strategic Autonomy: A Debate that Is Moving Towards an Assertive Europe', *European Issues*, no. 582, 1 February 2021, https://www.robert-schuman.eu/en/european-issues/0582-europe-as-a-power-european-sovereignty-strategic-autonomy-a-debate-that-is-moving-towards-an.

18   See *ibid*.

19   Pascal Lamy, 'Union européenne: vous avez dit souveraineté?', *Commentaire*, no. 169, Spring 2020, https://eduscol.education.fr/document/29809/download.

20   See Anu Bradford, *The Brussels Effect: How the European Union Rules the World* (New York: Oxford University Press, 2020).

21   Daniel Fiott (ed.), 'European Sovereignty: Strategy and Interdependence', *Chaillot Paper*, no.

169, July 2021, p. 37, https://www.iss.europa.eu/sites/default/files/EUISSFiles/CP_169.pdf.

22   *Ibid*.

23   *Ibid*.

24   John Pocock, *The Machiavellian Moment: Florentine Political Thought and the Atlantic Republican Tradition* (Princeton, NJ: Princeton University Press, 2016), p. viii.

25   'L'Europe face à la puissance, une conversation avec Hans Kribbe', *Le Grand Continent*, 15 February 2021, https://legrandcontinent.eu/fr/2021/02/15/leurope-face-a-la-puissance-une-conversation-avec-hans-kribbe. See also Hans Kribbe, *The Strongmen: European Encounters with Sovereign Power* (Montreal: McGill-Queen's University Press, 2020).

26   Giulia Paravicini, 'Angela Merkel: Europe Must Take "Our Fate" into Own Hands', *Politico*, 28 May 2017, https://www.politico.eu/article/angela-merkel-europe-cdu-must-take-its-fate-into-its-own-hands-elections-2017/.

27   European Commission, 'EU–China Strategic Outlook: Commission and HR/VP Contribution to the European Council', 12 March 2019, p. 1, https://ec.europa.eu/info/publications/eu-china-strategic-outlook-commission-contribution-european-council-21-22-march-2019_de.

28   Barbou des Places, 'Taking the Language of "European Sovereignty" Seriously', p. 292.

29   European Union, 'Shared Vision, Common Action: A Stronger Europe – A Global Strategy for the European Union's Foreign and Security Policy', June 2016, p. 4. While 'strategic autonomy' was over time used with

broader scope, it was further qualified in the wake of the pandemic outbreak. 'Open strategic autonomy' was meant to account for the need to act in concert with partners across the board, especially in the fields of economy and trade, without resorting to protectionism.

30 Fiott, 'European Sovereignty', p. 8. See also Suzana Anghel, 'Strategic Sovereignty for Europe', European Parliamentary Research Service Ideas Paper, September 2020, https://www.europarl.europa.eu/RegData/etudes/BRIE/2020/652069/EPRS_BRI(2020)652069_EN.pdf; and Mark Leonard and Jeremy Shapiro, 'Empowering EU Member States with Strategic Sovereignty', European Council on Foreign Relations Paper 289, June 2019, https://ecfr.eu/wp-content/uploads/1_Empowering_EU_member_states_with_strategic_sovereignty.pdf.

31 Olaf Scholz, 'Europe Is Our Future', speech at Charles University, Prague, 29 August 2022, https://www.bundesregierung.de/breg-en/news/scholz-speech-prague-charles-university-2079558.

32 Christoph Heusgen, 'It's Presumptuous to Talk About European Sovereignty', *Internationale Politik Quarterly*, 6 January 2022, https://ip-quarterly.com/en/its-presumptuous-talk-about-european-sovereignty.

33 Leonard and Shapiro, 'Empowering EU Member States with Strategic Sovereignty'.

34 Pierre Vimont, 'Les intérêts stratégiques de l'Union européenne', Le Rapport Schuman sur l'Europe, l'état de l'Union 2016, pp. 109–10.

35 Richard Youngs, 'The EU's Strategic Autonomy Trap', Carnegie Europe, 8 March 2021, https://carnegieeurope.eu/2021/03/08/eu-s-strategic-autonomy-trap-pub-83955.

36 Fiott, 'European Sovereignty', p. 2.

37 Josep Borrell, 'Embracing Europe's Power', Project Syndicate, 8 February 2020, https://www.project-syndicate.org/commentary/embracing-europe-s-power-by-josep-borrell-2020-02.

38 Charles Michel, 'Strategic Autonomy for Europe, the Aim of Our Generation', speech at the Bruegel think tank, European Council, 28 September 2020, https://www.consilium.europa.eu/en/press/press-releases/2020/09/28/l-autonomie-strategique-europeenne-est-l-objectif-de-notre-generation-discours-du-president-charles-michel-au-groupe-de-reflexion-bruegel/.

39 Some might question how the EU can aspire to act as a power as such if the very constraining of power – specifically that of France, Germany and the United States – is intrinsic to the European project. Macron's call for European sovereignty inevitably revived these lingering suspicions. European states are quick to surmise that behind French calls for a powerful Europe is a desire to shape Europe as 'France writ large'. De Gaulle famously likened Europe to a lever by which France could avoid being dominated by the US and Russia.

40 Raymond Aron, *Paix et guerre entre les nations* (Paris: Calmann-Lévy, 1962), pp. 82–3.

41 Bart Szewczyk, *European Sovereignty, Legitimacy, and Power* (London: Routledge, 2021), p. 3.

42  Lefebvre, 'Europe as a Power, European Sovereignty, Strategic Autonomy'.

43  Mateusz Morawiecki, 'Historical Challenges and False Directions for Europe at the Crossroads', EURACTIV, 8 August 2022, https://www.euractiv.com/section/europe-s-east/opinion/historical-challenges-and-false-directions-for-europe-at-the-crossroads/.

44  See Nicole Gnesotto, *La puissance et l'Europe* (Paris: Presses de Sciences Po, 1998).

45  Gabriel Robin, *Entre empire et nations: penser la politique étrangère* (Paris: Odile Jacob, 2004).

46  This was requested in a resolution adopted by the European Parliament on 9 June 2022. The Conference on the Future of Europe has made a similar request, Borrell has actively supported the idea and Scholz advocated it in his Charles University speech.

47  The day after the outcomes of the Conference on the Future of Europe were made public, 13 member states, mainly from Eastern, Central and Northern Europe, cautioned against 'unconsidered and premature attempts to launch a process towards treaty change'. They also emphasised that the EU had demonstrated, during crises including the Ukrainian one, its ability to deliver within the current treaty framework. See 'Non-paper by Bulgaria, Croatia, the Czech Republic, Denmark, Estonia, Finland, Latvia, Lithuania, Malta, Poland, Romania, Slovenia, and Sweden on the Outcome of and Follow-up to the Conference on the Future of Europe', Europa, 9 May 2022, https://www.europa-nu.nl/9353000/1/j4nvih7l3k-b91rw_j9vvj9idsjo4xr6/vlstn1p5intb/f=/non_paper.pdf.

48  See Matina Stevis-Gridneff, 'Top E.U. Official Is Becoming an Unexpected Wartime Leader', *New York Times*, 14 September 2022, https://www.nytimes.com/2022/09/14/world/europe/eu-ursula-von-der-leyen-russia-war.html.

49  Julien Freund, *L'essence du politique*, 3rd ed. (Paris: Dalloz, 2003), p. 127.

# The Energy Transition, Protectionism and Transatlantic Relations

## Nicholas Crawford

Over the past two years, relations between the European Union and United States have improved dramatically. President Joe Biden's deft handling of the transatlantic relationship since January 2021 has contrasted starkly with Donald Trump's confrontational approach. Biden's team has resolved some long-standing US–EU disputes, rallied NATO and the EU in defending Ukraine against Russian aggression, and worked to more closely align European allies and the United States on China.

Among the many issues on which Trump clashed with his European counterparts was climate change and the energy transition. Most pointedly, he scrapped the United States' commitment to the Paris Agreement on climate change and its goal of keeping global warming below 2 degrees Celsius. One of Biden's first actions as president was to rejoin the agreement. Later in 2021, he announced that the United States would target net-zero carbon emissions by 2050, in line with Europe's goals. This augured well for US–EU cooperation in this field.

The energy transition has, however, again emerged as a source of transatlantic tension in the wake of Congress's passage of the Inflation Reduction Act of 2022 (IRA), which offers a huge raft of subsidies for the United States' clean-energy industries. With this act, the United States is finally getting as serious as the EU about transition policy, but it also marks a new divergence in their approaches. To many Europeans, the enormous scale

**Nicholas Crawford** is IISS Research Associate for Geo-economics and Strategy.

**Survival** | vol. 65 no. 2 | April–May 2023 | pp. 75–102        https://doi.org/10.1080/00396338.2023.2193101

of the IRA subsidies, and controversial discriminatory measures in favour of domestic manufacturing, threaten the competitiveness of Europe's own clean-energy industries.

Warnings that the IRA could cause a new trade war between the United States and the EU and undermine Biden's rapprochement with Europe are overblown, however. The IRA's impact on EU industry will fall far short of the damage that some EU leaders have claimed will ensue. And the EU is unlikely to retaliate with a subsidy package that resembles anything like the IRA.

## Geopolitical internationalism, geo-economic nationalism

Climate change and the energy transition have been important in the realignment of the United States and its allies in Europe since 2021. Besides rejoining the Paris Agreement and setting the 2050 net-zero goal, the Biden administration has set several ambitious targets for the deployment of renewables.

However, the energy transition places a strain on the industrial competitiveness of any advanced economy and introduces new economic-security concerns. Europe and the United States are determined, for instance, to ensure that cutting emissions does not allow imports from more fossil-fuel-friendly countries to undercut domestic industry. Furthermore, like allied governments in Europe, the Biden team is resolved to break the United States' dependence on China for many of the clean-energy technologies and critical minerals required to achieve the transition. The EU and United States want to secure a share of these green-technology industries for themselves.

The energy transition therefore increases the pull of protectionism and presents a stern test of Europe's and the United States' ability to reconcile their economic self-interests with their internationalist foreign policies. The EU has wrestled with this challenge since launching its Emissions Trading System in 2005. It proposes now to introduce a carbon-border-adjustment mechanism to put imports to the bloc on a level playing field with goods produced under the Emissions Trading System, and although ostensibly protectionist, the EU has carefully calibrated this policy in an attempt to comply with international trade law.

Many Americans, including some in the administration, have advocated a 'friend-shoring' policy in clean-energy industries as a way of reconciling geopolitical internationalism with the United States' economic-security needs.[1] By requiring the US to work with allies, such a policy would help to diversify manufacturing and critical-mineral supply chains away from China without invoking protectionist measures. The policy would not, however, guarantee that the United States would be the main source of its own energy-transition resources or technologies.

But the Biden administration has an additional goal. After two decades of erosion in US manufacturing, with the loss of many jobs to China, the Biden administration wants to use the energy transition – and its wider foreign- and economic-security policies – to rebuild US manufacturing industries and create new middle-class jobs. Rather than friend-shoring, Biden's team and many in Congress are therefore determined to advance the transition by way of a 'reshoring' policy that brings manufacturing home. This is central to Biden's 'foreign policy for the middle class'.[2]

The IRA, passed in August, is the cornerstone of the Biden administration's effort to build a domestic clean-energy industry.[3] It provides for at least $369 billion in tax incentives for renewables and clean fuels to ensure that the value chain for these sectors is increasingly located within the United States. The act also includes several protectionist measures, including bonus tax credits for investors and manufacturers that use US-made equipment and materials, and a substantial consumer tax credit exclusively for electric vehicles assembled in North America with battery components and critical minerals sourced in North America or economies with which the United States has a free-trade agreement (which do not include the EU).[4]

The IRA therefore rankles with the EU, among other economies, on two levels. Firstly, through its subsidies for manufacturing clean-energy technologies and for mining and refining critical minerals in the United States, the Biden administration is using taxpayer money to skew production costs to the United States' advantage and Europe's disadvantage. Secondly, insofar as businesses and consumers receive smaller tax credits if they purchase clean-energy technologies or critical minerals from Europe, the administration is tilting purchase costs in the United States' favour too. Overall, therefore, the IRA appears to distort international trade even with allies, and to redirect investment away from Europe's clean-energy industries and towards the United States'.

In a meeting with US lawmakers in November 2022, French President Emmanuel Macron described the IRA as 'super-aggressive' towards European companies.[5] Issues around the IRA also prompted Thierry Breton, EU commissioner for internal market, to pull out of the second summit of the US–EU Trade and Technology Council, the forum in which the United States and EU meet to align policy on their economic security and trade relations with China.[6] Macron has warned that the IRA and other recent economic legislation, including the US CHIPS and Science Act, risk fragmenting the West.[7] One European commissioner has even suggested that the IRA could push Europe back towards a friendlier relationship with China.[8]

In the United States, several prominent voices have argued that the Biden administration is undermining its internationalist, alliance-building foreign policy with a nationalist, protectionist economic policy.[9] In their view, the IRA could undermine the US government's efforts to repair the damage Trump has done to transatlantic relations. Some have gone as far as to warn that the IRA could precipitate a new US–EU trade war, less than two years after the two sides resolved their long-running Airbus–Boeing dispute.[10]

The Biden administration and many US liberals do appear to be comfortable with discarding the rules of international trade, on the basis that 'globalization didn't work'.[11] In their eyes, globalisation's role in the United States' widening income inequality and the erosion of US manufacturing overshadows its contribution, over three decades, to keeping inflation low, maintaining steady Western GDP growth and raising living standards around the world. Instead, they claim that the World Trade Organization (WTO) should adapt to the United States' new proclivity for protectionism, even though the US has argued for decades that every country must follow the rules.[12] US Trade Representative Katherine Tai has advised the EU to respond to the IRA by introducing more subsidies itself.[13]

Following meetings with Macron in November 2022, Biden pledged to 'tweak' the IRA, but there is very little scope to do so. Every measure is written into the bill's text and can only be amended through a new congressional bill, for which there is no political appetite. Concessions to European industry are hardly a vote-winner for any US politician. Following the November 2022 midterm elections, the House of Representatives is now under the control of an 'America First' Republican Party, which makes concessions less likely still. The US government and the EU have established a joint Task Force on the Inflation Reduction Act, but it will only be able to look at the application of the act's rules and negotiate additional measures outside the scope of the IRA.

At the philosophical level, Biden's geopolitical internationalism and geo-economic nationalism clash. The IRA blatantly flouts international trade law, undermining the administration's claimed commitment to uphold the international order and the rule of law. There was already daylight between the United States and Europe in the international legal realm, with the US continuing to block appointments to the WTO Appellate Body, forcing the EU to work with other major economies to establish the Multi-Party Interim Appeal Arbitration Arrangement. The IRA widens the gap.

At a practical level, however, the IRA is unlikely to do severe harm to the administration's relationship with the EU or its internationalist approach in other areas. The IRA's impact in Europe will fall far short of European fears, which have gained amplitude due to the initial buzz around the act, the apparent scale of the subsidies and signals from companies about making new investments in the United States. Economic analyses of the IRA's impact on European industry only began to appear on desks in European economic ministries in February 2023, long after the early commotion. Despite sugges-tions that Brussels would respond with a subsidy package to rival the IRA's, potentially triggering a subsidy war, the measures it eventually agrees will be more limited, mainly repackaging existing funds and modestly adjust-ing state-aid rules. The IRA will not drive a wedge between Europe and the United States. In fact, a booming clean-energy industry on both sides of the Atlantic will benefit both.

## Four reasons not to worry

The European Commission and various EU member states have sounded the alarm about the impact of the IRA on European industry. But European industry has drummed up much of the concern to induce European governments to dole out more generous subsidies and back down on other policies they dislike. Perhaps the most prominent intervention has come from the chief executive of Iberdrola, one of Europe's largest power companies. He argued that while the United States passed the IRA, European governments were sowing uncertainty for renewables investors by discussing a tax on windfall profits made by companies like Iberdrola during the continent's energy crisis.[14] Yet Iberdrola has continued to invest heavily in Europe. Other industry leaders have called for more support as well, but such self-interested reactions are hardly surprising.[15] Some EU politicians may also be deliberately overstating their forecasts of the IRA's impact to corral EU members into advocating more interventionist policies that they, the politicians, had already favoured.[16]

In theory, the IRA's generous subsidies could distort trade in clean-energy equipment, offer an advantage to the United States' energy-intensive industries, and draw investors away from Europe's own clean-energy and energy-intensive industries. The challenge is to assess whether, which and how much European industries are likely to be affected. By looking at each affected industry, it is possible to get a clearer view of the extent of the IRA's effects. Reasons emerge for Europe not to worry.

*Reason 1: local production for local markets*
Electric vehicle (EV) manufacturing is one of the industries for which the IRA's support is most controversial. In large part, this is due to the requirement that many of the components and critical minerals used in the EVs be sourced from the United States or countries with which it has free-trade agreements. Apparently to the surprise of Democratic Senator Joe Manchin – one of the architects of the IRA – the EU has no free-trade agreement with the United States.

However, EV manufacturing is one of several industries in which products for the US market would have been made predominantly in North America once they reached scale, irrespective of the IRA. Large European automotive companies already manufacture models that sell best in North America. BMW Group has a major production plant in South Carolina; Mercedes-Benz has plants in Alabama, Michigan, North Carolina and

South Carolina; and Volkswagen Group has plants in Tennessee and Mexico. Volkswagen announced that production of the EV that sells best in the United States would begin at its Tennessee plant before the IRA was passed. BMW's plans for a new plant in Mexico also preceded the passage of the IRA.[17] The determinative factor in both decisions was not favourable federal law but rather sufficient US demand. Only cars that sell at low volumes (including the most expensive models) were likely to be produced in Europe for export to the United States, and that remains the case for high-end EVs after the IRA.[18]

Likewise, European automotive firms were bound to use Canadian-, Mexican- or US-made batteries for EVs sold in North America once demand reached a large enough scale, with or without the IRA. As McKinsey & Company, the consultancy, has reported, not having battery manufacturing close to car-making creates significant supply-chain risks.[19] Currently, batteries are often manufactured in Asia and transported to Europe and North America for installation in vehicles, but this is symptomatic of the relatively small scale of EV sales thus far. With growing demand for EVs, battery makers are already springing up closer to EV markets in Europe and North America. Both continents already host homegrown battery makers – Northvolt in Europe and iM3NY in the United States – and Asian giants of the industry. Envision AESC, LG Energy Solution, Samsung SDI and SK On all have operational plants in both Europe and the United States, and Panasonic and Tesla will within a couple of years.

The same holds for wind-turbine manufacturing. Europe's two largest wind-turbine makers, Vestas and Siemens Gamesa, already produce wind-turbine blades, nacelles and steel towers in the United States, which accounts for at least 70% of wind-turbine capital expenditure, because transatlantic shipment of these large parts is difficult. The third-biggest European wind-turbine brand, Nordex SE, produces parts for its US installations in Mexico, and will be affected, but the European industry overall probably will not. The IRA could prompt all three European firms to establish new or expanded manufacturing in the United States to their benefit; the additional production would not eat into markets served by their European plants.

*Reason 2: Europe's small role in some industries*

The second reason that the IRA will have limited impact on Europe is that, in several industries targeted by the IRA, Europe simply plays a very small role. This is true of solar-power equipment, geothermal-power equipment, and the mining and refining of critical minerals.

In the value chain for the solar-power industry, European manufacturers have a significant market share for only two segments – the manufacture of inverters, which allow solar farms to feed into the electricity grid, and the production of polysilicon, the basic material for photovoltaic cells. Europe plays almost no part in the other segments of the value chain, including the manufacture of photovoltaic cells and modules, silicon wafers, trackers and racking structures. In those segments where European manufacturers play a substantial part, the IRA's impact will not be big. Inverters account for only around 6% and polysilicon 2.5% of the cost of a solar farm, excluding installation and freight costs.[20] Under the terms of the IRA, solar developers in the United States need to source 75% of the components and materials (by value) from the United States to receive the domestic-content bonus credit, so European suppliers should remain competitive. US solar developers' priority will be sourcing photovoltaic modules and cells, electrical equipment and racking from within the United States.

Europe does not play a major role in the geothermal value chain either. There are no major EU-based companies that produce electrical submersible pumps or cooling towers; the main industry players are based in the United States.[21] There are important European generator and turbine makers, but they have supplied very few US geothermal plants, instead focusing on markets in Europe, the Middle East and Asia. US geothermal plants have mostly deployed generators and turbines made in the United States or Israel.[22] The only equipment the US frequently imports from Europe are heat exchangers, but these account for just 8% of the equipment costs.[23] US geothermal developers only need to source 40–55% of their manufactured components from the United States to benefit from the domestic-content bonuses, depending on the specific tax credit.[24]

Similarly, the EU currently has a minuscule share of the critical-minerals industry, and was never likely to export these resources to the United States.

The US has much larger identified resources than Europe, and for some time has been moving ahead faster with new mining and refining projects. Currently, Europe produces no cobalt or rare earths.[25] Norway has recently discovered substantial offshore rare-earth resources, but it will be a long time before it or any other European country can mine them at commercial scale.[26] Europe has 5.1 megatons of the 98 MT of lithium resources identified worldwide, and there are plans for lithium mines in Spain and Finland, but Portugal is the only European country to produce the mineral currently, accounting for less than 0.5% of global production in 2022.[27] In graphite too, Europe is a minor player. It produces almost no synthetic graphite currently and, despite ramping up production, will yield just 0.2 MT in 2025 compared to anticipated global production of 5 MT that year.[28] The EU, Norway and Ukraine together account for just 1% of global natural-graphite mining as well.[29]

Although it has trumpeted its plans for critical-mineral production, the European Commission acknowledges that Europe is fated to be a net importer of these materials. Commission officials recognise that, at best, it might supply 30% of EU demand for critical minerals from within the bloc by 2030.[30] The US is much richer in these resources. While it too will probably remain a net importer, a growing share of the United States' supply will be from Australia, Canada and Latin America rather than China, and certainly not from the EU.

*Reason 3: enough demand to go around*

The huge demand in both Europe and the United States for clean-energy technologies and clean fuels suggests that the IRA's distortion of trade and investment will be limited. The European market will absorb most of what European industry can produce, and the US market will do likewise for what the US industry can produce. There is no big need to trade across the Atlantic, and there will be plenty of opportunities for clean-energy investors to profit on both sides of the pond.

Meeting the EU's targets for deployment of renewables alone will be an enormous challenge for Europe's clean-energy industry. By 2030, the European Commission wants the bloc to almost quadruple its 2020 solar-photovoltaic capacity;[31] almost triple its 2021 wind-power capacity;[32] increase the number of zero-emission vehicles on the road from 2.9 million in 2022 to 30m in 2030;[33] and produce 10m tonnes of renewable hydrogen.[34] Producing that hydrogen will require the installation of 90–120 gigawatts of electrolysers, up from a capacity of less than 1 GW in 2022.[35] If Europe gets anywhere close to these targets, European clean-energy companies will have ample opportunity to expand.

The Biden administration, like the European Commission, has ambitious plans for the uptake of renewables and EVs. They include the addition of 30 GW of solar-photovoltaic capacity in 2021–25 and 60 GW per year in 2026–30,[36] 3–4 GW of offshore wind per year to reach 30 GW by 2030,[37] and 3.5 GW per year for five years to 2026.[38] It also expects 50% of new vehicles to be zero-emissions vehicles by 2030.[39] Furthermore, the energy-storage industry intends to add 100 GW of storage capacity in 2020–30.[40] The United States is currently a net importer of many clean-energy technologies, mainly from Asia, so it will be a huge challenge for the country to fully substitute for these imports.

Unsurprisingly, several companies in Europe announced new plans to invest in the United States following the passage of the IRA. After years of uncertainty about American policies on energy transition, the United States has suddenly become a more attractive place to invest in clean energy, imbuing investors with confidence that there will be demand for clean-energy and upstream technologies and materials. If Europe's firmer demand for clean energy had tilted the balance in its favour, the IRA may have tilted it slightly back towards the United States. But Europe remains an attractive destination for clean-energy investments alongside the United States.

### Reason 4: constraints on US industry

For all the subsidies the US government can provide, there will be limits to the speed at which US clean-energy industries can grow. The United States also has certain disadvantages compared with Europe. Together, these factors make it unlikely that the IRA will crowd out investment in Europe's clean-energy industry to the extent that some suggest.

Like most economies, the US faces a gap between supply and demand for skilled labour for the energy transition.[41] The IRA makes the employment and training of apprentices a condition for many of its tax benefits, and the Department of Energy has introduced pilot skills programmes such as its $5m 'Lithium-Battery Workforce Initiative'.[42] Nevertheless, it will take years for labour supply to catch up with demand. Relatedly, salaries in the renewables industry are 40% higher in the United States than they are in Europe.[43] Labour costs, though not the biggest expense for a clean-energy developer or equipment manufacturer, still matter. In addition, US equipment manufacturers are likely to face bottlenecks due to the unavailability of the necessary materials. The IRA provides credits for critical-mineral production, but it usually takes years for new mining and refining projects to come on stream.

The United States also has a higher weighted-average cost of capital (WACC) than much of Europe. The central-bank base rate in the United States currently stands at 4.5–4.75%, compared to 3.00–3.25% in the European Monetary Union. The IRA will reduce the risk profile of fledgling clean-energy projects in the United States. But even for utility-scale solar-photovoltaic projects – a relatively mature industry – post-tax WACC stood at 2.6–4.3% in Europe compared to 3.3–5.0% in the United States in 2020.[44] Given that WACC can constitute 20–50% of the levelised cost of energy for renewables projects, the difference affords Europe a material advantage over the United States, and will do so for as long as European Central Bank rates are substantially lower than the Federal Reserve's.[45]

## One reason to worry, a bit

For the US–EU dispute, the IRA's most consequential subsidy is the Clean Hydrogen Production Tax Credit.[46] It is extraordinarily generous and targets an industry that has been a political priority for the European Commission and several EU member states. Clean hydrogen and its derivatives are expected to be crucial in reducing the emissions of Europe's energy-intensive industries and long-distance transport. The IRA provision has fed anxiety about European de-industrialisation, with Europe's energy-intensive industries fearing for their competitiveness.[47] While this worry predates the IRA by several years, soaring energy prices in Europe in the wake of Russia's invasion of Ukraine have exacerbated it.[48] Especially exposed to rising energy prices are Germany's chemical, steel, aluminium and paper industries, whose competitiveness was built, in part, on decades of cheap coal and gas. In October 2022, German chemical giant BASF announced the permanent downsizing of its European operations, pointing out that energy prices in Europe were five to six times those in the United States.[49]

Part of Europe's answer to these concerns has been to press ahead faster with the production and adoption of green hydrogen. Although European governments acknowledge that the region will be a net importer of hydrogen in the long run, it aims to encourage enough domestic clean-hydrogen production through the 2020s to get the industrial adoption of hydrogen under way. Since 2021, the European Commission has approved around €17.9bn in funding for the hydrogen industry, including €10.6bn in state aid through its Important Projects of Common European Interest scheme, at least another €5.1bn from its Recovery and Resilience Fund, €1.2bn for its Clean Hydrogen Partnership and €1bn from the EU Innovation Fund.[50] The German government has budgeted €900m for its international hydrogen procurement as well.[51]

Europe thus hopes to be at the forefront of commercialising technologies for producing clean hydrogen (electrolysers), converting it into other clean fuels, and transporting it and its derivatives; and using hydrogen and clean fuels in energy-intensive industries, aviation, shipping and heavy-goods road transport. The EU's fear is that the IRA could undermine these plans, with the effects felt not only by the green-hydrogen and ancillary industries but also downstream in energy-intensive industries. With IRA subsidies of up to $3 per kilogram of clean hydrogen, the cost of clean-hydrogen production in the US could be cut immediately by almost 80%.[52] In fact, as the US Department of Energy is targeting clean-hydrogen production from renewables at just $1/kgH2 by 2031,[53] the new subsidies could bring production costs below zero.[54] Producing clean hydrogen in the United States is likely to be much more profitable than producing it in Europe, encouraging investors to shift from Europe to the US. The US company Plug Power, an industry leader across the hydrogen ecosystem, expects green-hydrogen production to be the segment of its business with the highest gross margin by 2026.[55] Combined with other IRA credits, the subsidy could have knock-on effects for ancillary and downstream industries too. The availability of cheap hydrogen is likely to boost US demand for fuel cells – especially those made in the United States, thanks to the added 10% tax incentive for purchasing fuel cells made domestically.[56] US fuel-cell makers will further benefit from a 30% investment credit on new manufacturing facilities.[57]

However, there are limits to the subsidy's impact on Europe's hydrogen industry. Firstly, demand from industry for clean hydrogen is likely to grow more slowly in the United States than in Europe. Incentives to make the switch to clean energy are weaker in the United States than they are in Europe. Fossil fuels remain relatively cheap in America, there is no US-wide carbon tax or emissions-trading scheme, and refitting plants to use hydrogen comes at considerable cost.

*Fossil fuels remain relatively cheap in America*

Secondly, the IRA subsidy does not discriminate against European electrolyser manufacturers, which could supply some of the United States' demand for the technology. As US developers will probably buy up a larger share of the electrolysers built in the United States, there may be enhanced export opportunities elsewhere in the world for Europe-based electrolyser makers.

Thirdly, the IRA's Clean Hydrogen Production Tax Credit is expected to expire in 2032.[58] This is roughly when the industry is forecast to mature and commercialise. Thereafter, although the costs of producing green hydrogen will always be lower in the United States, Europe and the US will be on a more level playing field.[59] Until around that time, the US Treasury is supposed to expend $13.1bn to support clean hydrogen under the IRA, and $8bn under the 2021 Infrastructure Investment and Jobs Act.[60] European governments' assistance to the hydrogen industry will be comparable, though it will extend to the manufacture of electrolysers and fuel cells, and the industrial adoption of hydrogen, as well hydrogen production itself. The disparity between US and European support for the industry may not be as large as claimed. The European Commission's planned €900m hydrogen auction –

the first of several – is likely to be a particularly effective tool to encourage continued investment in Europe's hydrogen industry.[61]

Fourthly, the IRA could actually help the EU meet its goal of importing 10 MT/year of hydrogen by 2030 as the United States will be producing cheaper clean hydrogen than any other country. It also presents an opportunity for Europe and the United States to collaborate on projects to ship hydrogen and its derivatives, accelerating the commercial maturation of hydrogen and clean-fuel transportation. Initiatives of this kind may constitute the best way for Europe and the United States to resolve their disagreements over the IRA.[62]

In the long term, Europe may indeed suffer the loss of some energy-intensive industries. The best guarantors of cheap clean energy for industry will be a year-round abundance of solar and wind resources, and less competition between population centres and industry for renewable electricity. Companies in energy-intensive sectors will have to work out whether to move renewable energy (such as hydrogen or its derivatives) from overseas markets to use in European industry, or whether European industry should move overseas towards cheaper clean energy. The chemical industry may end up overseas; others like steel and cement may remain. It will not be the IRA that determines the matter either way.

### No subsidy war, no trade war

Although the reality of the IRA may not be so awful, Europe's incendiary rhetoric has raised the spectre of a trade war. European Commission President Ursula von der Leyen has called for a 'European Sovereignty Fund'.[63] The head of the European Parliament's Committee on International Trade has suggested that the EU bring a legal case against the United States before the WTO.[64] And Macron has revived his idea of a 'Buy European Act' and argued that the EU should reserve its subsidies for European manufacturers.[65]

EU leaders have, however, threatened much more than they are likely to deliver. There are major obstacles to the introduction of big new spending packages on clean-energy industries in Europe at both the national and the EU level. The EU is already meting out generous support for clean-energy industries through a constellation of instruments that includes the Innovation

Fund, the Just Transition Fund, REPowerEU, InvestEU, and the Recovery and Resilience Facility. The European Commission approved €51bn in aid schemes in 2022 alone.[66] The mechanisms the EU uses are different from the United States', but they reflect the political and economic possibilities and realities of a multinational bloc. The same realities will prove an obstacle to replicating the IRA or pursuing anything close to a US–EU trade war.

*Moving old money around*

In February 2023, the European Commission circulated the first draft of its response to the IRA, titled 'A Green Deal Industrial Plan for the Net-Zero Age'. It contains – quite wisely – many uncontroversial proposals focusing on reducing impediments to the bloc's energy transition that have little to do with the IRA, but should make Europe's clean-energy industries more attractive to investors. However, it also suggests increased public funding for Europe's clean-energy industries through two more controversial measures.

Firstly, the European Commission has suggested loosening the EU's state-aid rules to 1) allow EU member states to simplify aid, including eliminating open tenders in some cases; 2) permit national governments to offer investment tax incentives at standardised rates to clean-energy industries; 3) raise the ceiling on how much aid any one company can receive; 4) permit governments to respond to a company's plans to relocate to a third country due to the offer of subsidies by temporarily matching the aid promised by that foreign government, namely the United States; and 5) allow governments to provide more financial aid to industry without first seeking approval from the European Commission. Secondly, it proposes the establishment of the European Sovereignty Fund, intended as a joint EU fund to provide financial assistance to industrial projects in critical and emerging technologies for the energy and digital transitions.

There are political obstacles to both measures. France and Germany are supportive of the state-aid rule changes, which is no surprise, but many other member states oppose them.[67] Loosening the rules would allow governments with the deepest pockets (namely, France and Germany) to dole out much more support than smaller states can, distorting trade and investment within the EU's internal market. There has been considerable discord among

EU members over Berlin's €177.5bn Climate and Transformation Fund, announced in July 2022 in response to the country's energy crisis, which includes €20bn for the hydrogen sector and industrial-emissions reduction for 2023–26. Eleven member states have penned a joint position paper cautioning against substantial changes to the rules.[68]

The EU is also unlikely to reach agreement on additional joint funding for the proposed European Sovereignty Fund. The EU's budget is set through 2027, and although it will be reviewed in 2023, there is little appetite among EU members to increase it, whether through national contributions or further joint EU debt. Ten countries have already expressed opposition.[69] Disagreements over the matter at a February 2023 meeting of the European Council saw the topic all but removed from the EU leaders' joint statement.[70] The so-called 'Frugal Four' states – Austria, Denmark, Germany and the Netherlands – routinely oppose bigger budgets and the issuance of joint EU debt, but many other European states have taken a similar line.[71]

There are economic constraints as well. Government net borrowing and public debt in the eurozone will not return to pre-pandemic levels for several years under the European Central Bank's current forecast horizon.[72] Additional spending to dampen the impact of energy inflation in Europe will make many governments reluctant to increase spending further or to reduce their tax revenue. And with inflation levels still high, governments may be nervous about introducing additional, debt-financed spending measures.[73]

Against this backdrop, compromise is likely on both reforms to state-aid rules and the European Sovereignty Fund. Some of the less controversial state-aid reforms may succeed, perhaps including the simplification of state-aid processes, the introduction of standard maximum rates for investment tax incentives and temporary anti-relocation aid. But the EU is unlikely to allow members to hand out much larger packages of state aid absent European Commission assessment of their impact on fairness within the internal market. As for the European Sovereignty Fund, the EU is likely to move money from elsewhere in the European Commission's budget and, potentially, to amalgamate several existing financing mechanisms, along the lines suggested by German Finance Minister Christian Lindner.[74]

*No trade-law war*

The EU would be disinclined to take Member of the European Parliament Bernd Lange's suggestion that the bloc bring a case against the United States before the WTO to force the US government to remove discriminatory measures. There would be little point to doing so. Since 2019, the United States has blocked the appointment of judges to the WTO Appellate Body, causing the international dispute-settlement procedure to grind to a halt. Even if the EU won an initial hearing at the WTO, the dispute would get stuck at the appeals stage and Brussels would be legally unable to impose retaliatory tariffs on the United States. It is loath to impose retaliatory tariffs illegally. Despite introducing a host of innovative instruments to deal unilaterally with trade distortions over recent years, it has taken pains to remain compliant with international trade law.[75]

The most likely alternative is for the EU to initiate an internal anti-subsidy investigation. It might then impose countervailing tariffs on imports from the United States that have been subsidised by the IRA and undercut European companies within Europe's home market. The EU can do this unilaterally in line with the WTO Agreement on Subsidies and Countervailing Measures, and it is generally uncontroversial. It has done so on 263 past occasions, including 15 times on biodiesel imports from the United States.[76]

Countervailing measures would be a tepid response to the IRA. Increasing import tariffs on subsidised clean technologies may protect domestic manufacturers within the EU market, but it would do little to address wider distortions of trade and investment caused by the IRA. Such tariffs would be much narrower in scope than the retaliatory tariffs applied during the Airbus–Boeing dispute. By the same token, they would allow the EU to respond substantively to the IRA without triggering retaliation from the United States and precipitating a trade war.

## No 'Buy European'

Macron's proposal for a 'Buy European Act' for preferential treatment of European manufacturers would not survive contact with reality. Any attempt to introduce such an act would cause Brussels prohibitively disruptive political, geopolitical and legal headaches. Whereas the Biden administration and the US Congress appear blissfully uninterested in the United States' breaches of international trade law, there is much more political opposition in the EU to undermining rules-based trade. Although Paris favours preferential treatment for domestically produced goods, Berlin is reportedly opposed.[77] Many other member states would likewise resist any derogation of international trade law. All three executive vice-presidents of the European Commission have publicly cautioned against mimicking the United States' discriminatory subsidies, as has the head of the European Parliament's Committee on International Trade.[78]

At the geopolitical level, Brussels's problem is that EU subsidies would trigger disputes with partners, including the United Kingdom under the terms of the EU–UK Trade and Cooperation Agreement. It would also clash with the EU's call on the global stage for compliance with international trade rules and castigation of China and the US for failing to do so. As Margrethe Vestager, European commissioner for competition and an executive vice-president of the European Commission, has warned, 'to do what the Americans are doing, and that we criticize them for, would be a response that would put us in the same position, so that we would also be criticized'.[79]

Moreover, the EU cannot ignore international trade law as easily as the United States can. Although the WTO Appellate Body is blocked, preventing countries from holding the US to account for its breaches of international trade law, the EU played a leading part in establishing an alternative body without US participation – the Multiparty Interim Appeal Arbitration Arrangement. Through this plurilateral arrangement, other parties, including Australia, Canada, China and Switzerland, can hold the EU to WTO law.

*     *     *

Geopolitical and economic constraints make it unlikely that the EU will embark on a trade war with the United States, at least during Biden's term as president. Brussels is more likely to seek to consolidate the improvement of its relations with the United States since the end of Trump's presidency. A trade war would become plausible only if, in a few years, the IRA has, in fact, caused real harm to European industry, and Europe's relations with the United States have deteriorated on other fronts, such that Europe has less to lose.

Meeting the China challenge is more important to Europe than counteracting the IRA. The Russia–Ukraine war has underlined how important it is for the EU to reduce its economic dependence on geopolitical adversaries, and it will take years for the West to disentangle itself from China in strategic industries, including many clean-energy industries such as critical minerals, solar photovoltaics and batteries. In reaching a truce in the Airbus–Boeing dispute, the EU and the United States agreed that it had been a costly distraction from the geo-economic problems caused by China, and that setting it aside would facilitate transatlantic cooperation in addressing them.[80] On the American side, the IRA is hardly an exemplar of such cooperation. At the same time, however, it has forged a consensus in the United States on the importance of clean industries, and that could open the door to improved cooperation with the EU.

Furthermore, since Russia's invasion of Ukraine, Europe has relied heavily on the United States to provide financial and military assistance to Ukraine, and sought Washington's help in boosting energy supplies to replace Russian oil and gas. Europe will also look to the United States to help shoulder the burden of bankrolling Ukraine's reconstruction. Though precipitated by a geopolitical emergency, Europe's heightened dependency on the United States will endure for some time, and cuts against sharp European antagonism towards the US over the IRA.

A calibrated and civilised dispute over the IRA may, in fact, provide the Biden administration with an opportunity to bring its geopolitical internationalism and geo-economic nationalism into closer alignment. The EU would likely accept modest concessions from the United States in clean-energy industries that involve no changes to the rules of the IRA, but rather take the form of cooperative initiatives to boost such industries on both sides of the Atlantic. A collaborative effort to commercialise the shipping of hydrogen and its derivatives would be a logical place to begin. Ultimately, strong clean-energy industries in Europe and the United States will be mutually beneficial as they try to reduce supply-chain dependence on China. In the longer term, world-leading clean-energy industries in both

Europe and the United States would enable the transatlantic partners to advance the energy transition in other parts of the world.

## Notes

1   See US Department of the Treasury, 'Remarks by Secretary of the Treasury Janet L. Yellen on Way Forward for the Global Economy', 13 April 2022, https://home.treasury.gov/news/press-releases/jy0714.

2   See Salman Ahmed and Rozlyn Engel (eds), 'Making U.S. Foreign Policy Work Better for the Middle Class', Carnegie Endowment for International Peace, 2020, https://carnegieendowment.org/files/USFP_FinalReport_final1.pdf; and Felicia Wong and Todd N. Tucker, 'A Tale of Two Industrial Policies', *Foreign Affairs*, 26 January 2023, https://www.foreignaffairs.com/united-states/tale-two-industrial-policies.

3   See Morgan D. Bazilian and Gregory Brew, 'The Inflation Reduction Act Is the Start of Reclaiming Critical Mineral Chains', *Foreign Policy*, 16 September 2022, https://foreignpolicy.com/2022/09/16/inflation-reduction-act-critical-mineral-chains-congress-biden/; Jeff D. Colgan and Nicholas L. Miller, 'The Rewards of Rivalry', *Foreign Affairs*, 1 November 2022, https://www.foreignaffairs.com/united-states/rewards-rivalry-us-china-competition-can-spur-climate-progress; Robert Johnston, 'Industrial Policy Nationalism: How Worried Should We Be?', Center on Global Energy Policy, 7 February 2023, https://www.energypolicy.columbia.edu/industrial-policy-nationalism-how-worried-should-we-be/; and Ilaria Mazzocco, 'Why the New Climate Bill Is Also About Competition with China', Center for Strategic and International Studies, 25 August 2022, https://www.csis.org/analysis/why-new-climate-bill-also-about-competition-china.

4   See 'An Act to Provide for Reconciliation Pursuant to Title II of S. Con. Res. 14' ('Inflation Reduction Act of 2022'), H.R. 5376, 117th Congress, 16 August 2022, §§13101, 13102, 13401, 13701, 13702, https://www.congress.gov/117/plaws/publ169/PLAW-117publ169.pdf.

5   See Leila Abboud, 'Emmanuel Macron Says US Climate Law Risks "Fragmenting the West"', *Financial Times*, 1 December 2022, https://www.ft.com/content/a1a03af2-831a-433c-8984-b99c84018a13.

6   See Jillian Deutsch, 'Top EU Official Pulls Out of US Summit over Climate Law Dispute', Bloomberg, 1 December 2022, https://www.bloomberg.com/news/articles/2022-12-01/top-eu-official-pulls-out-of-us-talks-on-climate-tax-law-worry.

7   See Abboud, 'Emmanuel Macron Says US Climate Law Risks "Fragmenting the West"'.

8   See Sam Fleming and Andy Bounds, 'Joe Biden's Green Subsidies May Backfire, Warns EU Commissioner', *Financial Times*, 30

December 2022, https://www.ft.com/content/07ce707d-1cf5-4e9e-ba43-4555ea13b290.

9   See Edward Alden, 'Biden's "America First" Economic Policy Threatens Rift with Europe', *Foreign Policy*, 5 December 2022, https://foreignpolicy.com/2022/12/05/biden-ira-chips-act-america-first-europe-eu-cars-ev-economic-policy/; Kori Schake, 'Biden's Foreign Policy Is a Mess', *Foreign Affairs*, 10 February 2023, https://www.foreignaffairs.com/united-states/biden-foreign-policy-mess; and Fareed Zakaria, 'American Protectionism Could Imperil a Golden Era of Western Unity', *Washington Post*, 8 December 2022, https://www.washingtonpost.com/opinions/2022/12/08/europe-us-protectionism-foreign-policy-ukraine/.

10  See Andrew Ross Sorkin et al., 'Could Biden's Climate Agenda Trigger a New Trade War?', *New York Times*, 6 December 2022, https://www.nytimes.com/2022/12/06/business/dealbook/biden-climate-trade-europe.html.

11  Wong and Tucker, 'A Tale of Two Industrial Policies'.

12  *Ibid*.

13  See Andy Bounds and Aime Williams, 'Top US Trade Official Urges EU to Join Forces on Subsidies amid Green Deal Tensions', *Financial Times*, 2 November 2022, https://www.ft.com/content/0e52d609-5cfe-453c-9baf-b33b66e941e9.

14  See Barney Jopson, 'US Beats EU as Magnet for Green Investment, Says Iberdrola', *Financial Times*, 9 November 2022, https://www.ft.com/content/7797bd70-645d-4ef9-a7ee-0c90aa1a09c6.

15  See Richard Milne, 'Northvolt's New Chair Urges Europe to Follow US Lead on Battery Subsidies', *Financial Times*, 15 December 2022, https://www.ft.com/content/4e39bb68-58bb-465d-b11c-4b426640409c; and Patricia Nilsson and Alexander Vladkov, 'German Car Industry Calls for European Policy to Counter US Subsidies', *Financial Times*, 11 January 2023, https://www.ft.com/content/4024a766-3578-403b-93be-5f5efbfd93f5.

16  See Samy Adghirni and Justin Sink, 'Biden Says He Won't Apologize for the Climate Law that Angers EU', Bloomberg, 1 December 2022, https://www.bloomberg.com/news/articles/2022-12-01/macron-blasts-new-us-subsidies-law-before-dinner-at-white-house; Charlemagne, 'Europe Should Not Respond to America's Subsidies Binge with Its Own Blunders', *The Economist*, 9 February 2023, https://www.economist.com/europe/2023/02/09/europe-should-not-respond-to-americas-subsidies-binge-with-its-own-blunders; Suzanne Lynch, Barbara Moens and Samuel Stolton, 'France and Germany Go It Alone as EU Summit Prepares to Tackle Fightback Against US', *Politico*, 8 February 2023, https://www.politico.eu/article/france-and-germany-go-it-alone-as-eu-leaders-meet/; Anne-Sylvaine Chassany, 'Macron Wants Tougher EU on Trade and Foreign Investment', *Financial Times*, 11 May 2017, https://on.ft.com/3YsxnOr; and Adam Tooze, 'An Arms Race on Industrial Policy Is the Last Thing Europe Needs',

*Financial Times*, 23 December 2022, https://www.ft.com/content/c609f8c6-9484-4c1f-945d-5dc5b208e615.

[17] See Christine Murray and Amanda Chu, 'BMW Plans €800mn Mexican EV and Battery Investment amid Subsidies Row', *Financial Times*, 3 February 2023, https://www.ft.com/content/10c8c436-416b-4fb6-b1a1-c7456780053c.

[18] European companies that may be worse affected are relatively small and have no production in North America, including Volvo and Jaguar Land Rover. These companies may end up selling in the US only high-value cars that would be ineligible for the IRA consumer tax credit anyway – SUVs priced at over $80,000 and other cars at over $55,000.

[19] See James Eddy, Alexander Pfeiffer and Jasper van de Staaij, 'Recharging Economies: The EV-battery Manufacturing Outlook for Europe', McKinsey & Company, May 2019, https://www.mckinsey.com/~/media/McKinsey/Industries/Oil%20and%20Gas/Our%20Insights/Recharging%20economies%20The%20EV%20battery%20manufacturing%20outlook%20for%20Europe/Recharging-economies-The-EV-battery-manufacturing-outlook-for-Europe-vF.pdf.

[20] International Energy Agency, 'Utility-scale PV Investment Cost Structure by Component and by Commodity Breakdown', 26 October 2022, https://www.iea.org/data-and-statistics/charts/utility-scale-pv-investment-cost-structure-by-component-and-by-commodity-breakdown.

[21] See Bram Vonsée, Wina Crijns-Graus and Liu Wen, 'Energy Technology Dependence: A Value Chain Analysis of Geothermal Power in the EU', *Energy*, vol. 178, 1 July 2019, p. 426.

[22] See Sertaç Akar et al., 'Global Value Chain and Manufacturing Analysis on Geothermal Power Plant Turbines', Technical Report NREL/TP-6A20-71128, National Renewable Energy Laboratory, September 2018, https://www.nrel.gov/docs/fy18osti/71128.pdf.

[23] Vonsée, Crijns-Graus and Wen, 'Energy Technology Dependence', p. 424.

[24] 'Inflation Reduction Act of 2022', §§13101, 13102, 13701, 13702.

[25] United States Geological Survey, 'Mineral Commodity Summaries 2023', January 2023, pp. 61, 143.

[26] See Nerijus Adomaitis, 'Norway Finds "Substantial" Mineral Resources on Its Seabed', Reuters, 27 January 2023, https://www.reuters.com/markets/commodities/norway-finds-substantial-mineral-resources-its-seabed-2023-01-27/.

[27] United States Geological Survey, 'Mineral Commodity Summaries 2023', p. 109.

[28] Rystad Energy, 'Fake It Till You Make It: Synthetic Graphite Holds the Key to Meeting Battery Demand Surge, Despite ESG Concerns', 10 November 2022, https://www.rystadenergy.com/news/fake-it-till-you-make-it-synthetic-graphite-holds-the-key-to-meeting-battery-dema.

[29] United States Geological Survey, 'Mineral Commodity Summaries 2023', p. 83.

[30] See Thierry Breton, 'Critical Raw Materials Act: Securing the New Gas & Oil at the Heart of Our Economy', European Commission,

14 September 2022, https://ec.europa.eu/commission/presscorner/detail/en/STATEMENT_22_5523; and Frédéric Simon, 'EU to Introduce Targets for Raw Materials Self-sufficiency', EURACTIV, 9 December 2022, http://www.euractiv.com/section/energy-environment/news/eu-to-introduce-targets-for-raw-materials-self-sufficiency/.

31  European Commission, 'EU Solar Energy Strategy', COM(2022) 221 final, 18 May 2022, https://eur-lex.europa.eu/resource.html?uri=cellar:516a902d-d7a0-11ec-a95f-01aa75ed71a1.0001.02/DOC_1&format=PDF.

32  Nick Ferris, 'Data Insight: The 2030 European Wind Gap', Energy Monitor, 6 April 2022, https://www.energymonitor.ai/tech/renewables/data-insight-the-2030-european-wind-gap/; and Global Wind Energy Council, 'Global Wind Report 2022', 4 April 2022, https://gwec.net/wp-content/uploads/2022/03/GWEC-GLOBAL-WIND-REPORT-2022.pdf.

33  European Alternative Fuels Observatory, 'European Union (EU27): Summary', data for 2022 AF Fleet (M1&N1) from 30 September 2022, https://alternative-fuels-observatory.ec.europa.eu/transport-mode/road/european-union-eu27; and European Commission, 'Sustainable and Smart Mobility Strategy: Putting European Transport on Track for the Future', COM(2020) 789 final, 9 December 2020, https://eur-lex.europa.eu/resource.html?uri=cellar:5e601657-3b06-11eb-b27b-01aa75ed71a1.0001.02/DOC_1&format=PDF.

34  European Commission, 'REPowerEU Plan', COM(2022) 230 final, 18 May 2022, https://eur-lex.europa.eu/resource.html?uri=cellar:fc930f14-d7ae-11ec-a95f-01aa75ed71a1.0001.02/DOC_1&format=PDF.

35  Range derived from calculations in Dawud Ansari, Julian Grinschgl and Jacopo Maria Pepe, 'Electrolyser for the Hydrogen Revolution', SWP Comment No. 57, September 2022, https://www.swp-berlin.org/publications/products/comments/2022C57_Electrolysers_HydrogenRevolution.pdf; Chris Goodall, 'Some Rules of Thumb of the Hydrogen Economy', Carbon Commentary, 11 June 2021, https://www.carboncommentary.com/blog/2021/6/11/some-rules-of-thumb-of-the-hydrogen-economy; and European Clean Hydrogen Alliance, 'European Electrolyser Summit: Joint Declaration', 5 May 2022, https://hydrogeneurope.eu/wp-content/uploads/2022/05/2022.05.05-EU-ELY-Summit_joint-declaration_signed-c70ff98b5001f55b76b50cf0221c895f.pdf.

36  US Department of Energy, 'Solar Futures Study', September 2021, https://www.energy.gov/sites/default/files/2021-09/Solar%20Futures%20Study.pdf.

37  Global Wind Energy Council, 'Global Wind Report 2022'.

38  Ibid.

39  White House, 'FACT SHEET: President Biden Announces Steps to Drive American Leadership Forward on Clean Cars and Trucks', 5 August 2021, https://www.whitehouse.gov/briefing-room/statements-releases/2021/08/05/fact-sheet-president-biden-announces-steps-to-drive-american-leadership-forward-on-clean-cars-and-trucks/.

40  US Energy Storage Association, '100 x 30: Enabling the Clean Power Transformation', August 2020, https://energystorage.org/wp/wp-content/uploads/2020/08/100x30-Empowering-Clean-Power-Transformation-ESA-Vision.pdf.

41  See US Department of Energy, 'America's Strategy to Secure the Supply Chain for a Robust Clean Energy Transition', 24 February 2022, p. 15, https://www.energy.gov/sites/default/files/2022-02/America%E2%80%99s%20Strategy%20to%20Secure%20the%20Supply%20Chain%20for%20a%20Robust%20Clean%20Energy%20Transition%20FINAL.docx_0.pdf.

42  See US Department of Energy, 'DOE Announces $5 Million to Launch Lithium-battery Workforce Initiative', 18 March 2022, https://www.energy.gov/articles/doe-announces-5-million-launch-lithium-battery-workforce-initiative.

43  Paul Daume et al., 'Renewable-energy Development in a Net-zero World: Overcoming Talent Gaps', McKinsey & Company, November 2022, https://www.mckinsey.com/~/media/mckinsey/industries/electric%20power%20and%20natural%20gas/our%20insights/renewable%20energy%20development%20in%20a%20net%20zero%20world%20overcoming%20talent%20gaps/renewable%20energy%20development%20in%20a%20net%20zero%20world%20overcoming%20talent%20gaps.pdf?shouldIndex=false.

44  International Energy Agency, 'The Cost of Capital in Clean Energy Transitions', 17 December 2021, https://www.iea.org/articles/the-cost-of-capital-in-clean-energy-transitions.

45  Ibid.

46  See David Matthews, 'US Inflation Reduction Act Could Torpedo EU Green Hydrogen Ambitions', Science|Business, 15 December 2022, https://sciencebusiness.net/news/Hydrogen/US-Inflation-Reduction-Act-could-torpedo-EU-green-hydrogen-ambitions.

47  See Thomas Moller-Nielsen, 'US Protectionism Poses "Existential Challenge" to Europe, Say EU Leaders', Brussels Times, 30 November 2022, https://www.brusselstimes.com/328633/us-protectionism-poses-existential-challenge-to-europe-eu-leaders-claim.

48  See Charlie Cooper and Giorgio Leali, 'Is This the End of Made in Europe?', Politico, 15 January 2023, https://www.politico.eu/article/end-made-in-europe-manufacturing-industry-struggle/; Peggy Hollinger et al., 'Will the Energy Crisis Crush European Industry?', Financial Times, 19 October 2022, https://www.ft.com/content/75ed449d-e9fd-41de-96bd-c92d316651da; European Commission, Directorate-General for Research Innovation, 'Re-finding Industry – Defining Innovation: Report of the Independent High Level Group on Industrial Technologies', 23 April 2018, https://op.europa.eu/en/publication-detail/-/publication/28e1c485-476a-11e8-be1d-01aa75ed71a1; Johanna Treck, 'Mittel-kaput? German Industry Stares into the Abyss', Politico, 10 November 2022, https://www.politico.eu/article/germany-industry-europe-energy-

prices-basf/; and Yanis Varoufakis, 'Is Europe Deindustrializing?', Project Syndicate, 23 January 2023, https://www.project-syndicate.org/commentary/underinvestment-in-cloud-capital-hurts-european-cars-and-energy-by-yanis-varoufakis-2023-01?barrier=accesspaylog.

49 See Ludwig Burger, 'BASF Seeks "Permanent" Cost Cuts at European Operations', Reuters, 26 October 2022, https://www.reuters.com/markets/europe/basf-says-european-operations-need-be-cut-size-permanently-2022-10-26/; and Treek, 'Mittel-kaput? German Industry Stares into the Abyss'.

50 European Commission, 'Questions and Answers on the EU Delegated Acts on Renewable Hydrogen', 13 February 2023, https://ec.europa.eu/commission/presscorner/detail/en/qanda_23_595.

51 European Commission, 'State Aid: Commission Approves €900 Million German Scheme to Support Investments in Production of Renewable Hydrogen', press release, 20 December 2021, https://ec.europa.eu/commission/presscorner/detail/en/ip_21_7022.

52 'Inflation Reduction Act of 2022', §13204. See also Oleksiy Tatarenko and Thomas Koch Blank, 'The Inflation Reduction Act: The Moment for US Green Steel and Fertiliser', Energy Monitor, 12 September 2022, https://www.energymonitor.ai/tech/hydrogen/the-inflation-reduction-act-the-moment-for-us-green-steel-and-fertiliser/.

53 US Department of Energy, 'Hydrogen Shot: An Introduction',

August 2021, https://www.energy.gov/eere/fuelcells/articles/hydrogen-shot-introduction.

54 See Andrew Mulder, 'US Green Hydrogen Costs to Reach Sub-zero Under IRA; Longer-term Price Impacts Remain Uncertain', S&P Global, 29 September 2022, https://www.spglobal.com/commodityinsights/en/market-insights/latest-news/energy-transition/092922-us-green-hydrogen-costs-to-reach-sub-zero-under-ira-longer-term-price-impacts-remain-uncertain; and Emma Penrod, 'Growing Scale, Inflation Reduction Act Subsidies Could Push Green Hydrogen Prices Negative: RE+ Panel', Utility Dive, 27 September 2022, https://www.utilitydive.com/news/ira-subsidies-green-hydrogen/632599/.

55 Andrew Marsh, 'Plug January Business Update', Plug Power web-cast, 25 January 2023.

56 'Inflation Reduction Act of 2022', §13102.

57 Ibid., §13501.

58 See Mulder, 'US Green Hydrogen Costs to Reach Sub-zero Under IRA'; and Yuanrong Zhou, 'Can the Inflation Reduction Act Unlock a Green Hydrogen Economy?', International Council on Clean Transportation, 3 January 2023, https://theicct.org/ira-unlock-green-hydrogen-jan23/.

59 See Nicholas Crawford, 'Hydrogen: Future Energy Interdependence', IISS Analysis, 16 December 2021, https://www.iiss.org/blogs/analysis/2021/12/hydrogen-and-future-energy-interdependence; and Hydrogen Council, 'Global Hydrogen Flows: Hydrogen Trade as a Key Enabler for

Efficient Decarbonization', October 2022, https://hydrogencouncil.com/wp-content/uploads/2022/10/Global-Hydrogen-Flows.pdf.

60 Congressional Budget Office, 'Estimated Budgetary Effects of H.R. 5376, the Inflation Reduction Act of 2022', 3 August 2022, https://www.cbo.gov/system/files/2022-08/hr5376_IR_Act_8-3-22.pdf; Joint Committee on Taxation, 'Estimated Budget Effects of the Revenue Provisions of Title I – Committee on Finance, of an Amendment in the Nature of a Substitute to H.R. 5376, "An Act to Provide for Reconciliation Pursuant to Title II of S. Con. Res. 14", as Passed by the Senate on August 7, 2022, and Scheduled for Consideration by the House of Representatives on August 12, 2022', 9 August 2022, https://www.jct.gov/publications/2022/jcx-18-22/; and 'An Act to Authorize Funds for Federal-aid Highways, Highway Safety Programs, and Transit Programs, and for Other Purposes' ('Infrastructure Investment and Jobs Act'), H.R. 3684, 117th Congress, 15 November 2021, Subtitle B, https://www.congress.gov/117/plaws/publ58/PLAW-117publ58.pdf.

61 See Plamena Tisheva, 'EU Plans Pilot Green Hydrogen Auction in Autumn 2023', Renewables Now, 2 February 2023, https://renewablesnow.com/news/eu-plans-pilot-green-hydrogen-auction-in-autumn-2023-813378/.

62 See Rebecca Christie, 'Hydrogen Is Elemental to U.S.–EU Green Compromise', Reuters, 10 February 2023, https://www.reuters.com/breakingviews/hydrogen-is-elemental-us-eu-green-compromise-2023-02-10/.

63 European Union, '2022 State of the Union Address by President von der Leyen', 14 September 2022, https://ec.europa.eu/commission/presscorner/detail/ov/speech_22_5493/.

64 See 'Bernd Lange (SPD): "Ich schliesse eine Klage gegen die USA bei der WTO nicht aus"', interview with HR Info Radio, 4 December 2022, https://www.hr-inforadio.de/podcast/aktuell/bernd-lange-spd-ich-schliesse-eine-klage-gegen-die-usa-bei-der-wto-nicht-aus,podcast-episode-111552.html.

65 See Clea Caulcutt, 'Emmanuel Macron Calls for "Buy European Act" to Protect Regional Carmakers', Politico, 26 October 2022, https://www.politico.eu/article/emmanuel-macron-buy-european-act-cars-united-states-china/.

66 European Commission, 'A Green Deal Industrial Plan for the Net-zero Age', COM(2023) 62 final, 1 February 2023, https://commission.europa.eu/system/files/2023-02/COM_2023_62_2_EN_ACT_A%20Green%20Deal%20Industrial%20Plan%20for%20the%20Net-Zero%20Age.pdf.

67 See Lynch, Moens and Stolton, 'France and Germany Go It Alone as EU Summit Prepares to Tackle Fightback Against US'.

68 See Gabriela Baczynska, 'Eleven EU Countries Urge "Great Caution" in Loosening State Aid Rules', Reuters, 14 February 2023, https://www.reuters.com/world/europe/eleven-eu-countries-urge-great-caution-loosening-state-aid-rules-2023-02-14/.

69 See Jan Strupczewski, 'Seven EU Countries Oppose New EU Funding as Response to U.S. Subsidy Plan – Letter', Reuters, 27 January 2023,

https://www.reuters.com/markets/europe/seven-eu-countries-oppose-new-eu-funding-response-us-subsidy-plan-letter-2023-01-27/.

70   See Jonathan Packroff, 'Solidarity and Joint Borrowing Scrapped from EU Leaders Summit Statement', EURACTIV, 8 February 2023, https://www.euractiv.com/section/economy-jobs/news/solidarity-and-joint-borrowing-scrapped-from-eu-leaders-summit-statement/.

71   In Germany, the governing coalition is split on the matter, with the Greens open to joint EU debt, but the Free Democratic Party (FDP) staunchly opposed and Chancellor Olaf Scholz's Social Democratic Party somewhere in between. All three parties are faring poorly in polls, but the FDP most of all. Pollytix Strategic Research, 'Pollytix German Election Polling Trend', 17 February 2022, https://pollytix.eu/pollytix-german-election-trend/. Finance Minister Christian Lindner, the FDP leader, is under pressure to reassert his party's identity and demonstrate its sway on the coalition government to close the gap on the governing coalition. He has taken an increasingly hawkish line on fiscal policy and firmly opposes financing a European Sovereignty Fund. See Silvia Amaro, 'Germany Says Borrowing More Money to Compete with the U.S. Would Be a "Threat" to Europe', CNBC, 6 December 2022, http://www.cnbc.com/amp/2022/12/06/germany-eu-shouldnt-borrow-more-to-compete-with-us-green-subsidies.html; and Nikolaus J. Kurmayer, 'Germany Breathes Sigh of Relief at EU Green Industry Plan', EURACTIV, 1 February 2023, https://www.euractiv.com/section/energy-environment/news/germany-breathes-sigh-of-relief-at-eu-green-industry-plan/.

72   See European Central Bank, 'Eurosystem Staff Macroeconomic Projections for the Euro Area', December 2022, https://www.ecb.europa.eu/pub/pdf/other/ecb.projections202212_eurosystemstaff~6c1855c75b.en.pdf.

73   See Nicholas Crawford and David F. Gordon, 'The Geopolitics of Greenflation', Survival, vol. 64, no. 5, October–November 2022, pp. 91–112.

74   See Amaro, 'Germany Says Borrowing More Money to Compete with the U.S. Would Be a "Threat" to Europe'. Scholz and Economy Minister Robert Habeck have made suggestions along similar lines, stating that existing funds under the rubric of the EU Recovery and Resilience Fund should be used in response to the IRA first, before the EU discusses any additional funding packages. See Michael Nienaber, 'Germany Backs National Action in Green Subsidy Dispute with US', Bloomberg, 13 December 2022, https://www.bloomberg.com/news/articles/2022-12-13/germany-backs-national-action-in-green-subsidy-dispute-with-us; and Sabine Siebold, 'Scholz on Sovereignty Fund: Use Money from Existing Packages First', Reuters, 14 December 2022, http://www.reuters.com/world/europe/scholz-sovereignty-fund-use-money-existing-packages-first-2022-12-14/.

75   See Council of the European Union, 'Council Gives Final Approval

to Tackling Distortive Foreign Subsidies on the Internal Market', press release, 28 November 2022, https://www.consilium.europa.eu/en/press/press-releases/2022/11/28/council-gives-final-approval-to-tackling-distortive-foreign-subsidies-on-the-internal-market/; and European Parliament, 'International Public Procurement Instrument: Securing Fairness for EU Firms', press release, 9 June 2022, https://www.europarl.europa.eu/news/en/press-room/20220603IPR32143/international-public-procurement-instrument-securing-fairness-for-eu-firms.

76  European Commission, 'Database of All Subsidies Investigated by the EU in Its Anti-subsidy Investigations', 2 December 2022, https://circabc.europa.eu/ui/group/2e3865ad-3886-4131-92bb-a71754fffec6/library/0b8b5cb5-af24-40b9-9385-125ee7b9d61e/details?download=true.

77  See Nienaber, 'Germany Backs National Action in Green Subsidy Dispute with US'.

78  See Valdis Dombrovskis, Frans Timmermans and Margrethe Vestager, 'Europe Cannot Afford to Engage in Tit-for-Tat with the US', *Financial Times*, 26 January 2023, https://www.ft.com/content/0bf3708d-20fe-4700-8702-bd0f6ef5591e; 'Bernd Lange (SPD): "Ich schliesse eine Klage gegen die USA bei der WTO nicht aus"'; and Giorgio Leali, 'EU's Free-trading Vestager Warns Against Subsidy War with America', *Politico*, 1 December 2022, https://www.politico.eu/article/vestager-warns-against-imitating-us-amid-buy-european-debate/.

79  Quoted in Leali, 'EU's Free-trading Vestager Warns Against Subsidy War with America'.

80  See White House, 'On-the-Record Press Call by United States Trade Representative Ambassador Katherine Tai', press briefing, 15 June 2021, https://www.whitehouse.gov/briefing-room/press-briefings/2021/06/15/on-the-record-press-call-by-united-states-trade-representative-ambassador-katherine-tai/.

# Truman Redux? Biden's National Security Strategy

**Aaron Ettinger**

In 1969, Hans Morgenthau claimed that American foreign policy at the end of the 1960s was living on 'the intellectual capital which was accumulated in the famous fifteen weeks of the spring of 1947'.[1] He was referring to a sequence of events that began with president Harry Truman's address to the US Congress in March and ended with secretary of state George Marshall's Harvard commencement speech in June. Those two statements, along with the publication of George Kennan's 'X' article in July of that year, established the foundations of America's Cold War strategy: the Truman Doctrine, the Marshall Plan and containment. More broadly, the programmes devised during those 15 weeks established the parameters of a grand strategy featuring internationalism, formal multilateralism, military interventionism and US leadership that would endure for the next three-quarters of a century. Morgenthau's retrospective came with a warning, however: 'this capital has now been nearly exhausted', he said, adding that the 'obsolete' foreign policies of the late 1960s necessitated 'a task of renovation similar to that of 1947'.[2] Morgenthau would likely be disconcerted to find that US grand strategy in the 2020s still draws upon the same intellectual capital as did American policy in the 1940s.

The task of 'renovation' as advocated by Morgenthau not only remains unaccomplished, it was never even attempted until Donald Trump introduced

**Aaron Ettinger** is an assistant professor in the Department of Political Science at Carleton University, Ottawa, Canada.

**Survival** | vol. 65 no. 2 | April–May 2023 | pp. 103–122    https://doi.org/10.1080/00396338.2023.2193103

his presidency's haphazard 'America First' strategy. His successor, Joe Biden, seeks not to renovate but to restore the old programme at a unique moment in US foreign-policy history. The emergence of China marks the arrival of a peer competitor; Russia's invasion of Ukraine marked the return of conventional land warfare to Europe; and the effects of the COVID-19 pandemic, inflation and supply-chain shocks have left the 1990s vision of globalisation in tatters. Although the current era has yet to be given a label, it is plain that a new set of geopolitical configurations is emerging.[3] The Biden administration knows as much, yet remains intellectually indebted to the past: its 2022 National Security Strategy (NSS) is a close intellectual heir to Truman-era ideas.[4] Despite Biden's acknowledgement early in his presidency that the United States 'cannot pretend the world can simply be restored to the way it was 75, 30, or even four years ago', US policy is still rooted in received wisdom.[5]

> US policy is still rooted in received wisdom

This was evident very shortly after Biden's inauguration, when his administration released an interim NSS. This strategy was both a rebuke of Trump and a statement of restoration, inflected with internationalist shibboleths, campaign rhetoric and a desire to put the American house back in order.[6] The goal of consolidating liberal-democratic capitalism – in opposition to illiberal authoritarianism – was placed at the centre of US foreign policy. Over the first year of Biden's presidency, he set out to reclaim global leadership while promising major social spending at home. By his second year in office, these ambitions were being stymied by domestic opposition and illiberal authoritarianism on every continent. The American retreat from Afghanistan in August 2021, the Russian invasion of Ukraine the following February and the massive economic disruptions that followed appeared to spell the end of the restoration agenda. The full version of the NSS was delayed for months to accommodate these rapid changes in the configuration of global politics. It was finally released in October 2022.

I argue that the grand strategy articulated in Biden's 2022 NSS amounts to an inverted neo-Trumanite foreign policy for the 2020s, one that aims to manage the tense coexistence of cooperation and conflict, democracy and authoritarianism, great-power rivalry and global cooperation, all while fostering economic recovery in the US. The 2022 NSS is neo-Trumanite because it reflects three features of Truman's foreign policy, updated for the post-Cold War era. Firstly, it posits that an ideational conflict is taking shape between the forces of liberal-democratic capitalism and the triple threats of authoritarianism, inequality and exclusionary nationalism. The full NSS retreats somewhat from the interim strategy's excessive reliance on the democracy-versus-authoritarianism angle as both the principal strategic problem for US policy and the unifying concept of global politics writ large. Instead, the 2022 NSS treats ideological confrontation as a lens through which US foreign policy views cooperation and conflict among the world's great powers and non-state actors. Secondly, the NSS reflects the political-economic objectives underlying the Marshall Plan, which set out to restore market capitalism in Western Europe and East Asia. This time, however, economic reconstruction is intended to restore confidence in market economics among Americans by way of domestic infrastructure and social-spending programmes. Thirdly, it reaffirms the importance of US leadership of the international system – a novelty under Truman that has since become an article of faith in mainstream American foreign policy. Together, these features aim to restore the US-led liberal international order in response to challenges from Russia and China, powers that 'layer authoritarian governance with a revisionist foreign policy', according to Biden.[7] The 2022 NSS inverts the Truman paradigm because so much of the agenda is directed inward, at the reconstruction of the US economy and the reconsolidation of liberal-democratic capitalism. Unlike in the late 1940s, when the aim was to counter the influence of Soviet authoritarianism and economic despair in Europe, Biden's NSS seeks to address the risk of authoritarian drift at home. By rallying around democracy both domestically and among other democratic states, the strategy aims to check the influence of twenty-first-century authoritarianism in all its forms.

This is an extraordinarily ambitious agenda. The US does not enjoy the same relative advantages in material power it did in the late 1940s.[8] Today, the country's global influence is being attenuated by challengers, while at home, US public and elite opinion is split on fundamental questions related to the country's social contract. Furthermore, unlike during the Cold War, in which the US and the USSR embodied the conflict's ideological rivalry, in the 2020s, state and non-state rivals are forming complex, networked coalitions that are arrayed against each other both in real life and online. Much has changed since 1947, but the United States' ultimate objectives – security, prosperity and the defence of the 'blessings of liberty' – remain the same, as do the methods the country seeks to employ to achieve those objectives.

## Truman's foreign policy

National Security Strategies are required by law.[9] Each time one is published – there are have been 17 since 1987 – it is feasted upon by pundits and scholars in search of a 'doctrine' that can be situated in the grand sweep of American history. As a formal strategy document, the NSS provides a framework for understanding ends and means in foreign policy. It is a reference point for national-defence budgeting and creates a common basis for national-security coordination within the executive branch. Although the White House is not obliged to follow the programme laid out in the NSS, it is always useful for an administration to plan. Still, as boxer Mike Tyson once said, 'everyone has a plan until they get punched in the mouth'. Things happen, and new information can lead to unexpected shifts. This can be seen in the considerable revisions to the Biden administration's own NSS between the interim version and the final version one year later. In a more scholarly sense, the NSS has retrospective value as a window into a presidential administration's world view. More broadly, NSS documents are useful texts for comparing foreign policies across different eras of US history. The Biden administration's NSS displays clear connections with the same defining principles articulated in the 1940s, notably the need to safeguard liberal-democratic capitalism.[10]

These connections were quickly drawn in early commentary on Biden's foreign policy.[11] There seemed to be a clear parallel between the assertiveness of Josef Stalin's Soviet Union in the late 1940s and that of a rising China in the early 2020s – especially so after diplomatic meetings between the US and China in March 2021 turned acrimonious.[12] However, the China-as-Soviet Union analogy misses the broader point. Truman's foreign policy was not solely a matter of positioning the US against a great-power competitor with different ideological foundations. It was also intended to establish the conditions in which US allies and partners could recover after the war, re-establish the foundations for their own prosperity and make the world safe for liberal democracy and market capitalism.[13] To appreciate the Trumanite features of Biden's foreign policy, it is worth revisiting the features of its antecedent. Historians suggest that the United States' embrace of full-fledged internationalism in the 1940s was the product of at least five major transformations in US foreign policy: the Truman Doctrine, the Marshall Plan, counter-Soviet containment, the acceptance of US international leadership and the reorganisation of national defence.[14] While these features may have emerged most clearly in 1947, they had begun to develop following the failure to establish an acceptable post-war settlement between the Soviet Union and the US, and continued to evolve into the 1950s.

The ideological tenor of the rivalry was already taking shape in 1946. In February, Stalin delivered an address that proclaimed the superior viability and stability of the Soviet system, thereby framing world politics in explicitly ideological terms.[15] Kennan's 'Long Telegram' was composed in response and would be published the following year. Winston Churchill delivered his Iron Curtain speech in March 1946, one month after Stalin's address, as Truman looked on. Indeed, Truman was equally suspicious of the Soviet Union, having concluded that 'force is the only thing the Russians understand'.[16] This position aligned nicely with Churchill's, but departed from Franklin Roosevelt's view that 'we can and must, do business with Uncle Joe',[17] and with public opinion in the United States.[18]

Truman would give full voice to his Manichaean anti-totalitarianism in an address to the US House of Representatives in March 1947. A bankrupt Britain had withdrawn its support for the Greek government in its civil war against communist rebels, and Truman was requesting $400 million in aid to Greece. Needing to convince a sceptical, Republican-controlled House that the funds were necessary, Truman argued that the world had arrived at an inflection point in history at which 'nearly every nation must choose between alternative ways of life'.[19] The choice was between a way of life based on the will of the majority as expressed in free institutions, representative government, free elections, guarantees of individual liberty, freedom of speech and religion, and freedom from political oppression; and one based on the will of a minority forcibly imposed upon the majority. This alternative relied on terror and oppression, controls on the press and broadcasting, fixed elections and the suppression of personal freedoms.

This world view was novel. Though anti-communism had been woven into US foreign policy since 1918, it had not been presented so starkly as a globe-encompassing confrontation between liberal democracy and authoritarian communism.[20] Perhaps the most dramatic shift was the implication that the US needed to act as the patron of domestic democracy movements.

*Restoring European economic viability was the next step*

As Truman put it, 'it must be the policy of the United States to support free peoples who are resisting attempted subjugation by armed minorities or by outside pressures'.[21] The idea that the US should offer military and economic support to fledgling democracies as part of a global contest between democracy and authoritarianism came to be known as the Truman Doctrine.

Aid to Greece was only a start. Ideological confrontation would mean nothing to European democracies on the brink of hunger and deprivation. Restoring European economic viability was the next step. The Truman administration was increasingly alert to the fact that the US needed to secure and stabilise key industrial areas in Europe and East Asia, to bring, in Truman's words, 'production, freedom, and confidence back to the world'.[22] For his part, Marshall argued in 1947 that unchecked economic suffering might lead to 'economic collapse and the consequent elimination of any chance of democratic survival'.[23] The political imperatives animating what would become the European Recovery Program (more commonly known as the 'Marshall Plan') were always explicit. Chief among these was the perceived need to blunt the appeal of Soviet communism.

Marshall's commencement address at Harvard in June 1947 identified a dire economic situation in Europe: the continent's industrial and business capital had been damaged to such an extent that a normal economy could not function. Foodstuffs and manufactured goods could not reach their markets; European societies could not generate currency to purchase US products; and there was an overall loss of confidence in the European system of exchange. Marshall argued that US assistance was needed to ensure the 'return of normal economic health in the world, without which there can be no political stability and no assured peace'.[24] He claimed that this policy was 'directed not against any country or doctrine but against hunger, poverty, desperation and chaos'. It was intended to 'permit the emergence of political and social conditions in which free institutions can exist'. As John Lewis Gaddis has argued, the US could not merely position itself as an ideological opponent to communism, it had to offer a positive and viable alternative.[25] In short, liberal democracy had to prove it could deliver. The European Recovery Program provided the capital that Western European countries needed to rebuild their economies, for their own sake and as a matter of primary importance to American security.[26] Gradually, economic recovery permitted deeper participation in the emerging liberal order led by the US.[27]

That order entailed the construction of permanent global institutions that would be venues for economic, security and political co-management. At the helm was the United States, which established the rules while offering to smaller countries the benefits of access and influence.[28] International commerce would be conducted through the Bretton Woods system, the General Agreement on Tariffs and Trade and other emerging rule-sets of capitalist exchange. Security cooperation was formalised in a series of alliances, the most significant of which was NATO, which bound European and North American states in a mutual-defence pact. The United Nations, a universal-membership organisation, became the emblematic institution of the post-war order and a crucial forum in which smaller states could exert themselves.

Ultimately, Truman's foreign policy was two-pronged: it sought to contain and confront the Soviet Union, while rebuilding and consolidating countries belonging to the liberal-democratic world. He framed the confrontation with the Soviet Union in ideological terms, with security interests roiling beneath the rhetoric. Though sometimes predating the 'famous fifteen weeks', initiatives toward formal multilateralism, the domestic reorganisation of the US defence establishment and commitments to international leadership were subsumed under the rubric of the Cold War.[29] This ideational framing proved highly influential, guiding US foreign policy for the next 40 years.

## An 'inverted neo-Trumanite' NSS

When the Cold War ended in the early 1990s, US foreign policy recommitted itself to completing the task of world order begun in the 1940s.[30] The ensuing decades saw the erosion of America's position, however. Economic crises, failed wars, democratic backsliding, unrealised promises of prosperity and the accompanying grievances established the conditions for the emergence of Trump, a president who sought to dismantle the liberal international order.

The first year of Biden's presidency was preoccupied with demonstrating that the US was returning to active global leadership after the Trump interregnum. The White House's release of an interim NSS was a novel step that was preceded by two speeches. In an address at the State Department on 4 February 2021, Biden declared that 'America is back', a direct counterpoint to Trump's incantation of 'America first' in his own inauguration address. Biden promised a return to the kind of diplomacy that had atrophied under Trump, noting that 'diplomacy is back at the centre of our foreign policy'.[31] The speech was notable mostly because of how conventional it was. Biden did not make any radical or bold claims; rather, he spoke of his enthusiastic desire to return to a pre-Trump status quo. Two weeks later, Biden's speech at a virtual session of the Munich Security Conference emphasised NATO unity and solidarity, noting that the transatlantic relationship 'must remain the cornerstone of all that we hope to accomplish in the 21st century, just as we did in the 20th'.[32]

The release of the interim NSS in March 2021 offered the most elaborate and integrated vision of the Trumanite themes that had been taking shape over the previous 12 months. The most striking feature of the strategy was the way in which it pitted democracy against authoritarianism, a formulation Biden had avoided throughout much of 2020.[33] Strategic competition with China, which had been the centrepiece of Trump's NSS and National Defense Strategy, did not disappear, but neither did it top the list of problems confronting the US. Instead, China was presented as a problem-subset of authoritarianism, nationalism and illiberalism. Much like Truman had done 75 years earlier, the Biden administration posited a clash of systems, except this time the clash was both between states and within them. States and non-state actors alike were cast as players in an ideational confrontation that was seen to touch on every aspect of foreign policy.

Biden spent much of the summer of 2021 on an energetic diplomatic offensive to restore confidence in US leadership. His purpose was to rally the democratic members of the transatlantic community as part of a collective pushback against a suite of illiberal and transboundary global challenges. In June 2021, at the start of a presidential trip to Europe, Biden and British prime minister Boris Johnson signed a 'New Atlantic Charter'.[34] This bilateral memorandum bore a striking resemblance to the 1941 Atlantic Charter signed by Roosevelt and Churchill – even the layout and typesetting of the 2021 document resembled its predecessor's. A more modest version of Woodrow Wilson's Fourteen Points, the 1941 charter had established eight general principles for peaceable international relations, open trade and national self-determination that were expected to organise world politics after the presumed defeat of Nazi Germany. The New Atlantic Charter also contained eight points affirming the necessity of democratic values and cooperative global governance, while also gesturing to global health, environmental issues, technology, misinformation, alliances and more.

The G7 summit in the United Kingdom followed the release of the New Atlantic Charter. On this occasion, the meetings were productive enough to yield a mammoth 14,046-word leaders' declaration.[35] The size and scope of the communiqué suggested that the leaders took an expansive view of the G7's remit, covering issues from mental health to outer-space policy, and did so without much disagreement. The first priority established by the document was, appropriately, ending the COVID-19 pandemic and distributing vaccines to the developing world. Economic recovery and climate change were also emphasised. The communiqué reflected progressive values and the language of Biden's democracy agenda. Australia, India and South Korea were invited to the summit as well, prompting speculation about the emergence of a 'D10' group of democracies. This formulation drew an implicit distinction between summit participants and China, though explicit references to China were limited to a statement about the country's importance as a cooperative partner on important issues, a call to determine the origins of COVID-19, a statement on human rights, and an expression of concern about the East and South China seas.[36]

After the G7 summit, Biden arrived in Brussels for the annual NATO summit with every intention of reinforcing US commitment to the Alliance. Contrary to his predecessor, Biden began by affirming the centrality of Article 5 to US national security – a balm to relations that had been damaged by Trump. The summit's final communiqué duly affirmed the centrality of Article 5, as well as Alliance members' commitment to upholding the rules-based international order. The communiqué was notable for its stern language about Russia as posing a security threat to Europe. References to China, which was accurately labelled a 'strategic competitor', were far less numerous, and less censorious.

The internationalist capstone to Biden's first summer as president was his address to the 76th Session of the UN General Assembly in September. Unlike Trump's addresses, which had presented 'sovereignty' as a new anchor for international relations,[37] Biden's speech was a statement of restoration. It turned on the idea of rebuilding a cooperative world order, led by the United States.[38] Biden appealed to the traditional tenets of the international system, mentioning specifically the United Nations Charter and the Universal Declaration of Human Rights. He stressed the centrality of multilateralism, allies, collective action and engaging deeply with the rest of the world. All this was consistent with his previous foreign-policy statements going back at least as far as his time as vice president in the Obama administration.

There were, however, two neo-Trumanite elements detectable below the surface of an otherwise conciliatory address. The first was an oblique reference to China and Russia. Biden said that the US would 'stand up for our allies and our friends and oppose attempts by stronger countries to dominate weaker ones, whether through changes to territory by force, economic coercion, technological exploitation, or disinformation'.[39] This was comparable to Truman's expressed support for free peoples who were resisting subjugation by outside pressures. Biden made explicit his willingness to work with strategic adversaries on certain key issues, but he was clearly sending a message to China, and to a lesser extent Russia. The second neo-Trumanite element was Biden's emphasis on democracy. Echoing Truman's warning about a choice between alternative ways of life, Biden spoke as if the choice had already been made in favour of democracy. In his words, 'the democratic world is everywhere', visible in 'the anti-corruption activists, the human rights defenders, the journalists, the peace protestors on the frontlines of this struggle in Belarus, Burma, Syria, Cuba, Venezuela, and everywhere in between'. For Biden, the ubiquity of the democratic world required the United States to prove wrong the world's authoritarians, those who 'seek to proclaim the end of the age of democracy'.[40] But even as Biden was delivering his speech, the political winds were shifting.

## Foreign policy in troubled times

As the first summer of the Biden administration ended, its foreign-policy decisions began to diverge from its conciliatory aspirations. This was seen most vividly in the abrupt US withdrawal from Afghanistan after 20 years of war and nation-building.[41] The chaotic scenes in Kabul and the subsequent Taliban conquest provoked plenty of hand-wringing in Western capitals. Biden was chided for not consulting allies prior to the withdrawal, though this complaint was overstated. European allies had every reason to anticipate the withdrawal – Biden had long campaigned to 'end the endless war' and had promised to fulfil Trump's pact with the Taliban.[42] In September, Biden ran afoul of France and other allies when the US, along with Australia and the United Kingdom, announced a security pact that entailed the cancellation of a French contract to sell diesel submarines to Australia. Biden issued a personal apology to French President Emmanuel Macron.[43]

At the COP26 Climate Summit in Glasgow in November 2021, long-standing differences between developed and developing countries resulted in a final agreement that did not seem to go far enough to address what Biden had described as 'an existential threat to human existence as we know it',[44] though some progress was made on the role of business in reducing carbon emissions. A meeting of North American leaders that same month felt like an achievement in itself given the tensions that had built up during the Trump years, but it did not resolve long-simmering irritants related to, for example, US–Mexico border security or auto-sector subsidies vis-à-vis Canada.[45] Between COP26 and the 'Three Amigos' summit, Biden held virtual bilateral talks with Chinese President Xi Jinping, which may not have resulted in any breakthroughs but, at the very least, did not make things worse.[46] In December, Biden hosted a virtual Summit for Democracy organised around three main themes: strengthening democracy and defending against authoritarianism; fighting corruption; and promoting respect for human rights. Biden's opening remarks sought to rally democracies to guard against backsliding and to make the case for his legislative agenda regarding voting rights and a large domestic-spending bill.[47] The 'Build Back Better' bill – a $2.2 trillion Marshall Plan for the US economy – was then making its way through the US Congress. It had been pitched as a way of rebuilding the American middle class in the style of the New Deal. The White House also believed that by improving the United States' economic stability, this would preclude the kind of populist backlash that had made 'America First' nationalism palatable. The bill would stall in the Senate at the end of 2021, undermining the economic pillar of Biden's neo-Trumanite policy. It would, however, be revived in 2022 as the 'Inflation Reduction Act'.

Then came Russia's invasion of Ukraine in February 2022. This outrage galvanised Western democratic solidarity like few other events since the end of the Second World War.[48] The consequences of Russia's revanchist authoritarianism were soon revealed to the world – bombed-out cities, desperate refugees and bodies in the streets. The invasion also led to fuel and food shortages that raised the spectre of competing political pressures in Europe. The continent's dependence on Russian oil was exposed, and by extension, its vulnerability to Russian reprisals. With differing levels of exposure to these risks, individual European states might have prioritised their own national interest over any collective action. But the war seemed to have a clarifying effect for European priorities. The US and its NATO partners committed weapons and money to support Ukraine's defence forces, while carefully avoiding direct confrontation with Russia's forces. Individual countries imposed their own sanctions on Russian exports and pressured international businesses to leave Russia. By mid-2022, Finland

and Sweden, long resistant to NATO membership, had applied to join the Alliance. Not only did Vladimir Putin's war reanimate the West, it also gave new life to Biden's foreign policy. His larger strategy did not change, but the broader strategic environment did. It was in this context that the full NSS was released in October 2022.

Gloomier than the interim version in its outlook, the 2022 NSS clarified the grand-strategic problems faced by the US, the country's objectives and the ways in which it might achieve them. Describing the post-Cold War era as having ended, it predicted that the 2020s would be a decisive decade in which the terms of geopolitical competition would be established. US leadership was seen as necessary to manage great-power competition while simultaneously nurturing global cooperation. Biden's introductory letter walked the fine line between these two imperatives by distinguishing between a responsible US and 'those who do not share our vision for a world that is free, open, prosperous, and secure'[49] – meaning Russia and China – while also leaving the door open to cooperation.

*Putin's war gave new life to Biden's foreign policy*

Implicit in this construction was an acknowledgement that the liberal international order is no longer the only political operating system available.

References in the 2022 NSS to the goal of building a world that is 'free, open, prosperous, and secure' are consistent with the NSS canon. Such a world, according to the 2022 version, requires self-determination, territorial integrity, political independence at home and in foreign policy, international institutions, the free flow of information, human rights and a fair global economy.[50] However, two strategic challenges threaten these features: 'major power' competition and transboundary threats that can only be overcome through international cooperation. The major powers in question are identified as Russia and China. Russia poses an obvious threat to Europe, given its war in Ukraine, coercive oil diplomacy and non-conventional operations worldwide. But China represents a greater long-term challenge as a competitor with the intent and wherewithal to reshape the international order.[51] On transboundary problems, the NSS speaks to issues that have long been mentioned in US strategic documents: climate change, disease, terrorism, food insecurity and economic instability. Strategies in the 1990s tended to link such issues with globalisation.[52] The 2022 NSS makes the point that transboundary problems are not secondary to great-power competition but 'at the core of national and international security and must be treated as such'.[53] These two challenges are inextricably linked because managing transboundary problems means cooperating with other states – including not just the United States' two main geopolitical competitors, but also smaller states that do not share US commitments to liberal democracy, or countries that are suspicious of American intentions. The NSS is clear that the US does not wish to divide the world into Cold War-style blocs. Rather, the aim is to support the autonomy and right of smaller states to make choices that serve their own interests in the hope that these will be best served within the liberal international order.

The way in which the NSS sets up a competition between two systems – democracy and authoritarianism – that are each working to demonstrate their superior ability to solve problems and deliver peace, order and prosperity recalls Truman's choice between competing ways of life and Gaddis's characterisation of the meaning of the Marshall Plan. The interim NSS positioned democracy versus authoritarianism in the abstract as the chief problem of US grand strategy. In the final version, the dimensions of this confrontation are spelled out more precisely. 'The most pressing strategic challenge facing [the US] vision', says the NSS, 'is from powers that layer authoritarian governance with a revisionist foreign policy'.[54] Those powers, it says, seek to subvert the global order by 'weaponizing information to undermine democracies and polarize societies'.[55] The objective is not necessarily to defeat authoritarian competitors but to show that 'democratic governance consistently outperforms authoritarianism in protecting human dignity, leads to more prosperous and resilient societies, creates stronger and more reliable economic and security partners for the United States, and encourages a peaceful world order'.[56] A related passage concedes that some countries may be uneasy with the competition between the US and the world's largest autocracies, but specifies that the creation of rigid ideological blocs is not the goal. Instead, 'we are trying to support every country, regardless of size or strength, in exercising the freedom to make choices that serve their interests'.[57] Unlike previous strategies, the 2022 NSS does not articulate any desire to actively spread democracy. Rather, it emphasises persuasion by offering a demonstrably superior alternative.

Domestically, the NSS seeks to head off the authoritarian challenge through a series of reforms. The tacit premise is that the anti-democratic, authoritarian, nationalist character of the American right wing – with Trump as its leader – threatens the US constitutional order. Indeed, the 2021 Capitol Hill insurrection appeared to prove as much. According to the NSS,

> the future of America's success in the world depends upon our strength and resilience at home – and especially the strength of our middle class, which is critical to our national security as an engine of economic growth and a key source of democratic vibrance and cohesion.[58]

Accordingly, the NSS aims to promote measures that strengthen the middle class; uphold the integrity of elections; expand voting rights and democratic participation; alleviate inequalities; and lean on pluralism, inclusion and diversity as sources of national strength. The assumption is, of course, that anti-pluralism, exclusion and monoculture are sources of national weakness. In fact, the NSS includes a passage about counter-terrorism in its section on strengthening democracy, suggesting that the Biden administration regards domestic threats to democracy as a variety of terrorism.

A second echo of Trumanism can be found in the NSS's attitude towards international cooperation. Importantly, the NSS concedes that the liberal international order is not the only mechanism for achieving order. This is a striking departure from post-Cold War strategies, which upheld the rules-based international order as the only acceptable framework for world politics. Biden's NSS introduces the idea of dual-track cooperation: deep, institution-alised cooperation with long-term allies and ad hoc cooperation with any other partner willing to play ball. While the former is a common US foreign-policy practice, liberal internationalism has not normally been presented alongside transactionalism as equally viable options. Since the end of the Second World War, there has been a US expectation of cooperation through international institutions or through coalitions of the willing. However, this articulation of a dual-track system signals a more pragmatic approach. It accepts that there is limited appetite for formal multilateralism and concedes that ad hoc cooperation is both inevitable and better than nothing.

The third neo-Trumanite element is an emphasis on domestic revitalisation as necessary for restoring US strength in the world. This is the 'inverted' element of the NSS. In 1946, the Marshall Plan supplemented containment with a plan to rebuild the economies of Western Europe and Japan. In 2022 the reconstruction effort is directed inward, toward remaking the US economy after the distortions of an era bookended by the Great Recession and the COVID-19 pandemic. This means massive state-led reinvestment and a reconfiguration of trade rules to benefit the US middle classes, thereby restoring domestic confidence in market capitalism and democratic government. The NSS aims at investing in physical infrastructure and regional economic-development schemes, along with investments in areas where the private sector has not mobilised to protect core economic and national-security interests.[59] Most striking is the 'bottom-up and middle-out approach' to public investment, meaning investments in healthcare, education, skilled immigration and more.[60] In practical terms, protectionism is evident in the provisions of landmark pieces of legislation such as the Inflation Reduction Act and the CHIPS and Science Act, which aims to consolidate US microchip manufacturing, as well as in Biden's continued non-participation in the Comprehensive and Progressive Agreement for Trans-Pacific Partnership. While such legislation can irk US allies, it has not precipitated any major crisis among adherents to the liberal international order.[61]

*     *     *

In early 2022, Putin and Xi released a joint rebuke of US leadership of the international order.[62] The statement claimed that 'international relations [were] entering a new era' in which, it was implied, US leadership would no longer be assumed. However, the document's contradictions and implausible claims inadvertently did Biden's work for him. It demonstrated that there was in fact an axis of authoritarianism, just as Biden and other Democrats had been saying.[63] A few weeks later, Russia's invasion of

Ukraine not only served as proof of Biden's overarching concept, it also reanimated the transatlantic community, and the liberal international order more generally. It gave the US an opportunity to act alongside its European allies in a manner that affirmed Biden's democracy-versus-authoritarianism world view. The West's response to Russia's invasion showed that the liberal international order still had life. It signalled ongoing acceptance – in the West, at least – of norms that have underpinned the liberal international order for decades: a rejection of wars of conquest and an embrace of sovereignty, humanitarianism, democratic restraint and internationalism. It is possible that the 2022 NSS would have sent a different message had Russia rolled to an easy win in Ukraine,[64] but Ukrainian resistance, and the American response, reinforced a tradition in US foreign-policy thinking – born during those famous 15 weeks and still potent after 75 years.

## Notes

1   Hans J. Morgenthau, *A New Foreign Policy for the United States* (New York: Frederick A. Praeger, 1969), p. 3.
2   *Ibid.*
3   White House, 'Interim National Security Strategic Guidance', March 2021, p. 7.
4   White House, 'National Security Strategy', October 2022.
5   White House, 'Interim National Security Strategic Guidance', p. 7.
6   See Joseph R. Biden, 'Why America Must Lead Again', *Foreign Affairs*, vol. 99, no. 2, March/April 2020, pp. 64–76.
7   *Ibid.*, p. 8.
8   See G. John Ikenberry, *Liberal Leviathan: The Origins, Crisis, and Transformation of the American World Order* (Princeton, NJ: Princeton University Press, 2011), p. 163.
9   See 'Goldwater–Nichols Department of Defense Reorganization Act of 1986', H.R. 3622, 99th Congress,

12 September 1986, https://www.congress.gov/bill/99th-congress/house-bill/3622.
10  See Melvyn P. Leffler, *Safeguarding Democratic Capitalism: U.S. Foreign Policy and National Security, 1920–2015* (Princeton, NJ: Princeton University Press, 2017).
11  See George F. Will, 'Biden's Trumanesque Foreign Policy', *Washington Post*, 24 March 2021, https://www.washingtonpost.com/opinions/bidens-trumanesque-foreign-policy/2021/03/23/ed46fad4-8c05-11eb-a6bd-0eb91c03305a_story.html; David Adesnik, 'Biden Revives the Truman Doctrine', *Foreign Policy*, 29 March 2021, https://foreignpolicy.com/2021/03/29/biden-truman-doctrine-russia-china-national-security-strategic-guidance-global-fight-freedom/; and Deborah Welch Larson, 'The Return

of Containment', *Foreign Policy*, 15 January 2021, https://foreignpolicy.com/2021/01/15/containment-russia-china-kennan-today/.

12  See Lara Jakes and Steven Lee Myers, 'Tense Talks with China Left U.S. "Cleareyed" About Beijing's Intentions, Officials Say', *New York Times*, 19 March 2021, https://www.nytimes.com/2021/03/19/world/asia/china-us-alaska.html.

13  See Leffler, *Safeguarding Democratic Capitalism*.

14  See Melvyn P. Leffler, *A Preponderance of Power: National Security, the Truman Administration, and the Cold War* (Stanford, CA: Stanford University Press, 1992); John Lewis Gaddis, *The Cold War: A New History* (New York: Penguin Press, 2005); Seyom Brown, *Faces of Power: Constancy and Change in United States Foreign Policy from Truman to Obama*, 3rd ed. (New York: Columbia University Press, 2015); and Hal Brands, *What Good Is Grand Strategy? Power and Purpose in American Statecraft from Harry S. Truman to George W. Bush* (Ithaca, NY: Cornell University Press, 2014).

15  Josef Stalin, 'Speech Delivered by J.V. Stalin at a Meeting of Voters of the Stalin Electoral District, Moscow', 9 February 1946, available from the Wilson Center Digital Archive, http://digitalarchive.wilsoncenter.org/document/116179.

16  Brown, *Faces of Power*, p. 19.

17  *Ibid.*

18  See Henry R. Nau, *Conservative Internationalism: Armed Diplomacy Under Jefferson, Polk, Truman, and Reagan* (Princeton, NJ: Princeton University Press, 2013), pp. 150–1; and Lamont Colucci, *The National Security Doctrines of the American Presidency: How They Shape Our Present and Future*, vol. 2 (Denver, CO: Praeger, 2012), pp. 317–18.

19  US House of Representatives, 'Address of the President of the United States', 80th Congress, 1st Session, Doc. No. 171, 1947.

20  On Woodrow Wilson's attitude towards the Bolshevik revolution, see George C. Herring, *From Colony to Superpower: U.S. Foreign Relations Since 1776* (Oxford: Oxford University Press, 2008), p. 415.

21  US House of Representatives, 'Address of the President of the United States'.

22  Quoted in Brands, *What Good Is Grand Strategy?*, p. 27.

23  Quoted in Wallace J. Thies, *Why NATO Endures* (Cambridge: Cambridge University Press, 2009), p. 94.

24  George C. Marshall, 'The Marshall Plan Speech', 5 June 1947, available from the George C. Marshall Foundation, https://www.marshallfoundation.org/the-marshall-plan/speech/.

25  See Gaddis, *The Cold War*.

26  See William O. Walker III, *The Rise and Decline of the American Century* (Ithaca, NY: Cornell University Press, 2018), p. 30.

27  See Ikenberry, *Liberal Leviathan*, p. 199.

28  *Ibid.*

29  See G. John Ikenberry, *A World Safe for Democracy: Liberal Internationalism and the Crises of Global Order* (New Haven, CT: Yale University Press, 2020), pp. 182–4; and Stephen Wertheim, *Tomorrow, the World: The Birth of U.S. Global Supremacy* (Cambridge, MA: Harvard University Press, 2020).

30  See Ikenberry, *Liberal Leviathan*, p. 222.

31  White House, 'Remarks by President Biden on America's Place in the

World', 4 February 2021, https://www.whitehouse.gov/briefing-room/speeches-remarks/2021/02/04/remarks-by-president-biden-on-americas-place-in-the-world/.

32 White House, 'Remarks by President Biden at the 2021 Virtual Munich Security Conference', 19 February 2021, https://www.whitehouse.gov/briefing-room/speeches-remarks/2021/02/19/remarks-by-president-biden-at-the-2021-virtual-munich-security-conference/.

33 Bernie Sanders and Elizabeth Warren had been much clearer about this ideational binary. See Aaron Ettinger, 'Principled Realism and Populist Sovereignty in Trump's Foreign Policy', *Cambridge Review of International Affairs*, vol. 33, no. 3, 2020.

34 Joe Biden and Boris Johnson, 'New Atlantic Charter and Joint Statement Agreed by the PM and President Biden', 10 June 2021, https://www.gov.uk/government/publications/new-atlantic-charter-and-joint-statement-agreed-by-the-pm-and-president-biden.

35 Trump-era joint communiqués ran to only 4,011, 4,152 and 790 words. On one occasion there was no joint communiqué at all.

36 G7, 'Carbis Bay G7 Summit Communiqué', 11–13 June 2021.

37 See Ettinger, 'Principled Realism and Populist Sovereignty in Trump's Foreign Policy'.

38 White House, 'Remarks by President Biden Before the 76th Session of the United Nations General Assembly', 21 September 2021, https://www.whitehouse.gov/briefing-room/speeches-remarks/2021/09/21/remarks-by-president-biden-before-the-76th-session-of-the-united-nations-general-assembly/.

39 *Ibid.*

40 *Ibid.*

41 For more on the US presence in Afghanistan, see Carter Malkasian, *The American War in Afghanistan: A History* (Oxford: Oxford University Press, 2021).

42 Quoted in Karen DeYoung, 'In Allied Capitals, a Nuanced, Cautious View of Biden', *Washington Post*, 17 October 2021, https://www.washingtonpost.com/national-security/biden-foreign-policy-allies/2021/10/16/c066cc3a-2eab-11ec-baf4-d7a4e075eb90_story.html.

43 See Natasha Bertrand et al., 'Even Biden Caught Off Guard by His Administration's Foreign Policy Crises', CNN, 24 September 2021, https://www.cnn.com/2021/09/24/politics/biden-foreign-policy-crises-off-guard/index.html.

44 Quoted in Ivana Kottasová and Angela Dewan, 'Was COP26 Successful? Here's How Climate Summits Make a Difference', CNN, 15 November 2021, https://www.cnn.com/2021/11/14/world/does-cop26-matter-for-climate-intl/index.html.

45 See Katie Rogers and Natalie Kitroeff, 'At Summit, U.S., Canada and Mexico Avoid Thorny Questions', *New York Times*, 18 November 2021.

46 See Kevin Liptak, '"Healthy Debate," But No Breakthroughs in Biden's Critical Talks with China's Xi Jinping', CNN, 16 November 2021, https://www.cnn.com/2021/11/15/politics/joe-biden-xi-jinping-virtual-summit/index.html.

47 White House, 'Remarks at the Virtual Summit for Democracy Opening

Session', 9 December 2021, https://
www.whitehouse.gov/briefing-room/
speeches-remarks/2021/12/09/remarks-
by-president-biden-at-the-summit-for-
democracy-opening-session/.

48 See James Traub, 'There Is a West',
*Foreign Policy*, 7 March 2022, https://
foreignpolicy.com/2022/03/07/
there-is-a-west/.

49 White House, 'National Security
Strategy', p. 2.

50 *Ibid.*, p. 6.

51 *Ibid.*, p. 3.

52 See Aaron Ettinger, 'US National
Security Strategies: Patterns of
Continuity and Change, 1987–2015',
*Comparative Strategy*, vol. 36, no. 2,
2017, pp. 115–28.

53 White House, 'National Security
Strategy', October 2022, p. 6.

54 *Ibid.*, p. 8.

55 *Ibid.*, pp. 17–18.

56 *Ibid.*, p. 8.

57 *Ibid.*, p. 9.

58 *Ibid.*, p. 14.

59 *Ibid.*

60 *Ibid.*, p. 15.

61 See Edward Alden, 'Biden's
"America First" Economic Policy

Threatens Rift with Europe', *Foreign
Policy*, 5 December 2022, https://
foreignpolicy.com/2022/12/05/
biden-ira-chips-act-america-first-
europe-eu-cars-ev-economic-policy/.

62 President of Russia, 'Joint Statement
of the Russian Federation and the
People's Republic of China on the
International Relations Entering a
New Era and the Global Sustainable
Development', 4 February 2022, http://
en.kremlin.ru/supplement/5770.

63 See Elizabeth Warren, 'A Foreign
Policy for All', *Foreign Affairs*, vol.
98, no. 1, 2019, pp. 50–61; and Bernie
Sanders, 'A New Authoritarian Axis
Demands an International Progressive
Front', *Guardian*, 13 September 2018,
https://www.theguardian.com/
commentisfree/ng-interactive/2018/
sep/13/bernie-sanders-international-
progressive-front.

64 See Anne Applebaum, 'The Brutal
Alternate World in Which the U.S.
Abandoned Ukraine', *Atlantic*,
22 December 2022, https://www.
theatlantic.com/ideas/archive/2022/12/
zelensky-congress-speech-us-ukraine-
support/672547/.

# The US and South Korea: The Trouble with Nuclear Assurance

## Adam Mount

Nuclear-weapons experts often cite former UK defence minister Denis Healey's maxim about the challenge of extended deterrence during the Cold War: 'it takes only five per cent credibility of American retaliation to deter the Russians, but ninety-five per cent credibility to reassure the Europeans'.[1] The usual implication is that this disparity is an inevitable feature of extended deterrence and that US officials should work harder to bolster nuclear assurance – that is, the practice of conducting exercises and consultations to attempt to convince concerned allies that the United States remains resolved to guarantee their security with nuclear weapons.

Today, US officials regularly warn that extended deterrence is at risk in Europe, the Middle East and Asia.[2] The worry is particularly urgent in South Korea, where recent trends have increased demands for nuclear assurance. North Korea has rapidly expanded and diversified its nuclear arsenal. Its intercontinental ballistic-missile systems have caused South Korean analysts to ask whether Washington would trade Seoul for Seattle. Its programme to deploy sophisticated tactical nuclear weapons, which the regime says could be used pre-emptively for coercion and war termination, raises serious questions about whether the alliance is prepared to deter early nuclear use and coercion in a limited conflict.[3] At the same time, the

Adam Mount is a non-resident Senior Fellow at the Federation of American Scientists. A previous version of this paper was presented to the Forum on Republic of Korea–US Nuclear Strategy at the Sejong Institute in Seoul in November 2022.

**Survival** | vol. 65 no. 2 | April–May 2023 | pp. 123–140    https://doi.org/10.1080/00396338.2023.2193104

Trump administration's erratic demands of Seoul have amplified concerns about US extended-deterrence commitments in the long run. In response, American and South Korean officials have rushed to highlight nuclear-assurance measures and their commitment to extended deterrence.[4]

In South Korea, interest in an indigenous nuclear-weapons programme has continued to increase. Public polls have often found robust support for nuclear armament, and in recent years supportive statements from elites have grown more frequent and urgent.[5] They are no longer confined to fringe groups on the right wing. Successive leaders of the conservative ruling party have endorsed the idea, and a party committee has proposed clandestine steps to explore 'the optimal course for nuclear armament'.[6] The national conversation now includes specific recommendations for how to produce fissile material, sequence acquisition and defray the costs of a nuclear-weapons programme.[7] The idea has even gained traction with some prominent progressives and former military officers.[8] For the United States, nuclear assurance is the preferred answer: the 2022 Nuclear Posture Review states that one of the three main roles of US nuclear weapons is to convince allies they can 'remain secure without acquiring nuclear weapons of their own'.[9]

In early 2023, the problem escalated when South Korean President Yoon Suk-yeol stated in apparently improvised remarks to his foreign and defence ministries that 'if problems become more serious, South Korea could deploy tactical nuclear weapons here, or we could acquire our own nuke as well', noting that 'it would not take long' and that his government was then consulting with the United States on 'joint planning and joint execution' with respect to 'US nuclear assets'.[10] When asked by reporters if the allies were discussing joint nuclear exercises, US President Joe Biden answered 'no'.[11] Though the exchange between presidents was unusual, the friction behind it was not unfamiliar.

## Misplaced faith

For both the United States and its allies, nuclear assurance is the vital mechanism that underwrites nuclear deterrence and non-proliferation. As each of these challenges has intensified, experts and officials have doubled down on nuclear assurance, seeking new mechanisms. Proposals range from expanded consultative meetings, to new alliance-planning mechanisms that mirror NATO's Nuclear Planning Group (NPG), to outlandish nuclear-sharing proposals.

A close examination of the South Korean case casts doubt on the effectiveness of nuclear assurance as a mechanism for strengthening both extended deterrence and non-proliferation. Over the long run, nuclear weapons cannot resolve an ally's anxieties about extended nuclear deterrence. Urgent demands for nuclear assurance are not an inevitable part of the normal business of a healthy alliance, but represent a failure of the alliance to perform its central function: the maintenance of a credible combined-deterrence posture.

In practice, nuclear assurance does more harm than good to extended deterrence. As Lauren Sukin and Toby Dalton have argued, 'increasing the salience of nuclear weapons in Northeast Asia may not only fail to address' Seoul's concerns, 'but could also backfire', fuelling nuclear-proliferation risks and weakening extended deterrence.[12] By reinforcing the fiction that the alliance is dependent on nuclear weapons to protect South Korea, it serves the interests of factions within both countries invested in such weapons, but prevents the alliance from prioritising its more effective, flexible and credible conventional forces. Because the United States can never convince a sceptical ally that it will use nuclear weapons on its behalf, efforts to raise the salience of nuclear weapons only increase such an ally's anxieties. The goal should be the opposite: to assure Seoul that the alliance is sufficiently capable that its security does not depend on US nuclear use.

In the rush to strengthen nuclear assurance, it is easy to forget that Healey was not arguing that it is a necessary tool to address an ally's anxieties. He was making the opposite point: the European allies were worrying too much about the credibility of the American deterrent. In practice, the allies were more concerned about US political leadership than a deficit of nuclear assurance.[13] No nuclear-assurance measure can assuage an ally that is fundamentally concerned about whether a US president will defend them. An alliance that depends on nuclear assurance is a weak and fragile one. A strong US–South Korea alliance requires a commitment to reduce its reliance on nuclear assurance and nuclear deterrence in general.

## Evaluating nuclear-assurance proposals

Recommendations to improve US nuclear assurance to South Korea fall into three categories. Firstly, there are a range of proposals to expand or strengthen combined exercises with nuclear-capable assets. To take one example, the alliance could conduct exercises in which South Korean Air Force tactical aircraft support US nuclear-capable bombers, analogous to NATO's *SNOWCAT* exercises.[14] The idea is deserving of careful consideration if it could help to reduce alliance friction for a significant amount of time. However, the positive effects on deterrence or military operations would be minimal and the exercises largely performative. In an escalating conflict, if the US president did issue an order for nuclear release to a bomber, support missions would undoubtedly be assigned to US units.

Secondly, there are a variety of schemes for redeploying US nuclear-capable assets or nuclear munitions to bases on or near the Korean Peninsula.[15] These proposals would usually diminish political support for the alliance and weaken regional stability with little or no offsetting operational benefit.[16] Forward-deploying nuclear-capable assets would expose them to attacks from an enemy's theatre systems, presenting a tempting target for pre-emptive strikes that could unnecessarily escalate a conflict. If a US president were ever forced to employ a nuclear weapon, tactical dual-capable systems would be the last option they would choose. Proximity of nuclear-capable assets is only a political virtue in talks with allies; in a fight with an enemy, it is a military liability.

Thirdly, there are implausible proposals for nuclear-sharing arrangements. Some of these ideas, like a scheme to deploy dual-key warheads on South Korean submarines, would violate the Nuclear Non-Proliferation Treaty commitments of both countries and still fail to provide South Korea's presidents with additional confidence that a nuclear warhead would be used when and where they think it is necessary.

Importantly, none of these three types of measures would convince sceptical South Korean officials that the United States would use a nuclear weapon on their behalf. US extended-nuclear-deterrence guarantees are about as credible as they can ever be. It does not matter that US officials believe that they would trade Seattle for Seoul (as I do).[17] It does not matter that this is a slogan rather than a plausible contingency. What matters is that US officials can never prove it.

Redeploying warheads or nuclear-capable platforms would impose high costs in terms of Chinese economic coercion; acquisition and military construction; political support for the alliance in both countries; their diplomatic standing; and regional stability, with scant benefit.[18] For these reasons and others, successive US administrations have consistently rejected such measures.[19] Mooting and formally requesting them causes significant strain between the allies and distracts them from important conversations on plausible assurance mechanisms and combined military planning. Each of these ideas depends on three fallacies: that the alliance is reliant on nuclear deterrence, that nuclear assurance is the only available policy option, and that nuclear-assurance measures can actually satisfy South Korea. If these assumptions were valid, they might be worth the costs, but it is increasingly clear that they are not.

## Understanding allied anxieties

Nuclear assurance assumes that an ally holds modest and rational concerns about the resolve of a US president to employ nuclear weapons and that these concerns can be periodically addressed through rhetoric, consultations, exercises or minor adjustments to posture. Unfortunately, this is not an accurate description of the tensions within the US–South Korea alliance. Seoul's anxieties are not modest and transient; they are severe, persistent and growing. They have not proven tractable over decades of efforts to strengthen nuclear assurance. This is because, for many South Koreans, anxieties about US extended deterrence stem not from a rational calculation about deterrence credibility but rather from emotional dread of North Korea's growing nuclear arsenal. Photos of submarines, intricate consultations behind closed doors, confident op-eds from US officials, or even announcements of shifts in US nuclear posture will not dispel that emotion. Many South Koreans simply do not trust the commitment of US politicians and no amount of tinkering with the details of extended deterrence will persuade them.

In other words, such intense and persistent anxieties about the credibility of US extended deterrence imply that the US ally experiencing them believes that the existing deterrence posture is inadequate to defend its interests. If allies are anxious about extended nuclear deterrence, they doubt that the US nuclear posture is sufficient to protect them from aggression. Allied anxieties are therefore fundamentally concerns about deterrence, not assurance.

The fundamental flaw in nuclear assurance is that it does not contribute directly to deterrence. The existing menu of nuclear-assurance options is unlikely to affect an adversary's calculus in a crisis. They do not convey additional resolve to use a nuclear weapon. Instead, these types of demonstrations have become routine and performative.[20] If nuclear-assurance measures would affect North Korean leader Kim Jong-un's calculations in a crisis at all, they would likely have been factored in at the outset. In staging routine demonstrations of nuclear-capable assets, nuclear-assurance exercises have probably degraded the alliance's ability to credibly signal with nuclear forces in a crisis without resorting to escalatory measures.

Nuclear-assurance measures are designed to speak to leaders in Seoul, not Pyongyang. Yet, because it does not strengthen deterrence, nuclear assurance also does not assure anxious allies for long. In this sense, nuclear-assurance measures are wasting assets and successive rounds have diminishing returns. While the first combined exercises with a nuclear-capable B-52H bomber may have had some assurance effect, these missions, now routine, may even be detrimental to assurance because they seem to imply that US officials are unwilling to do more than they have in the past. In private, American officials commonly characterise these kinds of actions as pouring water into a bucket with a hole in the bottom.

Nuclear assurance can provide temporary relief for a chronic problem, but sustained use will require higher and more damaging doses to have the same effect. Like a patient addicted to opioids, an alliance that is reliant on nuclear assurance to feel healthy will have less incentive and less ability to treat the underlying problem.

Nuclear assurance is unsatisfying to allies not because of a lack of attention or resolve on the part of US officials, or because new North Korean threats have altered the structure of extended nuclear deterrence. As an adversary's nuclear capabilities expand, US attention and resolve increase rather than decrease. Extended nuclear deterrence and thus nuclear assurance are unsatisfying because nuclear weapons are blunt instruments, poorly suited for escalation management or termination of a limited conflict with a nuclear-armed adversary like North Korea.

## Inherited shortcomings of nuclear deterrence

Often, debates about nuclear assurance seem to rely on the assumption that an unambiguous, irreversible US commitment to nuclear employment would resolve an ally's anxieties. There are many good reasons why the United States cannot commit to employ nuclear weapons. The most commonly cited one is that US nuclear use can only occur at the sole discretion of the president. Fundamentally, the system of sole authority means that no one can be certain that a president will or will not use a nuclear weapon in any given contingency, and there is nothing the United States can do to convince allies otherwise.

In practice, a presidential decision to order nuclear use is not a standing order linked to a predetermined set of circumstances, but would be made in the context of an ongoing crisis. Each scenario is unique. The decision to use a nuclear weapon depends critically on a wide range of factors, including the credibility and immediacy of the initial North Korean threat and the risk of subsequent nuclear attacks; the yield, location, casualties and damage of nuclear first use; the state of the crisis or conventional conflict; the readiness and vulnerability of allied and North Korean forces; the global diplomatic context; and many others.[21]

US nuclear use carries potentially momentous costs for the United States and its allies. It could elicit further North Korean nuclear attacks; inflict unintended effects on civilian populations, an ally or a neighbouring country; have vast economic consequences, including for the ally in whose defence the weapon was used; or disrupt or degrade allied conventional operations necessary to prevail in an ongoing conflict. Some of these costs may depend on the characteristics of the detonation and the conflict, but some are fixed and would be incurred by any use of a nuclear weapon. Only in extraordinary cases would the benefits of nuclear use outweigh the costs. In most cases, if conventional forces can inflict the physical effects necessary to protect the interests of the alliance, a US president, as well as an ally's leader, would prefer to avoid nuclear use.

Allies should not understand US extended-deterrence guarantees as a commitment to nuclear use. Rather, US extended deterrence should be understood as a commitment to the security of an ally by the most effective available means, including, as a last resort, nuclear weapons. The United States is morally obligated to serve the objective of the alliance – South Korea's security – and not to use a particular means of securing that objective when there are multiple options for doing so. In short, the US commitment to use a nuclear weapon is inherently uncertain because it may not be in the United States' or South Korea's interest to do so.

Fortunately, the cases in which the security of an ally would depend on US nuclear use are very rare. The most pressing and difficult challenge to allied deterrence posture is the threat that North Korea could employ a tactical nuclear weapon for coercive purposes in a limited conflict. It calls for conventional forces sufficient to deny the regime its objectives, prevail in the conflict and impose costs on the regime with the means that produce the lowest risk of a nuclear exchange that could be catastrophic for all sides.[22] Strong conventional options for deterring and responding to North Korean nuclear use provide the presidents of both allied countries with effective options that avoid nuclear use and its costs. A strong alliance should seek to minimise its dependence on nuclear weapons to promote the development of more flexible and credible non-nuclear options.

The idea that the credibility of US extended deterrence rises and falls with US resolve to use a nuclear weapon assumes that nuclear use is necessary to attain the alliance's objectives and deter North Korean nuclear use. One corollary is that an alliance that is dependent on nuclear assurance assumes or prefers that US presidents will find themselves in the worst possible situation: a crisis in which they have no better option than to order the use of a nuclear weapon. This assumes the operational weakness of the alliance and is especially inappropriate on the Korean Peninsula, where Washington and Seoul enjoy overwhelming conventional superiority.

The central challenge for the US–South Korea alliance is not to maximise the credibility of extended nuclear deterrence but to maintain an effective overall deterrence posture. Allied concerns about deterrence can be effectively addressed only by strengthening that posture, in particular by investing in credible and capable conventional forces and thus minimising the alliance's dependence on nuclear weapons.

## Nuclear assurance as a political agenda

Given its disadvantages, why does the alliance rely so heavily on nuclear assurance? The main reason is that it satisfies the political interests of factions in both countries. In the United States, the primary effect of nuclear assurance is to maintain reliance on nuclear weapons as the central instruments of deterrence, which helps protect funding for nuclear-modernisation programmes. US officials and experts who share this agenda can participate in consultative mechanisms focused on nuclear assurance, creating opportunities to coordinate with allied officials who can then broadcast their shared views on questions of US nuclear-weapons policy, large and small. In this way, US officials can bootstrap their arguments, amplifying them for senior civilian officials reflexively concerned with the interests of allies.[23] Officials who are convinced that only a nuclear weapon can deter nuclear use, or are uninterested in the niceties of nuclear deterrence, have little reason to reassess nuclear assurance, which, after all, has gotten us this far.

In South Korea, nuclear assurance is similarly useful for groups who believe that nuclear weapons are indispensable to security. For advocates of a South Korean nuclear programme, it is helpful that nuclear assurance is a bottomless pit that can never be filled. Whether or not the United States responds to calls for nuclear assurance, South Korean politicians will understandably remain unsatisfied. The inevitable failure of nuclear assurance bolsters calls for nuclearisation. Such dynamics help explain empirical evidence that extended nuclear assurance may increase rather than decrease proliferation pressures.[24]

The growing debate on nuclearisation could be devastating to an alliance seeking to strengthen its deterrence posture against rapidly evolving threats. It is not a harmless intellectual exercise; it would force US functional and regional officials to divert their attention away from improving deterrence and towards non-proliferation efforts to prevent South Korea from making a mistake that could inflict enormous economic, diplomatic and stability costs on both countries.[25] US officials should resist any efforts by South Korean officials to blackmail the United States into extending stronger assurance measures by hinting at the possibility of an indigenous nuclear programme.

A recent proposal demonstrates how different factions make use of nuclear-assurance arguments to advance their prior beliefs. In early 2023, a task force of US Korea experts chaired by John Hamre, in the past an advocate for forward deployment of US nuclear warheads to South Korea, recommended that the alliance 'lay the pre-decisional groundwork for possible redeployment'.[26] The report recommended a series of consultations, studies, training exercises and, if threat levels continued to escalate, construction of storage facilities. Some advocates of nuclear assurance may read the plan as a way to reduce proliferation pressures by meeting South Korean requests. Advocates of nuclear sharing in Washington and Seoul would see it as a road map. In practice, the plan would build momentum for redeployment, raising expectations in Seoul and precluding a broader conversation on non-nuclear-deterrence options. At the same time, the steps would do nothing to increase South Korea's control over a US president's decision to authorise nuclear deployment or release, so their assurance value would be fleeting. The prospect may make sense from a nuclear-assurance perspective, but it will harm the alliance in the long haul.

Seeing nuclear assurance as a political device helps explain why nuclear assurance is ineffective even for allies who value nuclear deterrence highly. The practice of nuclear assurance cultivates the misconception that the alliance's deterrence posture depends primarily on nuclear weapons. Nuclear assurance is not designed to solve an alliance's assurance problems, but to maintain them at a useful level.

### Better coordination for deterrence and assurance

As North Korea's strategic and tactical nuclear forces have advanced, they have acquired new systems and new missions. It is becoming increasingly difficult for the alliance to maintain a credible deterrence posture, as it is forced to plan for a rapidly expanding set of contingencies. Meeting this challenge will require significant adjustments in how the alliance plans for conflict and how its senior officials coordinate on nuclear-weapons policy. Although US officials have invested considerable effort in assuring South Korea in recent years, South Korean officials have regularly expressed frustration that existing deterrence dialogues are too vague to inform their planning for new contingencies for nuclear escalation.

The central problem with the existing framework is that it is designed to provide assurance rather than to strengthen deterrence through planning and adaptation. Meetings tend to concentrate on general informational briefings about US nuclear-force structure and policy. South Korean officials are invited to tour US Strategic Command and to familiarise themselves with the capabilities of B-2 bombers.

For US officials, these dialogues are opportunities to demonstrate to their South Korean counterparts that US nuclear forces are capable and maintained at a state of high readiness, discuss additional nuclear-assurance measures with them, and inform and consult with them on changes to US nuclear-weapons policy. But they do little to enlighten wary South Korean officials about when, why and how a US president would order the use of nuclear weapons in South Korea's defence. US officials are understandably reluctant to provide any of its allies with the employment options that would be available to a president in a crisis. One reason is that looking closely at plans for plausible contingencies would reveal that nuclear employment is usually unnecessary and detrimental to the alliance's military objectives. Rather than see this as good news for the alliance, US officials focused on assurance may worry that they could be compounding Seoul's anxieties if they give any hint that the president might not need to use a nuclear weapon in their defence.

In recent years, some US and South Korean experts have called for a mechanism similar to NATO's NPG.[27] The idea is that the allies should jointly develop plans for nuclear employment, including target identification and selection. However, the recommendation is based on mistaken assumptions about the function of the NPG, which, despite its name, does not perform nuclear planning. Like South Korean officials, non-US NATO officials routinely complain that they have little visibility on US planning and targeting. The problem is not that the South Korean officials are being denied access to nuclear planning enjoyed by other US allies, but that there is no nuclear planning that would reassure them, because nuclear weapons are not central to their defence. South Korea doesn't need an NPG; it needs something better.

The NPG recommendation has essentially the correct goal. South Korea's preferences about when, where and why the United States should employ a nuclear weapon on its behalf should be powerful – even, in some cases, decisive – factors in US nuclear planning and for a president's decision on nuclear use. To better inform a president considering nuclear employment, the United States should add a step to the nuclear-employment authorisation procedure that prompts the US president to consult with their counterpart in Seoul, and the alliance should stand up a secure communications channel to enable these consultations.[28] Establishing and rehearsing the use of this channel could provide the leaders of both countries with greater confidence in and visibility of their ally's interests and procedures in a crisis.

The fact remains that if the United States simply reasserts its reliance on nuclear weapons, this will only exacerbate South Korean anxieties in the long run. In turn, if South Korea merely seeks symbolic demonstrations that the US president is resolved to use nuclear weapons, it is bound to be disappointed. Alliance coordination should be designed first and foremost to strengthen the alliance's deterrence posture.[29] As the North Korean nuclear threat grows more complex, alliance planning must become more detailed and rigorous. Given North Korea's plans for coercive nuclear use for war fighting and escalation control, it is no longer sufficient to hope that the threat of US nuclear employment, no matter how credible, will deter North Korea's nuclear use. Washington and Seoul should be clear with each other about when, why and how they see nuclear use as necessary to secure a favourable outcome in an armed conflict.

## Making new dialogue fruitful

The allies' announcement that they will conduct tabletop exercises as part of extended-deterrence dialogues is a promising development.[30] They should examine in detail a wide range of contingencies for limited nuclear use and explicitly discuss the benefits and costs of a US nuclear response. South

Korean officials should describe precisely the effects that they hope a specific nuclear-employment operation would have on the conflict, on the risk of a wider nuclear exchange and on alliance credibility. In cases in which they recommend nuclear use, they should be asked to specify a target, yield and delivery vehicle, and explore the risks of the option together with US planners. Because the costs of nuclear use extend beyond the military situation on the peninsula, the exchange should include not only the usual nuclear-weapons experts, but also officials who manage conventional forces, diplomats and presidential advisers.

The dialogues should examine contingencies in which the allies' preferences diverge or their military strategies conflict. Iterated games should explore the escalation risks of postures that depend on nuclear retaliation, pre-emptive counterforce and leadership targeting. Both sides should candidly compare their plans, assessments of North Korean forces and psychological profiles of Kim Jong-un to determine whether the sides disagree about the costs and risks of such steps. In particular, threats of decapitation or nuclear first use carry significant risks of unintended escalation, and reflect the alliance's failure to develop capabilities and plans to deter the regime by denying its objectives. Furthermore, officials should discuss limits on nuclear targeting imposed by the US interpretations of the law of armed conflict and set aside concepts that rely on the use of nuclear weapons to punish the regime by targeting civilians or national infrastructure so as to cause a humanitarian crisis. Overall, the new table-top exercises should help the alliance minimise its reliance on dangerous and unreliable policies.[31]

A more effective deterrence dialogue would understand assurance in a broader sense. Assurance requires hat South Korean leaders have confidence not only that US presidents would employ a nuclear weapon when it is required, but also that they would not do so when it was not required – a particularly acute concern during the Moon and Trump administrations.[32] Behind closed doors, US officials have often worried about the escalation risks behind South Korean concepts to retaliate against any North Korean attack with three times the force. On the principle that conventional forces can have strategic effects, US officials would benefit from more information on South Korean plans for utilising its stand-off strike capabilities under its 'Korea Massive Punishment and Retaliation' concept. Both Seoul and Washington should commit to consulting each other before executing strikes on North Korea that could have strategic consequences for both countries.

Where possible, US officials should share detailed information about the capabilities and limits of the United States' nuclear and non-nuclear forces, as well as the attributes of North Korean targets that could inform nuclear-use decisions. In any event, there is no reason that US officials should not candidly discuss categories of targets and US interests in hypothetical contingencies. Participants should together examine the relative utility of hypothetical nuclear and non-nuclear operations with estimates of blast effects against categories of targets in the context of a conflict, to compare their thinking on what is necessary and sufficient to inflict the physical and cognitive effects required to prevail.

Discussions along these lines would make it clear to both sides that nuclear forces have extremely limited utility in plausible contingencies and drive more robust planning on conventional deterrence of North Korean aggression and nuclear use. The objective should be to prove not that the United States would use a nuclear weapon, but that it would not need to do so – that is, to reduce rather than reinforce the alliance's reliance on nuclear weapons. US officials have understandably been hesitant to have these kinds of detailed conversations about nuclear use, but the result has been misconceptions and miscommunications that have weakened the alliance. Though a US ally will never choose when a US nuclear weapon is used, a candid and detailed nuclear-planning process can better inform the decisions of both countries. This is what it should mean to be a US ally: the United States should work tirelessly with its allies to defend them without being forced to resort to nuclear use. But if a US president must consider nuclear use, they should do so in consultation with an allied leader who has been prepared and informed to help them make that mortal decision.

\* \* \*

Nuclear assurance is not durably credible to Seoul because it can only demonstrate capability to use nuclear weapons, not resolve. Nuclear weapons are inherently incapable of assuring an ally because they would only be used as a last resort, in the event the alliance had failed to maintain more effective, more credible and less costly measures. At best, nuclear assurance is a means to the end of a more effective deterrence posture – a helpful stopgap to buy time for the alliance to adapt its posture to new threats. At worst, nuclear assurance is a political charade that keeps up the pretence that the alliance is reliant on nuclear weapons, even at the expense of deterrence credibility, alliance cohesion and proliferation risk. With every passing year, there is more and more evidence that nuclear assurance is not the cure to the alliance's problems, but the cause of it. To prevent a crisis within the US–South Korea alliance, American officials should concentrate less on nuclear assurance and more on a combined deterrence posture that reduces the alliance's reliance on nuclear weapons. Ultimately, deterrence is the best assurance.

## Notes

1   Denis Healey, *The Time of My Life* (London: Michael Joseph, 1989), p. 243.

2   See, for example, Duk-kun Byun, 'N. Korean Nuclear Threat Poses Serious Challenge to U.S. Extended Deterrence: Campbell', Yonhap News Agency, 8 December 2022, https://www.msn.com/en-xl/news/other/n-korean-nuclear-threat-poses-serious-challenge-to-us-extended-deterrence-campbell/ar-AA154oZ0.

3   See Adam Mount and Jungsup Kim, 'North Korea's Tactical Nuclear Threshold Is Frighteningly Low', *Foreign Policy*, 8 December 2022, https://foreignpolicy.com/2022/12/08/north-korea-tactical-nuclear-threat/.

4   See 'Special Contribution by U.S. Secretary of Defense Lloyd Austin', Yonhap News Agency, 31 January 2023, https://en.yna.co.kr/view/AEN20230130008500325; and 'Yoon Calls for Effective Extended Deterrence During Meeting with U.S. Defense Chief', Yonhap News Agency, 31 January 2023, https://en.yna.co.kr/view/AEN20230131012400320.

5   See Toby Dalton, Karl Friedhoff and Lami Kim, 'Thinking Nuclear: South Korean Attitudes on Nuclear Weapons', Chicago Council on Global Affairs, 21 February 2022, https://globalaffairs.org/research/public-opinion-survey/thinking-nuclear-south-korean-attitudes-nuclear-weapons.

6   See Editorial Board, 'Ruling Party's Dangerous Calls for Tactical Nukes in S. Korea', *Hankyoreh*, 13 October 2022, https://english.hani.co.kr/arti/english_edition/english_editorials/1062545.html; and Kim Sang-jin, 'Ruling Party

Special Committee on North Korea Nuclear Response "We Need to Promote a Secret Nuclear Armament Project"', *JoongAng*, 23 November 2022, https://www.joongang.co.kr/article/25120044#home.

7   See Sang-Ho Yun, 'S. Korea Capable of Developing Nuclear Prototype Within Six Months', *Dong-A Ilbo*, 13 January 2023, https://www.donga.com/en/home/article/all/20230113/3890542/1.

8   In this context, it is not clear that the recommendation of South Korea's former top military commander for nuclear latency is a distinct proposal. See Da-gyum Ji, 'Ex-commanders of S. Korea, US Divided on S. Korea's Nuclear Acquisition', *Korea Herald*, 26 October 2022, https://www.koreaherald.com/view.php?ud=20221026000604.

9   US Department of Defense, '2022 Nuclear Posture Review', pp. 7–8, https://s3.documentcloud.org/documents/23205180/2022_national_defense_strategy_npr_mdr.pdf.

10  Jeongmin Kim, 'FULL TEXT: Yoon Suk-Yeol's Remarks on South Korea Acquiring Nuclear Arms', NK PRO, 13 January 2023, https://www.nknews.org/pro/full-text-yoon-suk-yeols-remarks-on-south-korea-acquiring-nuclear-arms/.

11  Soo-Hyang Choi and Trevor Hunnicut, 'Biden Says U.S. Not Discussing Nuclear Exercises with South Korea', Reuters, 2 January 2023, https://www.reuters.com/world/asia-pacific/south-korea-us-eye-exercises-using-nuclear-assets-yoon-says-newspaper-2023-01-02/.

12  Lauren Sukin and Toby Dalton, 'Reducing Nuclear Salience: How

to Reassure Northeast Asian Allies', *Washington Quarterly,* vol. 44, no. 2, Summer 2021, p. 147.

13  Healey, *The Time of My Life*, p. 243.

14  See David Santoro, 'Deterring North Korea: The Next Nuclear-tailoring Agenda', *War on the Rocks*, 8 August 2017, https://warontherocks.com/2017/08/deterring-north-korea-the-next-nuclear-tailoring-agenda/.

15  Recent examples include redeployment of US dual-capable tactical aircraft, strategic bombers or B61 gravity bombs to the peninsula or Guam. The perennial US reiteration that it maintains 'the capability to forward deploy strategic bombers, dual-capable fighter aircraft, and nuclear weapons to the region and globally' is a way of finessing these recommendations without rejecting them. See US Department of Defense, 'Nuclear Posture Review', p. 15.

16  See Bruce Klingner, 'The Case Against Nukes in South Korea', *Diplomat*, 18 October 2017, https://thediplomat.com/2017/10/the-case-against-nukes-in-south-korea/.

17  See Zachary Keck, 'The U.S. Will Trade Seattle for Seoul', *Foreign Policy*, 17 October 2022, https://foreignpolicy.com/2022/10/17/south-korea-nuclear-weapons-deterrence-france-cold-war-north-korea-threat/.

18  See Klingner, 'The Case Against Nukes in South Korea'.

19  See William Gallo, 'US Rules Out Redeploying Tactical Nukes to South Korea', Voice of America, 24 September 2021, https://www.voanews.com/a/us-rules-out-redeploying-tactical-nukes-to-south-korea/6243767.html.

20  See Van Jackson, 'The Trouble with the US Bomber Overflight Against North Korea', *Diplomat*, 12 January 2016, https://thediplomat.com/2016/01/the-trouble-with-the-us-bomber-overflight-against-north-korea/.

21  See Vince A. Manzo and John K. Warden, 'After Nuclear First Use, What?', *Survival*, vol. 60, no. 3, June–July 2018, pp. 133–60; and Adam Mount, 'The Strategic Logic of Nuclear Restraint', *Survival*, vol. 57, no. 4, August–September 2015, pp. 53–76.

22  See Adam Mount, 'Conventional Deterrence of North Korea', Federation of American Scientists, December 2019, https://fas.org/wp-content/uploads/2019/12/FAS-CDNK.pdf.

23  To give one example, in advance of the Nuclear Posture Review, US officials sent to allies a questionnaire that became a powerful instrument for those within the Pentagon trying to prevent Biden from shifting to a 'sole purpose' declaratory policy. See Demetri Sevastopulo and Henry Foy, 'Allies Lobby Biden to Prevent Shift to "No First Use" of Nuclear Arms', *Financial Times*, 30 October 2021, https://www.ft.com/content/8b96a60a-759b-4972-ae89-c8ffbb36878e.

24  See Lauren Sukin, 'Credible Nuclear Security Commitments Can Backfire: Explaining Domestic Support for Nuclear Weapons Acquisition in South Korea', *Journal of Conflict Resolution*, vol. 64, no. 6, July 2020, pp. 1,011–42.

25  See Lauren Sukin, 'How Bad Would a Nuclear-armed South Korea Be? Let Us Count the Ways', *Bulletin of the Atomic Scientists*, 21 October 2021, https://thebulletin.org/2021/10/how-bad-would-a-nuclear-armed-south-korea-be-let-us-count-the-ways/; and Lauren Sukin and Toby Dalton, 'Why South Korea Shouldn't Build Its Own Nuclear Bombs', *War on the Rocks*, 26 October 2021, https://warontherocks.com/2021/10/why-south-korea-shouldnt-build-its-own-nuclear-bombs/.

26  See John J. Hamre et al., 'Recommendations on North Korea Policy and Extended Deterrence', CSIS Commission on the Korean Peninsula, 19 January 2023, p. 18, https://csis-website-prod.s3.amazonaws.com/s3fs-public/2023-01/230119_Korean_Commission_2023.pdf?VersionId=93zTcEue3STUbr6v8IfjQ6z6B_3mNTr4.

27  See, for instance, Brad Roberts, 'Living with a Nuclear-arming North Korea: Deterrence Decisions in a Deteriorating Threat Environment', Stimson Center, 4 November 2020, https://www.stimson.org/2020/living-with-a-nuclear-arming-north-korea-deterrence-decisions-in-a-deteriorating-threat-environment/; and Wie Sung-lac, 'Time for a Reinforced Nuclear Deterrence', *Korea JoongAng Daily*, 3 August 2022, https://koreajoongangdaily.joins.com/2022/08/03/opinion/columns/nuclear-deterrence-South-Korea/20220803200927697.html.

28  For more on this recommendation, see Adam Mount and Pranay Vaddi, 'Better Informing a President's Decision on Nuclear Use', Lawfare, 9 November 2020, https://www.lawfareblog.com/better-informing-presidents-decision-nuclear-use.

29  See S. Paul Choi, 'Deterring North Korea: The Need for Collective Resolve and Alliance Transformation', 38 North, 23 July 2020, https://www.38north.org/2020/07/spchoi072320/.

30  See US Department of Defense, '54th Security Consultative Meeting Joint Communiqué', 3 November 2022, https://www.defense.gov/News/Releases/Release/Article/3209105/54th-security-consultative-meeting-joint-communique/.

31  See James M. Acton and Ankit Panda, 'North Korea's Doctrinal Shifts Are More Dangerous than Missile Launches', *Foreign Policy*, 4 November 2022, https://foreignpolicy.com/2022/11/04/north-korea-nuclear-doctrine-more-dangerous-than-missile-launches/.

32  Thanks to a South Korean military officer for valuable conversations on both points.

# Assessing Proliferation Risks in the Middle East

**Aya Kamil, Zuha Noor and Daniel Serwer**

The United States has long been concerned with nuclear proliferation in the Middle East. It went to war in 2003 on the (false) premise that Iraq was close to building nuclear weapons. In 2004, the Brookings Institution warned of a 'nuclear tipping point' that might be reached due to some combination of changes in US policy, the breakdown of the global non-proliferation regime, the erosion of regional security, domestic imperatives and the increased availability of technology.[1] In 2010, Richard L. Russell contributed an article to *Joint Forces Quarterly* called 'Off and Running: The Middle East Arms Race', in which he noted that a desire among regional governments to deter adversaries, compensate for conventional-weapons shortcomings, enhance war-fighting capabilities, garner domestic political power, and augment their international standing and leverage, especially in relation to the United States, could compel an arms race.[2]

Iran has long been a proliferation concern, but some experts concluded in 2012 that the other main potential proliferators – who were then thought to be Egypt, Saudi Arabia, Turkiye and the United Arab Emirates (UAE) – would not follow Israel's lead in acquiring nuclear weapons.[3] All were interested in civilian nuclear power and had signed the Nuclear Non-Proliferation Treaty (NPT), which put their nuclear facilities under International Atomic

**Aya Kamil** is a junior fellow at the Carnegie Endowment for International Peace. **Zuha Noor** is a senior at the University of Pennsylvania. Kamil and Noor worked on this paper while research assistants at the Middle East Institute. **Daniel Serwer**, the lead author for this article, is a scholar at the Middle East Institute, a professor at Johns Hopkins University and a senior fellow at its Foreign Policy Institute. He spent seven years in US embassies as a science counselor focused on non-proliferation issues.

**Survival** | vol. 65 no. 2 | April–May 2023 | pp. 141–164          https://doi.org/10.1080/00396338.2023.2193105

Energy Agency (IAEA) safeguards. Iran's policy, which aimed to acquire enrichment technology, was more ambiguous, but was still subject to IAEA safeguarding and avowedly peaceful. The reasons for opting not to develop nuclear weapons varied by country, but typical factors included the countries' historical and strategic choices, their relations with the United States and a lack of national-security problems that nuclear weapons would solve. Iran signed and implemented the Joint Comprehensive Plan of Action (JCPOA) in 2015, which was intended to delay any effort on its part to develop nuclear weapons. Israel lived up to expectations by continuing to follow a policy of neither admitting to nor denying its nuclear status, thus maintaining its policy of nuclear opacity.[4]

If a wider nuclear arms race was 'off and running' a decade ago, it is still a well-kept secret. The only publicly known effort to acquire a significant amount of fissionable (bomb-making) material in the Middle East during the past two decades, other than by Israel or Iran, was Syria's clandestine construction of a suspected plutonium-production reactor, the technology for which was provided by North Korea. Israel destroyed the reactor in an air raid in 2007, as it had done to a reactor in Iraq in 1981. Syria, like Iraq, is no longer in a position to contemplate a nuclear option.

That is no reason for complacency. Much has changed in the past ten years. While the US has not withdrawn from the Middle East, it relies much less than it used to on the region's oil. Washington has long wanted to shift military attention to the Indo-Pacific. It would like its Middle Eastern allies to carry more of their own security burdens. The drawdowns of US forces from Iraq and Syria, as well as the chaotic evacuation from Afghanistan and the election of Donald Trump, who sought to reduce American commitments abroad and even suggested that some allies obtain nuclear weapons, have shaken Middle Eastern confidence in American regional commitments.

Russia and China are challenging US hegemony in the region. Moscow successfully intervened militarily in Syria starting in 2015 to protect the Assad regime, and has also cooperated with the Organization of Petroleum Exporting Countries (OPEC) to sustain oil prices. The state-owned Russian firm Rosatom has contracts to build civilian nuclear-power plants in Egypt, Iran, Jordan and Turkiye. The Chinese are major consumers of Middle

Eastern oil and gas (along with South Korea and Japan), as well as financiers of infrastructure projects in the region. The Americans are not alone in wanting to pay more attention to the Indo-Pacific. Gulf oil and gas producers are also looking east for energy customers and technology suppliers.

A changing geopolitical picture has been accompanied by a shift in the Middle East's balance of power.[5] Iran and its proxies in Gaza, Iraq, Lebanon, Syria and Yemen are more emboldened and aggressive than they were ten years ago. The United States' withdrawal from the JCPOA in 2018 freed Iran to pursue higher levels of uranium enrichment. It is now approaching the nuclear threshold, at which point it will have sufficient quantities of highly enriched uranium to build one or more nuclear weapons. It will remain close to that threshold whatever is done, or not done, to revive the JCPOA – a challenging diplomatic task that seems unlikely to succeed. Tehran's supply of drones and missiles to Russia for use in Ukraine, as well as its brutal repression of domestic protests, have dampened American enthusiasm for the task. Washington's inability to guarantee that Iran will benefit from sanctions relief has likewise limited Tehran's interest. Hawkish attitudes in both capitals appear likely to prevail.

*Iran is approaching the nuclear threshold*

Turkiye, still embedded in NATO and supportive of Ukraine, has nevertheless increasingly courted Russia and intervened repeatedly in Syria and Iraq to counter Kurdish opponents who are allied with the US in the fight against the Islamic State (ISIS). The country's previously secular politics have become less democratic and more Islamist. They could even be described as 'neo-Ottoman' in the sense that Turkiye now seeks to project power in the region rather than maintain its (unsuccessful) policy of 'zero problems with neighbours'. Ankara wants Moscow and Damascus either to permit a further Turkish incursion into Syria or to repress Turkiye's US-allied Kurdish opponents.

Some Gulf monarchies, much like Egypt and Jordan before them, have begun to normalise relations with Israel, despite its undeclared nuclear status and its continued occupation of Palestinian territories. These monarchies seek internal-security and air-defence technologies in exchange for improved political relations, including the diplomatic recognition of Israel in the cases of the UAE and Bahrain. Other Arab states have found themselves marginalised. The implosion of Syria and Yemen into civil wars will leave them fragmented and sidelined for a generation at least. Iraq is still preoccupied with internal reconstruction after the American invasion in 2003. Both Jewish Israelis and the Arab monarchies disregard Palestine, split between Hamas in Gaza and the Palestinian Authority in the West Bank, even if the Palestinian cause remains popular among Arabs and Muslims generally, as was evident at the Qatar-hosted World Cup in 2022.

The question is whether any of these changes are likely to drive nuclear development in the Middle East. Will leaders in Turkiye or the Arab states seek to complete the work left unfinished by Saddam Hussein, Bashar al-Assad and Muammar Gadhafi? How will Iran's growing nuclear capabilities, regardless of its ultimate intentions, affect thinking among its rivals and near neighbours, particularly Turkiye and Saudi Arabia?[6] What will Egypt's attitude be? How will success or failure in the negotiations to revive the Iran nuclear deal affect regional ambitions? Will Pakistan or North Korea be prepared to provide nuclear technology to regional partners? Can the US, which has been the mainstay of non-proliferation not just in the Middle East but globally, continue to hold the line against nuclear-weapons ambitions in the region, despite its declining stature there? Will Russia and China, both far more active in the Middle East than they used to be, help or hinder nuclear-weapons development?

The answers to these questions are important. One-on-one nuclear face-offs (as between the US and the Soviet Union/Russia, the US and China, China and India, and India and Pakistan) have so far proven manageable and even favourable to non-proliferation (as was the case for Argentina and Brazil). But the prospect of a Middle Eastern nuclear regatta with three or more participants in close proximity is daunting. There have been no comparable cases of multiple adversaries in the same region gaining nuclear weapons. Multilateral deterrence would be a dicey affair, due to greater uncertainties and short lead times for crucial decisions. The possibility of loose nukes, or nuclear weapons in the hands of extremist groups, would grow. The nuclear question in the Middle East is a long-standing one for good reason. Further proliferation there could make the region's current problems, severe as they are, seem minor. Prevention based on careful analysis is the best way forward.

## Turkiye

Turkish President Recep Tayyip Erdoğan's 2019 statement at the World Economic Forum in Sivas, Turkiye, generated concern about his nuclear ambitions. 'Some countries have missiles with nuclear warheads', he said, 'not one or two. But (they tell us) we can't have them. This, I cannot accept.'[7] He went on to say that 'there is no developed nation in the world that doesn't have them', implying that Turkiye would not be left out of the nuclear club. In 2006 (while Erdoğan was prime minister), General Hilmi Özkök, then Turkiye's military chief of staff, stated:

> If the problem [of the proliferation of weapons of mass destruction] cannot be resolved despite the intense diplomatic efforts of the international community, I see a strong likelihood that we will face some important decision stages in the near future. Otherwise, we will face the prospect of losing our strategic superiority in the region.[8]

Erdoğan is not the first president of Turkiye to express an interest in nuclear weapons. In 1966, Cevdet Sunay, who had served as chief of staff before becoming president, instructed the Energy Ministry's General Directorate of Minerals Research to cooperate with Refik Tulga, his successor as chief of staff, and a physicist at Middle East Technical University to 'develop the atomic bomb'.[9]

Changing priorities and administrations ended that nuclear-weapons programme, but not the presence of nuclear weapons on Turkish soil. As a member of NATO, Turkiye has hosted American nuclear weapons since 1961. There are currently 50 B61 non-strategic nuclear warheads at Incirlik Air Base. The US National Nuclear Security Administration is modernising these, with deployment expected by 2024. They are presumably under dual-key control. These American weapons have appeared for decades to satisfy Turkiye's nuclear appetite. Ankara signed the NPT in 1969, though it waited until 1980 to ratify it. In 1990, the Turkish Atomic Energy Authority (TAEK) cancelled an agreement with Argentina to build a CAREM-25 nuclear reactor because TAEK's director said it was 'too small for electricity generation and too big for research or training, [but] very suitable for plutonium production'.[10]

Among its leading politicians, Turkiye today displays a left–right divide on nuclear weapons. Those belonging to right-leaning parties tend to be more vocal proponents of Turkiye acquiring nuclear weapons of its own. Members of the Nationalist Movement Party (MHP), for example, have favoured the acquisition of nuclear weapons, including party founder Alparslan Türkeş and Enis Öksüz, who said while serving as Turkiye's transportation minister that 'the others have it. Those who have it have not used them since the Second World War. It would be a [form of] security for Turkiye to have it too. It deters enemy adventurism.'[11] He followed this by admitting that although nuclear weapons are not a necessity and ideally should be abolished everywhere, because some countries possess them, it is only wise for Turkiye to work toward them too.

Centrist and left-leaning or Kemalist parties tend to be wary of both nuclear weapons and civilian nuclear power, and have raised concerns about Turkiye's civilian nuclear programme. The Kemalist Republican People's Party (CHP), nationalist İYİ Party and Kurdish People's Democratic Party (HDP) have criticised the government for contracting with Rosatom to build four commercial power reactors (totalling 4,800 megawatts) at Akkuyu to meet 10% of the country's electricity needs. Those advising caution on civilian nuclear power have a similar stance on nuclear weapons.

Frayed relations with the US could potentially influence Ankara's future nuclear appetite. While still vital to NATO, Turkiye has been following a far more independent and risky foreign policy than in the past. Challenged domestically by Kurdish rebels, Ankara has been conducting military operations against their compatriots in Syria and Iraq, which the rebels use as safe havens. Because some of the Syrian Kurds are allied with the US in its fight against Islamist extremists, Turkish shelling and incursions in Syria risk not only displeasing the Americans and undermining the fight against the Islamic State and al-Qaeda, but also causing harm to US troops deployed with the Kurdish-led Syrian Democratic Forces.

There are other sources of strain in the US–Turkiye relationship. Erdoğan was displeased with Washington's slow reaction to a 2016 coup attempt the Turkish president blamed on a political rival residing in the US. Turkiye has purchased S-400 air defences from Russia, precipitating Ankara's eviction from the American F-35 fighter project, in which the Turks were both customers and suppliers. An increasingly autocratic Erdoğan bridles at American criticism of Turkiye's human-rights record and sanctions-busting trade with Iran.

These irritants in the US–Turkish relationship have raised doubts in Ankara about Washington's commitments to Turkiye and could be used to justify seeking nuclear weapons. The consensus among security experts, however, is that Turkiye is still unlikely to pursue a nuclear-weapons programme, despite occasional declarations by its political leaders to the contrary. Sinan Ülgen considers Erdoğan's rhetoric just that: populist rhetoric that does not reflect actual nuclear activity. Ülgen and George Perkovich, joined by other analysts including Mustafa Kibaroğlu and Jessica Varnum, concluded in 2015 that despite its less traditional and more active security policies vis-à-vis Afghanistan, Libya and Syria, as well as its changing relationships with NATO and Russia, it stands to lose more than it could gain if it goes down the nuclear path.[12] Pursuing nuclear weapons cannot resolve Turkiye's major security issues, including Syria's disintegration, Kurdish insurgency and the need to manage an often tense relationship with the US and NATO.

*Turkiye is still unlikely to pursue nuclear weapons*

The ruling Justice and Development Party (AKP) has prioritised rejuvenating the economy. A serious nuclear-weapons programme and the global reaction it would elicit would obstruct this objective. Turkish analysts overwhelmingly contend that, despite a changing geopolitical context, a weapons programme would require a consensus among the relevant agencies and stakeholders, along with comprehensive planning for which there is no available framework.[13] Experts take a similar view of the possibility that Pakistan could share nuclear technology with Turkiye, as neither party could afford the possible international consequences.[14]

Turkiye boasts an impressive record of cooperation with international nuclear-regulatory regimes. It is a signatory to the NPT, the Comprehensive Nuclear-Test-Ban Treaty and the Partial Nuclear-Test-Ban Treaty, and has an overall track record of compliance with international anti-proliferation norms and standards. Turkiye completed a Safeguards Agreement with the IAEA in 1982 and ratified its Additional Protocol in 2001. The IAEA monitors all its nuclear facilities.

These include two research reactors.[15] One is a 250 kilowatt TRIGA Mark-II Training and Research Reactor. It is an open-tank-type reactor based at the Istanbul Technical University which features light-water coolant, a graphite reflector and solid-fuel elements. The second reactor is a light-water-moderated five megawatts thermal (MWt) TR-2 located at Çekmece Nuclear Research and Training Center (ÇNAEM). Its irradiated fuel is unsuitable for weapons and difficult to handle. ÇNAEM also houses a dedicated storage facility for spent fuel but does not house a reprocessing capability. It does, however, have a large hot cell, which facilitates the transport of radioisotopes, but might not be equipped to handle irradiated reactor fuel. While Turkiye could obtain reprocessing-grade hot-cell equipment from a foreign supplier to perform post-irradiated examination on spent fuel, it is unlikely to do so.[16]

Turkish scientists have, however, conducted computer simulations of reprocessing with the Purex process. German intelligence holds that Turkiye is working to acquire fuel-cycle technology, as it has refused to accept enriched uranium from Russia and a Japanese–French consortium.[17] But Turkiye's apparent lack of enrichment and reprocessing facilities means it is still a long way from developing a nuclear weapon.[18]

## Saudi Arabia

In 2018, Saudi Crown Prince Muhammad bin Salman (MbS) declared in an interview that 'Saudi Arabia does not want to acquire any nuclear bomb, but without a doubt, if Iran developed a nuclear bomb, we will follow suit as soon as possible'.[19] While he may have expressed himself more stridently than Erdoğan, this stance is largely similar to that of Turkiye. At a minimum, Saudi Arabia, like Turkiye, aims to use its own uranium resources for its civilian nuclear programme, which will necessitate gaining access to enrichment technology. Unlike in Turkiye, there are no US nuclear weapons deployed in Saudi Arabia that might be withdrawn if Riyadh opted to develop its own weapons.

There is little public discussion of nuclear weapons in Saudi Arabia beyond echoes of MbS's statement. In December 2022, for example, the Saudi foreign minister reiterated that 'all bets are off' if Iran acquires nuclear weapons[20] – which was itself an echo of what Saudi officials have been saying for at least two decades. There is no definite indication that the Saudis have acted on what remains a hypothetical syllogism.

The Kingdom signed the NPT in 1988 but has not signed an Additional Protocol, which would enable wider-ranging IAEA inspections. This limits IAEA access to nuclear facilities and raises questions about Saudi intentions. The country's official stance is outlined in the National Policy for the Atomic Energy Program of the Kingdom of Saudi Arabia, which sets out five principles:

1)   limiting all nuclear-development activities to peaceful purposes within the limits of legislation and international treaties and conventions;

2)   complying with the principle of transparency in all regulatory and operational aspects;

3)   applying nuclear-safety and -security standards in nuclear and radiological facilities, in accordance with an independent regulatory and monitoring framework;

4)   ensuring optimal use of the Kingdom's natural resources of nuclear material and applying the international best standards and practices for radioactive-waste management; and

5)   achieving sustainability by developing local content in the atomic-energy sector.[21]

The Kingdom recently inaugurated its first, low-power (30 MWt) research and training reactor. The country's reasons for introducing civilian nuclear energy include supporting desalination and electricity generation, diversifying the national energy mixture and decreasing domestic reliance on oil and gas.[22] The current target is to establish two power plants totalling 3,450 MW.

In addition, Saudi Arabia plans to extract uranium domestically as a step toward self-sufficiency in the production of nuclear fuel.[23] During the Future Minerals Summit held in January 2022, Energy Minister Abdulaziz bin Salman reiterated the Kingdom's intention to use its reserves of uranium ore to further develop its nuclear programme, thereby adding 17 gigawatts of capacity by 2040.[24] That would make it the regional leader in producing nuclear power. With Chinese assistance, Riyadh is building a facility at Al Ula to produce 'yellow cake', a uranium concentrate that represents an intermediate stage in manufacturing nuclear fuel but that has no direct use in a weapons programme. This was confirmed in January 2022 by the energy minister, who insisted Riyadh intends to exploit its 'huge amount of uranium'.[25]

Saudi–American nuclear cooperation stirred controversy in 2018 after the publication of a report indicating that the Trump administration had pursued a nuclear-reactor deal with Riyadh.[26] It was alleged the deal bypassed the 123 Agreement process stipulated by the US Atomic Energy Act, which requires that partner states 'adhere to a set of strong nonproliferation requirements'.[27] This deal appears to have evaporated with the end of the Trump administration.

## Egypt, Algeria and the UAE

Egypt launched an effort to acquire nuclear weapons in the 1960s, in accordance with president Gamal Abdel Nasser's long-term ambitions.[28] But the effort to match Israel's presumed capability was not well funded.[29] After the 1967 war with Israel, Nasser signed the NPT, but it was only after the 1973 war with Israel that president Anwar Sadat decided to terminate Egypt's then-frozen nuclear-weapons programme in exchange for US assistance.[30] Egypt ratified the NPT belatedly in 1981. Cairo has not signed an Additional Protocol with the IAEA, seeks control in principle over the entire fuel cycle and refuses to accept new technological restrictions until Israel gives up its nuclear weapons.

President Abdel Fattah Al-Sisi has, however, been clear about Egypt's current intentions. He has disavowed nuclear weapons, saying in 2021 that 'Germany does not have an atomic bomb and is still one of the great powers'.[31] Rather than trying to join the nuclear club, Cairo has preferred to aim at levelling the playing field by advocating a regional nuclear-weapons-free zone, as well as a prohibition on all nuclear weapons. Neither proposition is feasible, but both give Cairo a rhetorically aggressive diplomatic posture vis-à-vis Israel.

It is not clear whether Egypt would wish to remain non-nuclear if Turkiye or Saudi Arabia tried to acquire nuclear weapons. Cairo would hesitate to displease Saudi Arabia, but Egypt prides itself on being a leader in the Arab and Muslim worlds. A Saudi move toward nuclear weapons would at the least cause renewed discussion of the possibility in Egypt. As for Turkiye, Sisi and Erdoğan have been on bad terms until recently, as the former came to power in a coup against the Muslim Brotherhood, while the latter is heir to a Muslim Brotherhood political tradition. A Turkish move toward nuclear weapons, or a dramatic change of leadership in Egypt, could shift Cairo away from its current non-proliferation posture.

Egypt's civilian nuclear programme, which began in 1954, features two IAEA-safeguarded research reactors and a hot-cell laboratory located at Inshas in the Nile Delta.[32] In addition, Egypt is expanding its civilian nuclear programme to produce electricity. In December 2017, Sisi and Russian President Vladimir Putin signed an agreement initiating Egypt's nuclear-power plant at El-Dabaa. This project aims to construct four 1,200 megawatts electric (MWe) pressurised-water reactors using the Russian VVER-1200 (AES-2006) design.[33] Construction began in 2022. The project owner and operator is the Egyptian Nuclear Power Plants Authority. The main contractors are from the Rosatom group, which will provide engineering, procurement and construction services; nuclear-fuel supply; operational support and maintenance; and treatment of spent nuclear fuel.

The El-Dabaa project is an important component of bilateral economic cooperation with Russia, which will loan Egypt the $25 billion needed to finance it.[34] Egypt will begin repaying the loan in 2029, by which time the El-Dabaa nuclear reactors should have generated $17bn in revenue for the Egyptian government.[35]

President Sisi has also approved an agreement on nuclear energy with Saudi Arabia.[36] The agreement, signed in April 2016 during a visit to Cairo by Saudi King Salman, involves cooperation on peaceful uses of nuclear power, nuclear security and an exchange of information on nuclear safety. Egypt and Saudi Arabia are also working on connecting their power grids through a $1.6bn deal, approved by Egypt's cabinet in January 2015, which will enable them to share 3,000 MW of electricity.[37]

Algeria aroused international suspicions in the 1980s when it began to display signs of harbouring nuclear ambitions, presumably linked to a desire to counter a perceived threat from Libya's Gadhafi.[38] The US intelligence community intercepted secret agreements signed by Algeria with China and Argentina at the beginning of the 1980s to produce weapons-grade plutonium. Under a 1983 agreement, China provided Algeria with a nuclear reactor and a related research facility. In 1984, Algeria purchased 150 tons of uranium concentrate from Niger. It was also reported that Iraq had sent scientists and some uranium to Algeria. The reactor has a theoretical capacity to produce 3–5 kilograms of plutonium a year. Because the facility includes a hot cell, it might also have the ability to separate plutonium on a small scale. A large, heavy-walled building nearby that was spotted via satellite had no announced function but was 'believed to have been intended to be a full scale plutonium plant', according to the Federation of American Scientists Nuclear Information Project.[39] A Soviet-made SA-5 surface-to-air missile battery was detected nearby, apparently for aircraft or missile defence.

Algeria has two nuclear-research reactors.[40] The Argentinian company INVAP began constructing Algeria's first research reactor, Nur, in 1987. It was fully operational by 1989. This 1 MWt pool-type light-water reactor uses uranium fuel from Argentina enriched to 20%. Algeria uses this facility for laboratory-scale production of radioisotopes, research in neutron physics and the training of reactor operators. The complex also houses a fuel-fabrication plant.

Construction on the second reactor began in 1988 pursuant to Algeria's agreement with China. This 15 MWt heavy-water-moderated Es-Salam reactor, located at Ain Oussera, 140 kilometres south of Algiers in the Sahara Desert, is fuelled with 3% enriched uranium and first reached criticality in 1992. Compared with the Turkish reactor at ÇNAEM, this appears to have a higher productive capacity and also contains various other nuclear-related facilities, including an isotope-production plant, hot-cell laboratories and waste-storage tanks.

In February 1992, Algeria signed a facility-specific safeguards agreement with the IAEA. In 1995, Algeria concluded a full-scope safeguards agreement after it had ratified the NPT. In 2018, Algiers signed an Additional Protocol. Algeria today is a signatory to all major non-proliferation treaties and regimes, including the Treaty on the Prohibition of Nuclear Weapons and the African Nuclear-Weapon-Free Zone Treaty. Algiers has been a strong advocate for nuclear disarmament, as called for in Article VI of the NPT. It is no longer generally regarded as a proliferation risk.

The UAE has wanted to remove barriers to non-nuclear military assistance from the US. In its pursuit of a civilian nuclear programme, it has forsworn both enrichment and reprocessing.[41] It lacks the smaller research reactors that often provide training grounds for nuclear engineers, including on fuel-cycle technology. It has relied on South Korea's KEPCO to build its first four reactors at Barakah (southwest of Abu Dhabi), three of which are now in commercial operation. Abu Dhabi is an NPT signatory with full-scope safeguards and Additional Protocol agreements with the IAEA. It signed a 123 Agreement with the US in 2009. While the UAE is anxious to prove its technological mettle in outer space, Abu Dhabi has opted out of any nuclear-arms race in the Middle East.[42]

## Proliferation from Pakistan and North Korea

What of the possibility that Pakistan or North Korea could supply nuclear weapons or relevant technologies to Middle Eastern clients? Beginning in the mid-1980s, Pakistani scientist Abdul Qadeer Khan clandestinely exported nuclear equipment and technology to, at a minimum, Iran, Iraq, Libya and North Korea.[43] His motive appears to have been primarily financial, though some transactions may have involved barter for missile technology. The Khan network embarrassed Pervez Musharraf, then Pakistan's president, when it was uncovered in 2004,[44] but the state appeared to be at least passively involved in Khan's activities, with one report concluding that 'A. Q. Khan was able to manipulate the government, and the Pakistani authorities did not want to know what was going on'.[45]

Saudi Arabia and Pakistan have a generally cordial relationship that extends to cooperative military training, deployment of Pakistani troops to the Kingdom and export of Pakistani weapons. Saudi financial support for Pakistan's nuclear programme has been widely reported but not well documented.[46] The Pakistani parliament in 2015 voted against supporting Saudi Arabia in its war against the Houthis in Yemen. Today, the Pakistani establishment, burned by the A.Q. Khan affair, seems averse to the idea of transferring nuclear technology and expertise abroad, including to Saudi Arabia.

Turkiye and Pakistan also maintain cordial relations, including extensive cultural ties and military trade. Turkish businesses and people were implicated in A.Q. Khan's exports. Turkiye may have acquired centrifuge technology from the A.Q. Khan network, which purchased hardware for centrifuges in Turkiye. But as with Saudi Arabia, Pakistani nuclear exports to Turkiye would entail enormous risks, including the imposition of US and European sanctions.

North Korea signed the NPT in 1985 but withdrew from the treaty in 2003. IAEA inspectors stopped monitoring its nuclear facilities in 2009, when Pyongyang ceased all cooperation with the agency. North Korea no longer upholds, if it ever did, international commitments to the non-proliferation of nuclear weapons, regarding them as vital for its national security.[47]

North Korea has been an active exporter of missile technology since it developed its first short-range (60–160 km) missiles in 1976.[48] It is known to have dealt with Egypt, Iraq, Libya, Pakistan, Syria and Yemen, all of which modelled their own missiles on the North Korean *Nodong*. Sanctions have not been able to curb North Korea's missile trade, which supports the country's flailing, much-sanctioned economy.

There are no recent verifiable reports of Pyongyang selling nuclear weapons or technology to states or non-state actors, as it did to Syria in the early 2000s. But the UN Panel of Experts that monitors sanctions imposed on North Korea reported that Pyongyang had sold 'technology for weapons of mass destruction (WMDs) to buyers in the Middle East'.[49] North Korea's economy had been faltering even before the COVID-19 pandemic, which has only done further damage. This has prompted fears the country might resort to selling nuclear-weapons technology.

## Proliferation risks in the Middle East

From a realist perspective, the development of nuclear weapons can be a logical response to their possession by a rival or adversary. States generally seek to maximise their power vis-à-vis other states, so balancing a nuclear power with nuclear power is to be anticipated. This dynamic was observable after the Second World War, when first the Soviet Union and then China developed nuclear weapons to counter the United States.

This dynamic was not seen in the Middle East after Israel's development of nuclear weapons in the 1960s, however, for several reasons. While Cairo initially tried to follow suit, it was technologically handicapped, and in the end preferred to negotiate a peace treaty with Israel that removed both the incentive for war and presumably also the risk that Israel would use nuclear weapons against Egypt. The Egyptians also gained a relationship with the United States that has proven beneficial to its leadership, if not to the country's citizenry more generally. Under current conditions, Cairo is unlikely to put those gains at risk by moving definitively in the direction of nuclear weapons. But how it would respond to Ankara or Riyadh obtaining them is uncertain.

Turkiye and Saudi Arabia also failed to develop nuclear weapons in response to Israel. Instead, they have preferred to focus on civilian nuclear power.[50] But both Ankara and Riyadh regard indigenous uranium enrichment as essential to those efforts. They have criticised Israel vociferously for its nuclear weapons and advocate a regional nuclear-free zone that they know is not achievable. Saudi Arabia has also refused to negotiate an Additional Protocol with the IAEA. Despite the presence of multiple irritants in their relationships with Washington, Ankara and Riyadh have not wanted to place these relationships at risk by openly embarking on nuclear programmes that might lead to weapons. Clandestine efforts are always a possibility, but the Turks and Saudis would have to take into account the risk of disclosure.

Three Middle Eastern countries tried strenuously, but failed, to move in the direction of nuclear weapons, at least in part in response to Israel. All three were then, or are still, American adversaries. Iraq's programme, damaged when Israel destroyed its Osiraq reactor, imploded after the 1991 Gulf War. Baghdad is still far from being able or willing to resuscitate the effort. Israel destroyed Syria's plutonium-production reactor, and the country's subsequent wars and economic collapse now prevent it from re-embarking on a serious nuclear programme.

Iran's programme is ongoing, after stops and restarts for more than two decades.[51] Although there is still some hope Tehran can be dissuaded by hard-nosed diplomacy from making or deploying nuclear weapons,[52] it has shown no inclination to give up its technological progress in enrichment and will remain, at the very least, a nuclear-threshold state. It is also thought to be seeking alternative means of ensuring fuel supplies, if need be.[53] There are many 'nuclear latent' states with some or all of the technology required for building atomic weapons (between 20 and 30 in 2019).[54] Iran is more properly categorised as a 'nuclear hedging' state, one that is intent on at least acquiring all the technology required to enable it to make one or more nuclear weapons within a few months.

The question then is whether Egypt, Saudi Arabia or Turkiye, none of which responded to Israel's nuclear weapons with successful weapons programmes of their own, will respond to Iran's nuclear hedging. Washington will seek to restrain them, but at one time it also sought to restrain Israel, without success. Saudi Arabia has resisted a 123 Agreement with the US, which would impose tight restrictions on the use of US nuclear technology. So too has Egypt. Turkiye has such an agreement, but it is subject to a five-year 'rollover' in June 2023.

Egypt is likely far too dependent on US security cooperation and Russian civilian nuclear cooperation to risk losing both due to an expensive, long-shot effort to develop enrichment and reprocessing. Turkiye may be in a similar situation: would Erdoğan risk the loss of American nuclear weapons in order to gain his own? Saudi Arabia is dependent on US security protection, but the Saudis were sorely disappointed in the American failure to respond when Iran – through Houthi proxies – attacked Aramco oil facilities at Abqaiq and Khurais in 2019. The Kingdom has also defied the US by shrugging off human-rights violations, continuing the war in Yemen and cooperating with OPEC+ in an effort to maintain high oil prices.

To all appearances, neither Turkiye nor Saudi Arabia has yet acquired the facilities required to enrich uranium or reprocess plutonium in the quantities required for nuclear weapons. But Turkiye and Saudi Arabia maintain excellent ties with Pakistan, which could provide the technology required or even the weapons themselves. Pakistan, like North Korea, is in rough economic shape, especially after the massive flooding it experienced in summer 2022. Might the Pakistanis feel tempted or even obligated to help the Saudis if the Kingdom made a definitive move toward nuclear weapons and offered an attractive price? Might the North Koreans, who have little to fear from nuclear weapons in the Middle East, be prepared to sell nuclear technology to Saudi Arabia or Turkiye, as they already did to Syria?

Turkiye and Saudi Arabia are thus the leading potential nuclear-proliferation risks in the Middle East, behind Israel and Iran. Both have leaders who have spoken publicly about responding to Iranian nuclear weapons with acquisition efforts of their own. Neither has made all the commitments possible to IAEA inspections. Events in recent years have made both doubt the depth of Washington's commitment to their security. Ankara has contracted with Rosatom to build civilian nuclear-power plants, and Rosatom has submitted a bid to Saudi Arabia.[55] There is no indication that Russia or China would assist in a nuclear-weapons programme, but Pakistani or North Korean assistance cannot be ruled out.

## The way ahead

What can be done to discourage Ankara and Riyadh from nuclear programmes to match the rhetoric of their current political leaders and the accomplishments of two rival regional powers, Israel and Iran? If Turkiye or Saudi Arabia were to proceed in the direction of nuclear weapons, Egypt might not be far behind. Because of the United States' declining influence, countering proliferation in the Middle East will require a more concerted, multilateral intelligence and diplomatic effort than in the past. Washington will not be able to do it alone. It will need to cooperate with Russia and China, as well as its European allies.

The EU3+3 (France, Germany and the United Kingdom + China, Russia and the US) group that negotiated the 2015 JCPOA with Iran is one possible diplomatic format for such cooperation, but the war in Ukraine and geopolitical rivalry have dramatically reduced prospects for fruitful cooperation with Russia and China. Another possibility would be the

EU3 plus the US and Egypt, Saudi Arabia and Turkiye. That would have the virtue of pulling three potential Middle Eastern proliferators in the Western direction and giving them an opportunity to clarify their own intentions and security concerns. Researchers at the Carnegie Endowment for International Peace have identified the factors that influence nuclear decisions and the indicators that can signal potential proliferation in the hope of constructing a 'firewall' against it.[56] Keeping track of these factors and indicators, using both open-source and clandestine intelligence, is job #1. It will be especially important to keep a sharp eye on trade with Pakistan and North Korea, both of which are experts at deception and evading surveillance.

It will not suffice, however, to have early warning of Saudi or Turkish moves toward nuclear weapons. Prevention will be far easier than cure, and this will require close attention to Turkish and Saudi security perceptions, as well as a stronger security architecture for the region. Security assurances have long been a mainstay of non-proliferation among US allies in Europe and East Asia, but their effectiveness is declining, and not only in the Middle East.[57] American assurances may no longer suffice, but there is no multilateral security structure covering Egypt, Iran, Saudi Arabia and Turkiye, let alone Israel. The Organisation of Islamic Cooperation, to which the first four belong, is too weak to tackle an issue like nuclear weapons. Some sort of regional consultative mechanism is needed, if only to keep track of threat perceptions and ensure a minimum of transparency. The re-establishment of diplomatic relations between Saudi Arabia and Iran removes one obstacle to such a regional consultative mechanism.

Also needed are some specific diplomatic moves. The European Union and US should be working hard to get Egypt and Saudi Arabia to sign Additional Protocols with the IAEA. The Americans should continue their efforts to get them to sign bilateral 123 Agreements, and should renew the 123 Agreement with Turkiye. The diplomatic objective should be to encourage Egypt, Saudi Arabia and Turkiye to follow the precedents set by Algeria and the UAE in making a clean break with their nuclear-weapons ambitions and signalling this to the rest of the world. Such a step might be easier to take if they did so in unison, as the result of regional consultations.

This may never happen. Israel, which, as noted, has destroyed reactors in Iraq and Syria, and has attacked nuclear scientists and facilities in Iran, will likely continue to enforce its own opposition to nuclear proliferation in the Middle East. Any country in the region considering a nuclear-weapons programme has to take into account the risk of an Israeli attack. But Israeli muscle is facing tougher targets than in the past. Iran's nuclear programme is well ensconced underground. Turkiye and Saudi Arabia could follow suit, making complete destruction a difficult military objective. In any case, neither Egypt, nor Turkiye, nor Saudi Arabia are countries Israel would particularly want to attack, preferring commerce to conflict with each of them. Provoking a major regional power to retaliate would risk at least a generation of hostility.

The slow pace of nuclear proliferation in the Middle East has been a mostly unacknowledged blessing for more than 50 years. It would be best to keep it that way. The nuclear question needs a vigorous response.

## Notes

[1] Kurt M. Campbell et al., *The Nuclear Tipping Point: Why States Reconsider Their Nuclear Choices* (Washington DC: Brookings Institution Press, 2004).

[2] Richard L. Russell, 'Off and Running: The Middle East Nuclear Arms Race', *Joint Force Quarterly*, no. 58, 2010, pp. 94–9, https://ndupress.ndu.edu/portals/68/Documents/jfq/jfq-58.pdf.

[3] See Mehran Kamrava (ed.), *The Nuclear Question in the Middle East* (Oxford: Oxford University Press, 2012).

[4] See Avner Cohen, 'Israel and the Invention of Nuclear Opacity', in *ibid.*, pp. 189–224.

[5] See Vali Nasr, 'The Middle East's Next Conflicts Won't Be Between Arab States and Iran', FP, 2 March 2021, https://foreignpolicy.com/2021/03/02/the-middle-easts-next-conflicts-wont-be-between-arab-states-and-iran/.

[6] Clément Therme, Kjølv Egeland and Hebatalla Taha, 'Seizing Nuclear Tehran: Obstacles to Understanding Iranian Nuclear Activities', *Middle East Journal*, vol. 76, no. 2, Summer 2022, pp. 159–78.

[7] 'Erdoğan: Birilerinin elinde nükleer başlıklı füze var, ama benim elimde olmasın, ben bunu kabul etmiyorum', BBC News Türkçe, 5 September 2019, https://www.bbc.com/turkce/haberler-turkiye-49589110.

[8] Ezgi Yazigioglu, 'A Look upon Turkey's Future Nuclear Weapons Policy', IRIS Analyses, 25 September 2019, https://www.iris-france.org/140221-a-look-upon-turkeys-future-nuclear-weapons-policy/.

[9] See the memorandum prepared by Clarence Wendel for Parker T. Hart, then the US ambassador to Turkiye,

on 26 September 1966, available from the US National Security Archive, https://s3.documentcloud.org/documents/6536026/National-Security-Archive-Doc-14-Stuart-Rockwell.pdf.

10  Mustafa Kibaroglu, 'Turkey's Quest for Peaceful Nuclear Power', *Nonproliferation Review*, Spring–Summer 1997, p. 38.

11  'MHP, atom bombası istiyor', *Hürriyet*, 12 March 2000, https://www.hurriyet.com.tr/gundem/mhp-atom-bombasi-istiyor-39139480.

12  Sinan Ülgen and George Perkovich (eds), *Turkey's Nuclear Future* (Washington DC: Carnegie Endowment for International Peace, 2015).

13  See Yazigioglu, 'A Look upon Turkey's Future Nuclear Weapons Policy'.

14  Debalina Ghoshal, 'Will Turkey Acquire Nuclear Weapons from Pakistan?', Defense.info, 4 March 2020, https://defense.info/re-shaping-defense-security/2020/03/will-turkey-acquire-nuclear-weapons-from-pakistan/.

15  See Bruno Tertrais, 'The Middle East's Next Nuclear State', *Strategic Insights*, vol. 8, no. 1, January 2009, https://core.ac.uk/download/pdf/36704786.pdf.

16  See Mark Hibbs, 'Scratching Erdogan's Nuclear Itch', Arms Control Wonk, Carnegie Endowment for International Peace, 22 October 2019, https://carnegieendowment.org/2019/10/22/scratching-erdogan-s-nuclear-itch-pub-80178.

17  Hans Rühle, 'Is Turkey Secretly Working on Nuclear Weapons?', *National Interest*, 22 September 2015, https://nationalinterest.org/feature/turkey-secretly-working-nuclear-weapons-13898.

18  See Nuclear Threat Initiative, 'Turkey Overview', https://www.nti.org/analysis/articles/turkey-overview/.

19  'Saudi Crown Prince Says Will Develop Nuclear Bomb if Iran Does: CBS TV', Reuters, 15 March 2018, https://www.reuters.com/article/us-saudi-iran-nuclear-idUSKCN1GR1MN.

20  'Saudi Foreign Minister: "All Bets Off" if Iran Gets Nuclear Weapon', Reuters, 11 December 2022, https://www.reuters.com/world/middle-east/saudi-foreign-minister-all-bets-off-if-iran-gets-nuclear-weapon-2022-12-11/.

21  Kingdom of Saudi Arabia Nuclear and Radiological Regulatory Commission, 'National Policy for the Atomic Energy Program of the Kingdom of Saudi Arabia', p. 5, https://www.unodc.org/uploads/icsant/documents/Legislation/Saudi_Arabia/National_Policy_for_the_Atomic_Energy_Program.pdf.

22  *Ibid.*, p. 4.

23  See Emma Graham-Harrison, Stephanie Kirchgaessner and Julian Borger, 'Revealed: Saudi Arabia May Have Enough Uranium Ore to Produce Nuclear Fuel', *Guardian*, 17 September 2020, https://www.theguardian.com/world/2020/sep/17/revealed-saudi-arabia-may-have-enough-uranium-ore-to-produce-nuclear-fuel.

24  'Lsaeudiat takshif khutawatiha dimn barnamaj tatwir altaaqat alnawawiati' [Saudi Arabia unveils its roadmap for the development of nuclear energy], Al Ain News, 13 March 2022, https://al-ain.com/article/saudi-nuclear-energy-holding-company-objectives.

25  David Dalton, 'Saudi Arabia: Kingdom Aims to "Take Advantage"

of Uranium Resources as It Looks to Nuclear Energy', NUCNET, 14 January 2022, https://www.nucnet. org/news/kingdom-aims-to-take-advantage-of-uranium-resources-as-it-looks-to-nuclear-energy-1-5-2022.

26 See Nuclear Threat Initiative, 'Saudi Arabia Overview', https:// live-nuclear-threat-initiative. pantheonsite.io/analysis/articles/ saudi-arabia-overview/.

27 US National Nuclear Security Administration, '123 Agreements for Peaceful Cooperation', 7 December 2022, https://www.energy.gov/ nnsa/123-agreements-peaceful-cooperation. The Saudis are, however, still pursuing American security guarantees and civilian nuclear technology. See Dion Nissenbaum, Dov Lieber and Stephen Kalin, 'Saudi Arabia Seeks U.S. Security Pledges, Nuclear Help for Peace with Israel', *Wall Street Journal*, 9 March 2023.

28 See Maria Rost Rublee, 'Egypt's Nuclear Weapons Program', *Nonproliferation Review*, vol. 13, no. 3, 2006, https://www.tandfonline.com/ doi/abs/10.1080/10736700601071637.

29 See Khalil Shikaki, 'The Nuclearization Debates: The Cases of Israel and Egypt', *Journal of Palestine Studies*, vol. 14, no. 4, 1985, https://www.tandfonline.com/doi/ abs/10.2307/2537124.

30 See Rublee, 'Egypt's Nuclear Weapons Program'.

31 'Egypt's Sisi: Constructive Criticism Permissible for All, Affirming that He Can't Let People Live in Misery', Egypt Today, 25 April 2021, https://www.egypttoday.com/ Article/1/101250/Egypt%E2%80%99s-

Sisi-Constructive-criticism-permissible-for-all-affirming-that-he.

32 See Raymond Stock, 'As Obama Dithers, Egypt Ramps Up Its Nuclear Options', Middle East Forum, 9 January 2014, https://www.meforum. org/3716/egypt-nuclear-program.

33 'El Dabaa Nuclear Power Project', NS Energy, https://www. nsenergybusiness.com/projects/ el-dabaa-nuclear-power-project/.

34 'No Conflict Between Egypt and Russia on Dabaa Nuclear Plant: Electricity Ministry', Ahram Online, 11 January 2017, https://english.ahram.org.eg/ NewsContent/1/64/254845/Egypt/ Politics-/No-conflict-between-Egypt-and-Russia-on-Dabaa-nucl.aspx.

35 Gamal Essam El-Din, 'Egypt Approves Deal with Russia to Build First Nuclear Power Plant', Ahram Online, 6 September 2017, https://english.ahram. org.eg/News/276608.aspx.

36 'Sisi Approves Cooperation Agreement on Peaceful Use of Nuclear Energy with Saudi Arabia', Ahram Online, 28 September 2017, https://english.ahram. org.eg/NewsContent/1/64/277929/Egypt/ Politics-/Sisi-approves-cooperation-agreement-on-peaceful-us.aspx.

37 IEA, 'Egypt–Saudi Electricity Interconnection Project', 4 April 2022, https://www.iea.org/ policies/14291-egypt-saudi-electricity-interconnection-project.

38 See Federation of American Scientists Nuclear Information Project, 'Algeria Special Weapons', https://nuke.fas.org/ guide/algeria/index.html; and David Albright and Corey Hinderstein, 'Algeria: Big Deal in the Desert?', *Bulletin of the Atomic Scientists*, vol. 57, no. 3, May–June 2021, pp. 45–52.

39  Federation of American Scientists
    Nuclear Information Project, 'Algeria
    Special Weapons'.

40  Nuclear Threat Initiative, 'Algeria',
    https://www.nti.org/countries/algeria-5/.

41  Nuclear Threat Initiative, 'United
    Arab Emirates Overview', https://
    www.nti.org/analysis/articles/
    united-arab-emirates-overview/.

42  See UAE USA United, 'UAE Space
    Exploration', https://www.uaeusaunited.
    com/stories/uae-space-exploration.

43  See Michael Laufer, 'A.Q. Khan
    Nuclear Chronology', Carnegie
    Endowment for International
    Peace, https://carnegieendowment.
    org/2005/09/07/a.-q.-khan-nuclear-
    chronology-pub-17420.

44  See 'Evidence of A Q Khan Network
    Left Musharraf Embarrassed', Zee
    News, 22 September 2006, https://
    zeenews.india.com/news/south-asia/
    evidence-of-a-q-khan-network-left-
    musharraf-embarrassed_324486.html.

45  Bruno Tertrais, 'Kahn's Nuclear Exports:
    Was There a State Strategy?', in Henry
    D. Sokolski (ed.), Pakistan's Nuclear
    Future: Worries Beyond War (Carlisle, PA:
    Strategic Studies Institute, US Army
    War College, 2008), p. 30, https://www.
    jstor.org/stable/resrep12046.5?seq=7.

46  Mark Urban, 'Saudi Nuclear
    Weapons "On Order" from
    Pakistan', BBC News, 6 November
    2013, https://www.bbc.co.uk/news/
    world-middle-east-24823846.

47  See 'Kim Jong Un Says He Is Ready to
    Use His Nuclear Weapons', Sky News,
    15 August 2022, https://news.sky.com/
    story/kim-jong-un-says-he-is-ready-
    to-use-his-nuclear-weapons-12660403.

48  See Bertil Lintner, 'North Korea's
    Missile Trade Helps Fund Its Nuclear
    Program', YaleGlobal Online, 5 May
    2003, https://archive-yaleglobal.yale.
    edu/content/north-koreas-missile-
    trade-helps-fund-its-nuclear-program.

49  See Toby Dalton, 'The Most Urgent
    North Korean Nuclear Threat
    Isn't What You Think', Carnegie
    Endowment for International
    Peace, 15 April 2023, https://
    carnegieendowment.org/2021/04/15/
    most-urgent-north-korean-nuclear-
    threat-isn-t-what-you-think-pub-84335.

50  See Ludovica Castelli, 'Why Does
    Saudi Arabia Want to Acquire the
    Nuclear Fuel Cycle?', Stimson, 3
    March 2023, https://www.stimson.
    org/2023/why-does-saudi-arabia-want-
    to-acquire-the-nuclear-fuel-cycle/.

51  See Michael Eisenstadt, 'Iran's
    Nuclear Hedging Strategy: Shaping
    the Islamic Republic's Proliferation
    Calculus', Washington Institute for
    Near East Policy, 29 November 2022,
    https://www.washingtoninstitute.org/
    policy-analysis/irans-nuclear-hedging-
    strategy-shaping-islamic-republics-
    proliferation-calculus.

52  See Geoffrey Aronson, 'Jerusalem
    Declaration Signals Demise of
    the JCPOA', National Interest, 10
    August 2022, https://nationalinterest.
    org/blog/middle-east-watch/
    jerusalem-declaration-signals-demise-
    jcpoa%C2%A0-204124.

53  See Natasha Bertrand, 'Exclusive: Iran
    Is Seeking Russia's Help to Bolster Its
    Nuclear Program, US Intel Officials
    Believe', CNN, 4 November 2022,
    https://edition.cnn.com/2022/11/04/
    politics/iran-russia-nuclear-program.

54  See Ariel E. Levite, 'Nuclear Latency
    and Hedging: Concepts, History,
    and Issues', Woodrow Wilson

International Center for Scholars, September 2019, pp. 21–42, https://www.wilsoncenter.org/sites/default/files/media/documents/book/nuclear_latency_and_hedging_-_concepts_history_and_issues.pdf.

55 See 'Russia Submits Bid for Saudi Arabia's Twin Nuclear Reactors', Neutron Bytes, 28 December 2022, https://neutronbytes.com/2022/12/18/russia-submits-bid-for-saudi-arabias-twin-nuclear-reactors/.

56 Toby Dalton et al., 'Toward a Nuclear Firewall: Bridging the NPT's Three Pillars', Carnegie Endowment for International Peace, March 2017, https://carnegieendowment.org/files/CP_301_Dalton_et_al_Firewall_Final_Web.pdf.

57 Ariel E. Levite, 'Why Security Assurances Are Losing Their Clout as a Nuclear Nonproliferation Instrument', *Bulletin of the Atomic Scientists*, 29 June 2022, https://thebulletin.org/2022/06/why-security-assurances-are-losing-their-clout-as-a-nuclear-nonproliferation-instrument/#post-heading.

# Reading Clausewitz: *On War* for 21st-century Practitioners

**James S. Powell**

**On War**
Carl von Clausewitz. Michael Howard and Peter Paret, eds and
trans. Princeton, NJ: Princeton University Press, revised edition,
1984. £38.00/$45.00. 752 pp.

'We can find many whose writings illustrate how successive generations have thought about war', observes the late Michael Howard, sounding a cheerful note for military historians whose livelihoods rely on this abundant material. 'But there are remarkably few', he continues, 'who can help *us* to think about it.'[1] With this qualification, Howard appeals not to the historian but to the contemporary practitioner in making the case for the enduring relevance – even necessity – of Carl von Clausewitz's *On War*. Though cultivated in a distant and distinct milieu, the ideas of the nineteenth-century Prussian military theorist still offer insight and explanation in the complex realm of national security. For Clausewitz remains one of the few, writes Howard, to 'have penetrated below the ephemeral phenomena of their own times and considered war, not just as a craft, but as a great socio-political activity'.[2] When it comes to war, 'there is no systematic study comparable to that of Clausewitz'.[3] His work ought to be read widely.

**James S. Powell** is Assistant Professor of Military and Security Studies at the US Air Command and Staff College.

**Survival** | vol. 65 no. 2 | April–May 2023 | pp. 165–190        https://doi.org/10.1080/00396338.2023.2193106

Neither debates as to its meaning nor unseemly appropriations of its insights have eroded *On War*'s relevance. Hew Strachan takes Howard and co-translator Peter Paret to task for shading their 1976 interpretation of Clausewitz's ideas too starkly with post-Vietnam Cold War considerations, a restrictive approach when viewed from the far side of 9/11 and America's military interventions in Iraq and Afghanistan.[4] Yet in critiquing Howard and Paret, Strachan spares Clausewitz. An author has limited liability for the inferences drawn by readers across generations. Evincing an enthusiasm on a par with Howard's, Strachan exhorts national-security practitioners

'not to ditch *On War*, but to read more of it and to read it with greater care'.[5] *On War* persists as an enlightening work because Clausewitz 'emphatically sought to understand war in terms as broad as possible'.[6] Looking back on US security policy in the post-9/11 period, Strachan detects a dearth of 'self-awareness and strategic sensitivity' that 'greater attention' to *On War* might have offset.[7]

At its core, *On War* represents one man's attempt to reflect on his personal experience and then to apply critical thinking and historical analysis towards developing a theory that explained war and its conduct during the tumultuous Napoleonic era. Clausewitz entered Prussian military service as an officer-cadet at the age of 12 and saw combat in the wars against Revolutionary France and Napoleon Bonaparte. A defining moment came in October 1806 when Napoleon's Grande Armée destroyed the vaunted Prussian army in a campaign that reached its climax on battlefields at Jena and Auerstädt. Though continuing his military service, Clausewitz spent the rest of his life grappling with the transformation in warfare that this traumatic event seemed to affirm.[8]

Strikingly cogent in places, *On War* is a rewarding but challenging book. Writing in the style of his times, Clausewitz used the dialectic method, which presents opposing but related ideas in an effort to edge towards the truth. He crafted *On War* over many years and, while this process of thinking and writing makes the text remarkably rich and intriguing, that process also suggests an evolving perspective. Clausewitz died at 51, leaving behind notes indicating plans to revise his work. Which thoughts had crystallised and which were still subject to revision remains unclear. Scholars have debated 'what Clausewitz really meant' ever since.[9] For practitioners, disagreements over interpretation and understanding compound the challenge of determining how best to harness the book's utility and inform one's thinking. That Clausewitz himself anticipated such debates soothes more than it enlightens. Still, it helps to approach *On War* as 'unprejudiced readers in search of truth' (p. 70), the kind of readers for whom the author wrote.

## The utility of theory

Practitioners might start with a consideration of how theory benefits them in their roles as planners and advisers. As a sustained argument distinguishing war in the abstract from war in practice, Book 1, Chapter 1, summarises the problem Clausewitz faced as a military theorist: how might theory provide a useful guide for action given its obvious differences with war's observed and experienced reality (pp. 75–89)? Elaborating on his purpose in Book 2, Chapter 1, the author dares those responsible for waging war to wade into the 'confusing welter of ideas' (p. 132) that shape and describe the phenomenon. He warns of the dangers associated with generalisation, as well as the human tendency to generalise in the absence of thorough enquiry. Indeed, Clausewitz argues that analysis itself is impossible apart from theoretical understanding. 'The primary purpose of theory', he writes, 'is to clarify concepts and ideas that have become … confused and entangled. Not until terms and concepts have been defined can one hope to make any progress in examining the question clearly and simply and expect the reader to share one's views' (p. 132).

Yet for all this utility, theory not only has its limitations but is also subject to misapplication, as Clausewitz explains prior to a discussion of war's complex and dynamic nature:

> Theory should cast a steady light on all phenomena so that we can more easily recognize and eliminate the weeds that always spring from ignorance; it should show how one thing is related to another, and keep

the important and the unimportant separate … Theory cannot equip the
mind with formulas for solving problems, nor can it mark the narrow
path on which the sole solution is supposed to lie by planting a hedge of
principles on either side. But it can give the mind insight into the great
mass of phenomena and of their relationships, then leave it free to rise to
the higher realms of action. (p. 578)

Evoking garden imagery, Clausewitz assigns to theory the task of eliminating 'weeds' that clutter and obfuscate. While such pruning produces
helpful distinctions and cultivates a sense of relative importance among the
greenery, it falls short of providing a definitive path to success. We look
to theory in vain if we expect to find a hedge-marked lane leading to the
desired outcome. Theory instead lifts one's gaze to 'higher realms of action',
giving practitioners an awareness of these 'realms' while introducing them
to the challenges of navigating there.

Clausewitz's contrast between theory, on the one hand, and 'method
and routine', on the other, illustrates how thinking at the tactical and
strategic levels qualitatively differ. Book 2, Chapter 4, starts with the hier-
archy of law, principle, rule, method and routine in warfare. The author
does not condemn the practice of deriving routines and methods from
principles. He only declares that reliance on routine is more appropriate at the tactical level. Leaders who depend largely on their experience,
along with prescriptive guidance disseminated from their organisations' higher echelons, benefit from routine as Clausewitz describes it.
Contemporary battle drills, for instance, 'steady' the 'judgment' of
military officers and 'also guard them against eccentric and mistaken
schemes'. Thus, it is no surprise that tactical commanders can often
succeed by merely avoiding error. Routine, however, is far less useful
at the strategic level, where success does not conform to any detailed
recipe. According to Clausewitz:

War, in its highest forms, is not *an infinite mass of minor events*, analogous
despite their diversities, which can be controlled with greater or lesser
effectiveness depending on the methods applied. War consists rather of

*single, great decisive actions*, each of which needs to be handled individually. War is not like a field of wheat, which, without regard to the individual stalk, may be mown more or less efficiently depending on the quality of the scythe; it is like a stand of mature trees in which the axe has to be used judiciously according to the characteristics and development of each individual trunk. (p. 153, emphasis in original)

In short, context matters in war, not least at its highest levels. As one scales the professional ladder towards greater responsibilities, it is not enough to master more complicated battle drills. Strategic leaders who slavishly adhere to routine run the risk of applying military force in a manner ill-suited to the context in which they find themselves. Imitating the methods of history's great captains without an appreciation of context demonstrates 'the most extreme poverty of the imagination' (p. 155). Theory, says Clausewitz, not only acts as a safeguard against this danger but also provides a basis for sound analysis leading to appropriate action.

Before deciding on a particular course of action, seasoned practitioners often rely on intuition stemming from long years of experience, but theory serves to expose the limits of experience. To be sure, experience is indispensable in continuing professional education. Clausewitz's life as a soldier, for instance, deeply informed his thinking and writing. So while we ought not dismiss experience, neither should we regard judgements derived from our personal past as infallible or perpetually relevant. Theory helps us make sense of what we have seen and done, and helps us learn from it. A quotation often attributed to Frederick the Great illustrates the importance of balancing experience with reflection, practice with theory, doing with thinking:

What good is experience if it is not directed by reflection? ... Thought, the faculty of combining ideas, is what distinguishes man from a beast of burden. A mule who has carried a pack for ten campaigns under Prince Eugene will be no better a tactician for it, and it must be confessed ... that many men grow old in an otherwise respectable profession without making any greater progress than this mule.[10]

Some may see incongruity in theory's dual role as prompt for reflection and guide to action. To address it, students of policy and strategy might categorise a particular theory according to its author's purpose and thus distinguish between theories of phenomenon and theories of action.[11] Clausewitz himself presents war as a phenomenon and tries to explain what it is. In contrast, military theories of action focus more on how best to wage war. In *On War*, Clausewitz delves into the latter, of course, but he begins his enquiry with an earnest exploration of the former. Such categorisations highlight the varied intentions animating the writings of military theorists like Clausewitz and, say, Giulio Douhet, and thus help practitioners make sense of the diverse array of theoretical constructs introduced to them throughout their professional education.

## The second definition of war emphasises politics

Furthermore, theories provide a framework for fully understanding complex phenomena. In composing *Young Men and Fire*, Norman Maclean's classic account of the deadly Mann Gulch wildfire, the author realised that a genuine grasp of the event would elude him until he appreciated fire as a unique phenomenon. He discovered the need to begin his enquiry by outlining a theory of fire. Only through this preliminary lens could he explain the fire at the centre of his story and assess the actions of the 15 smokejumpers deployed to fight it under the specific conditions on that Montana day in August 1949.[12] This enabled the author to reconstruct in meticulous detail the behaviour of both the fire and the men as the fire overwhelmed them, killing all but three. A study of *On War* analogously supports the national-security practitioner.

Clausewitz's discussion of theory and its utility also offers an entry point for engaging with his two famous definitions of war, found in Book 1, Chapter 1. The first appears as a blunt, unabashed declaration: 'War is thus an act of force to compel our enemy to do our will' (p. 75). But the second definition shifts the focus, emphasising not violence but politics: 'War is merely the continuation of policy by other means' (p. 87).[13] These definitions carry different implications, reconcilable only by recalling the purpose of Clausewitz's enquiry. The first definition suggests that wars are inherently escalatory and destructive. The second implies that, because war aims to achieve some political objective, there may well be constraints on its violence.[14]

In fact, Clausewitz believed that neither definition of war was complete. *On War*'s Book 1, Chapter 1, is a sustained argument establishing the difference between theory and reality that goes to the heart of Clausewitz's understanding of the phenomenon of war. In theory, he says, 'there is no logical limit to the application of force' (p. 77). Yet in practice, he cannot help but observe limitations. While war in theory ought to gravitate towards extremes, war in practice seems subject to moderating forces such as politics, friction and uncertainty. This tension between Clausewitz's two definitions says something significant about war's enduring nature, to which he returns repeatedly.

The discussion of the 'trinity' – perhaps *On War*'s most referenced yet least understood passage – also aims to clarify the nature of war. In their canonical translation, Howard and Paret render trinity's German modifier *wunderlich* in the original text as 'paradoxical'. Criticising this word choice as too clinical or understated, other scholars favour 'strange' or 'wondrous' as more faithful to the sense of mystery Clausewitz ascribed to the complex interactions at work in war.[15] Regardless, the author's introduction of the trinity at the end of Book 1, Chapter 1, merits scrutiny as a framework for explaining the dynamics of war. The three elements of this trinity are 'primordial violence, hatred, and enmity'; the 'play of chance and probability'; and war's 'element of subordination, as an instrument of policy, which makes it subject to reason alone' (p. 89). In the next sentence, Clausewitz relates these three elements to the people, the army and the state, prompting some readers to associate violence (or passion) inextricably with the people, chance with the army and reason with the government.[16] Such an interpretation, however, imposes a far more rigid construct than Clausewitz intended. Nowhere in Book 1, Chapter 1, does Clausewitz tell us to *do* anything.[17] This critical section of *On War* is not about implementation, and the trinity is not something to apply prescriptively. Rather, it is a descriptive way of understanding the phenomenon of war and defining war's nature.

Clausewitz does suggest that all wars, regardless of time or place, include each element of the trinity – violence, chance and reason – and that these 'dominant tendencies' exist in a dynamic relationship. There is a balance among them, but the relationship is neither fixed nor arbitrary. In his seminal article on Clausewitz and complexity, Alan Beyerchen characterises the trinity as 'three interactive points of attraction that are simultaneously pulling the object in different directions'.[18] Thus, depicting the trinity as a simple triangle only muddles the concept for practitioners.

Michael I. Handel proposes a 'vector analysis' in which 'the nature of war is the outcome or "vector" of the three dominant tendencies'.[19] Through this approach, modern conventional war can be seen as three vectors of 'roughly equal' magnitude. A representation of guerrilla warfare, by contrast, might confer stronger influence on the role of the people and the passions that animate them.[20] Yet even this mode of visualisation risks reductionism. Perhaps a series of Venn diagrams rings truer, suggesting a propensity for the relative influence of violence, chance and reason in a particular war to expand or contract. For the practitioner, the trinity's value as a concept lies in its portrayal of the general phenomenon of war as 'a balance between … three tendencies, like an object suspended between three magnets' (p. 89).

## Clausewitz's dialectics

If the trinity indicates practitioners' subtle penchant for making the deliberately abstract inappropriately concrete, Clausewitz's use of a dialectical mode of argument encourages them to appreciate *On War* at a kind of meta level. His work reflects an intellectual journey – an ongoing interaction of thesis and antithesis.[21] As a result, several inconsistencies emerge. The author reconciles many of them through nuanced synthesis. Others he does not.[22] The details of these discrepancies matter far less for practitioners than discerning, more generally, the prevalence of tension among the related ideas presented in *On War*.

In Book 1, Chapter 2, for example, Clausewitz explores how the nature of war influences the application of military means towards political ends. In doing so, he briefly analyses not only means and ends, but also war and policy, tactics and strategy, physical and moral forces, and offence and defence. When we contemplate the meaning of these tandems of terms and how they relate to each other, we are compelled to hold the competing ideas in tension and to wrestle with their implications. What kinds of ends should states pursue in war, and what means are required to achieve them? How can an army's advantage in morale compensate for numerical inferiority? Does strategy or tactics matter more to military victory, and why? Clausewitz's discussion on the imperative of aligning means with ends, his designation of combat as the decisive means of war, and the weight he gives to moral forces as factors in determining a battle's outcome help frame a fruitful approach to these questions. More broadly, the hard thinking inherent in the dialectical process and the tensions that such thinking reveals provide lessons themselves. The crux of a strategic issue often lies in the tensions at play, and Clausewitz invites others to engage in this intellectual struggle.

## War and policy

His view of the relationship between war and policy deserves special attention. Though no doubt aware that war is a continuation of politics by other means, practitioners reading *On War* should aim to place this oft-cited axiom in context and extract its relevance. Firstly, as part of Book 1, Chapter 1, it constitutes another plank in Clausewitz's description of the nature of war. 'The political object is the goal, war is the means of reaching it, and means can never be considered in isolation from their purpose' (p. 87). In Book 2, Chapter 3, Clausewitz reinforces this point. A 'clash between major interests … resolved by bloodshed', war is 'part of man's social existence', while 'politics is the womb in which war develops' (p. 149).

This perspective has enormous implications for formulating strategy. As Clausewitz argues in Book 8, Chapter 6:

> That the political view should wholly cease to count on the outbreak of war is hardly conceivable unless pure hatred made all wars a struggle for life and death. In fact, as we have said, they are nothing but expressions of policy itself. Subordinating the political point of view to the military would be absurd, for it is policy that has created war. Policy is the guiding intelligence and war only the instrument, not vice versa. No other possibility exists, then, than to subordinate the military point of view to the political. (p. 607)

It follows that the interaction between war and policy also has implications for civil–military relations. Clausewitz suggests political awareness
(even acumen) as a required trait for senior military leaders and then deliv-
ers a stern warning to commanders tempted to complain about civilian
meddling in military affairs:

> No major proposal required for war can be worked out in ignorance of
> political factors; and when people talk, as they often do, about harmful
> political influence on the management of war, they are not really saying
> what they mean. Their quarrel should be with the policy itself, not with its
> influence. If the policy is right – that is, successful – any intentional effect it
> has on the conduct of the war can only be to the good. If it has the opposite
> effect the policy itself is wrong. (p. 608)

Thus, for practitioners crafting strategy in an unavoidably political environment, Clausewitz's view of war as an instrument of policy looms large. This
commonly referenced view seems easily and broadly affirmed today.[23] Yet
those charged with advancing national-security interests must guard against
the tendency to make the familiar trite.[24] Moreover, they must appreciate
the consequences of failing to follow the idea's logic. Consider historical
cases in which military concerns not only informed policy but came to dominate it. The German decision to invade France through Belgium in 1914 and
Japanese decisions vis-à-vis China and Southeast Asia prior to the Second
World War illustrate the dangers of upending the relationship between war
and policy.[25] Past leaders travelled along highly contingent paths to arrive
at these strategically damaging decisions, of course, but the unique circumstances of each episode still advertise dire possibilities.

Given the primacy of the political object, what then is the role of senior
military leaders in civil–military dialogue? Here, too, Clausewitz provides
grist for the mill. Much of civil–military relations centres on the alignment
of ends and means. Can the political ends be achieved with the military
means available? Statesmen and commanders answer this question together.
War may be subordinate to policy and its means directed towards policy's
ends. But the commander, says Clausewitz, 'is entitled to require that the

trend and designs of policy' be consistent with the means at hand (p. 87). Practitioners should understand that Clausewitz aptly calls for robust civil–military dialogue:

> No one starts a war – or rather, no one in his senses ought to do so – without first being clear in his mind what he intends to achieve by that war and how he intends to conduct it. The former is its political purpose; the latter its operational objective. This is the governing principle which will set its course, prescribe the scale of means and effort which is required, and make its influence felt throughout down to the smallest operational detail. (p. 579)

War's relationship to policy ought to be characterised not only by internal consistency with respect to ends and means, but also by consistency with war's nature. Herein lies another role for the senior military leader. If war serves as an instrument of policy and the conditions of specific wars are subject to change, then:

> The first, the supreme, the most far-reaching act of judgment that the statesman and commander have to make is to establish by that test the kind of war on which they are embarking; neither mistaking it for, nor trying to turn it into, something that is alien to its nature. (p. 88)

Without subverting policy's primacy, Clausewitz suggests that civilian leaders court disaster when they seek to wage war in a way that ignores the inescapable consequences of its nature:

> Only if statesmen look to certain military moves and actions to produce effects that are foreign to their nature do political decisions influence operations for the worse. In the same way as a man who has not fully mastered a foreign language sometimes fails to express himself correctly, so statesmen often issue orders that defeat the purpose they are meant to serve. Repeatedly that has happened, which demonstrates that a certain grasp of military affairs is vital for those in charge of general policy. (p. 608)

The traditional gap in the knowledge and experience of civilian leaders makes the provision of military advice by senior commanders an imperative. For an example of policy guidance that seemed to defy the dictates of war's nature, take H.R. McMaster's *Dereliction of Duty*, in which he discusses the Lyndon B. Johnson administration's call for 'graduated pressure' against North Vietnam in the mid-1960s. 'Graduated pressure defined military action as a form of communication', writes McMaster. As a strategy, it 'ignored the uncertainty of war and the unpredictable psychology of an activity that involves killing, death, and destruction'.[26] War, of course, entails communication of a kind with the enemy, but its nature demands much more. Graduated pressure overestimated the ability of Washington to send precise messages to Hanoi through aerial bombardments and troop deployments while assuming North Vietnamese leaders would receive those messages without misinterpreting them. More importantly, the approach underestimated the commitment of those leaders to political and territorial unification. Whether military pressure was graduated or not seemed irrelevant. Citing Clausewitz, McMaster argues that 'even though the Joint Chiefs of Staff believed that the concept of graduated pressure was inconsistent with the "nature of war", they planned for the war within the parameters of that concept'.[27]

If acquiescing to a use of force inconsistent with war's nature illustrates one possible military misstep, constraining the choices of civilian decision-makers errs in another direction. Named for General Colin Powell, who served as chairman of the Joint Chiefs of Staff from 1989 to 1993, the Powell Doctrine outlined a set of prerequisites for US military action overseas, in part with an eye to avoiding the mistakes of Vietnam. These included well-defined objectives, a calculated 'exit strategy', and broad domestic and international support – policy guidelines that seemed prudent enough for a general who, before he reached the chairmanship, had worked for several senior civilian officials in advisory capacities, including as national security advisor.[28] Yet historians criticise the Powell Doctrine for circumscribing the military options available to policymakers in the event of a brewing crisis or evolving contingency.[29] Its underlying assumptions 'made the senior officers of the army into doves, separated from their political masters', writes

Strachan. 'Because America's generals would only countenance the employment of military forces in the sorts of operations for which the army was optimized, they effectively rendered them unusable.'[30] Madeleine Albright, as secretary of state, observed as much in 1993 when Powell cautioned against intervening in the former Yugoslavia's civil war.[31]

The Powell Doctrine usurped political prerogatives by demanding 'clear and unambiguous objectives' for the military ahead of decisions to use force in what Powell himself described as 'murky, unpredictable circumstances'.[32] Consistent with the much-maligned Huntingtonian norm of separate political and military spheres, it also implied that political considerations held diminishing sway in discussions over how best to use force once war commenced.[33] Defending his views on the use of force, Powell takes aim at those who rely on 'a set of principles or a when-to-go-to-war doctrine' before offering a list of questions that functionally serves the same purpose.[34] He attributes US foreign-policy success during the George H.W. Bush administration to the careful alignment of military force and political objectives.[35] One could dispute Powell's assessment while agreeing with its basic – even Clausewitzian – rationale. Yet when Powell insists that his approach does not seek to restrict the use of force to 'occasions where the victory of American arms will be resounding, swift, and overwhelming', the general is less persuasive.[36] Indeed, that tailored, self-limiting application of the military instrument seems entirely compatible with the Powell Doctrine's intent.

Strachan again provides clarity by relating policy to war and connecting these terms to strategy. Paraphrasing Clausewitz while incorporating the nuance conveyed throughout *On War*, he explains, that 'policy which sees war simply as an instrument but fails to understand the nature of the instrument is bad policy. Strategy is therefore the product of the dialogue between politicians and soldiers, and its essence is the harmonization of the two elements, not the subordination of one to the other.'[37] It remains for statesmen and generals alike to manage the inherent tensions of such discourse in multiple situations – to temper or, if necessary, repair what has been called 'the broken dialogue'.[38] In any case, Clausewitz reminds us that, to bear the fruit of successful strategy, civil–military relations depend on a common understanding of the right relationship between policy and war in light of war's nature.

## Real and absolute war

From his view of war's relationship to policy, Clausewitz derives his distinction between absolute war and real war. Related to the contrast between war in theory and war in practice discussed in Book 1, Chapter 1, and then revisited in Book 8, the treatment of this distinction exemplifies his relentless pursuit of completeness and consistency even when they prove elusive. For the most part, when he uses the term 'absolute war', he is referring to an abstraction: what war would be like if it encountered no constraints. As he notes, war unfolds much differently in reality. There is, Clausewitz says, a 'gap between the pure concept of war and the concrete form that, as a general rule, war assumes'. Logically speaking, war ought to be 'a case in which two mutually destructive elements collide', but, in reality, it ramifies as 'tension between two elements, separate for the time being, which discharge energy in discontinuous, minor shocks' (p. 579).

From a sociological or historical perspective, notes Howard, Clausewitz believes 'all wars were the products of the societies that fought them'.[39] Cultural norms, predominant ideologies, technological advances, and political and economic institutions all lent to war in every age a certain shape and 'determined whether war would be total or limited, and what the limits would be'.[40] Metaphysically, Clausewitz saw a contrast between war in its natural state and war subject to the dictates of a logic outside itself. War in its ideal or natural form, explains Howard, accelerates along a path of escalation with 'no stopping-place short of the extreme'. Yet 'war was never a self-contained activity … unrelated to the events that had led up to it or to the situation it was intended to produce'.[41] It has always emerged in a political context. Thus, 'the reasoned decisions of the political leaders who called the war into being' invariably imposed limits – however slight or inconsistent – and disrupted what in theory would have been an inevitable slide into 'absolute war'.[42] These sociological and metaphysical aspects of Clausewitz's distinction between the conceptual and concrete, as Howard points out, are extrinsic to war. By contrast, a third – 'friction', essentially the discrepancy between plans and results – is a pervasive and unavoidable feature 'intrinsic to the conduct of war itself' and determined by limitations on the capability and will of humans to act.[43] Clausewitz considered friction multifaceted, affecting not only troop movements and military planning but also the decision-making and morale of leaders, as well as combatants.

Clausewitz's discussion of absolute and real war shines a light on the nature and character of war. Although change abounds in military affairs, much remains the same.

> We must ... be prepared to develop our concept of war as it ought to be fought, not on the basis of its pure definition, but by leaving room for every sort of extraneous matter. We must allow for natural inertia, for all the friction of its parts, for all the inconsistency, imprecision, and timidity of man; and finally we must face the fact that war and its forms result from ideas, emotions, and conditions prevailing at the time. (p. 580)

Those responsible for national-security planning must ask what kind of war they are dealing with. Charged with both diagnosis and prescription, they often struggle to account for both the enduring spirit or nature of war and the unique context of a particular military conflict. The intellectual balancing act is especially salient to the contemporary challenge of limited war, which derives much of its meaning from Clausewitz's analysis of absolute and real war. To cite one of his extended metaphors:

> Policy converts the overwhelmingly destructive element of war into a mere instrument. It changes the terrible battle-sword that a man needs both hands and his entire strength to wield, and with which he strikes home once and no more, into a light, handy rapier – sometimes just a foil for the exchange of thrusts, feints, and parries. (p. 606)

Such observations led Clausewitz to conclude, reluctantly, that wars were of two kinds.[44] He most clearly describes this duality in an 1827 letter to a Prussian staff officer. Wars intended 'to *crush* my opponent ... to make him *defenseless* and force him to accept my peace terms' radically differ, he wrote, from wars fought to gain 'some advantage by conquering a strip of land, occupying a fortress, etc., which I can retain or use in negotiations'.[45] Each kind of war called for a careful alignment of political purpose, available means and use of the military instrument. From this demand for internal consistency flowed the conclusion that commanders had to tailor the military instrument to prevailing political conditions. A universal application of armed force would not do. *On War*'s well-known reference to 'the first, the supreme, the most far-reaching act of judgment' ought to weigh heavily on civilian and military leaders alike. Clausewitz emphasises the criticality of understanding the situation, not least the political context, and determining which kind of war the contemplated one would be. 'We must not allow ourselves to be misled', he chided, 'into regarding war as a pure act of force and of destruction, and from this simplistic concept logically deduce a string of conclusions that no longer have anything to do with the real world'.[46] Decisions for how best to wage war in a given set of circumstances rest on recognising war's essential duality.

Correlating ends and means amid the dynamic conditions that distinguish a particular war while applying military force consistent with war's nature calls on the intellectual and moral faculties of both statesmen and commanders. Clausewitz's insights on this score have special relevance for practitioners navigating the troubled aftermath of America's post-9/11 conflicts in Afghanistan, Iraq and Syria, prompting several pointed questions. Why, for instance, do civil–military relations seem so strained in limited wars? And why does clarity of purpose in such conflicts seem so elusive? Clausewitz explains by contrasting real and absolute war:

> The more powerful and inspiring the motives for war, the more they affect the belligerent nations and the fiercer the tensions that precede the outbreak, the closer will war approach its abstract concept, the more important will be the destruction of the enemy, the more closely will the military aims and the political objects of war coincide, and the more military and less political will war appear to be. On the other hand, the less intense the motives, the less will the military element's natural tendency to violence coincide with political directives. As a result, war

will be driven further from its natural course, the political object will be increasingly at variance with the aim of ideal war, and the conflict will seem increasingly political in character. (pp. 87–8)

By referring to war approaching its 'abstract concept', Clausewitz evokes his idea of 'absolute war' wherein politics imposes minimal limitations upon a conflict's conduct and goals. When the reasons for war appear more compelling to a state and its people, they justify the commitment of more resources in pursuit of more ambitious ends, and thus facilitate a more natural alignment between political objectives and military aims. However, wars triggered by 'less intense' motives inject ambiguity into the dialogue between statesmen and commanders, generating a weaker consensus as to what a war's political objectives ought to be and how best to achieve them.

In these circumstances of what we would term limited war, the clarity that theoretically accompanies the aim of destroying the enemy's armed forces diffuses through branches of possibility, demanding greater sensitivity to political factors and a more calibrated application of the military instrument while inserting more links into a causal chain connecting the use of force with war termination. Thus, Clausewitz suggests that in limited wars, a counter-intuitive dynamic drives the relationship with policy. In wars requiring fewer resources, fuelled by less ambitious aims and waged with less at stake, statesmen and commanders find it harder to agree on specific goals, harder to design and focus military ways and means, harder to end hostilities on favourable terms, and harder to secure a meaningful victory recognised by all belligerents. Although wars in recent decades tend to reflect this logic, their repeated occurrence has not made their prosecution any easier.

## Friction and leadership

If war's relationship to policy constrains war in practice, so too does leadership. Clausewitz's analysis of 'genius' (principally in Book 1, Chapter 3) illustrates the close connection between war's nature and the indispensable attributes of the commander. Appreciating the politics of war benefits the senior military leader, to be sure. But what does Clausewitz mean when he warns that the commander – however politically astute – 'must not cease to be a general' (p. 112)? For one, regardless of the extent to which they understand the perspectives of statesmen, generals must master the task of applying military means to achieve the ends of policy in an environment fraught with danger, uncertainty and friction. Danger unnerves and distracts the novice while a persistent 'fog of ... uncertainty' obscures the process of decision-making (p. 101). Clausewitz prioritises friction as a factor that 'makes the apparently easy so difficult' (p. 121). It defies straightforward explanation, he says, being 'inconceivable' to the uninitiated, subtle but 'all-pervading', and the cumulative effect of 'countless ... minor incidents' combining 'to lower the general level of performance, so that one always falls far short of the intended goal' (p. 119).

At a time when contemporaries linked military success with adherence to rules and principles, Clausewitz introduced the problem of friction and warned of the implications that flowed from its ubiquity in war. Historian Williamson Murray rates the 'formulation and analysis of the concept of friction' as Clausewitz's 'greatest contribution'.[47] Howard suggests that his insight on how friction disrupts and dampens the pace and pulse of military campaigning puts Clausewitz 'in a class of his own'.[48] A by-product of war's innate chance and unpredictability, friction demands creativity from commanders. 'If Clausewitz was correct in singling out friction as the inescapable atmosphere of war', defence analyst Barry Watts argues, 'then any attempt to come to grips with war that generally omits friction is incomplete'.[49] Some scholars and practitioners have tried to do just that, proposing to eliminate friction from the battlefield through advances in surveillance and information technology, but contemporary warfare has exposed the futility of such aspirations.[50]

Friction persists and, to manage it, commanders – knowingly or not – take their cue from Clausewitz. A recent study of organisational change in wartime notes that militaries 'seek to impose as much order on the relentless chaos of war as possible'.[51] To counter the effects of friction, they formalise rank structures, communications procedures, doctrine and tactics. Yet these measures tend to hamper adaptation – the very process militaries need to thrive in a dynamic and unpredictable environment.[52] In war, such paradoxes are commonplace and seem to go hand in hand with Clausewitz's understanding of the phenomenon as volatile and complex.

National-security practitioners ought to empathise with past commanders forced to grapple with the implications of war's inherent complexity. Consider the strains that war heaps upon the intellect. In centuries past as well as in our own, both a lack and an abundance of information exacerbated the challenge of wartime leadership, requiring an 'eye of genius' that 'grasps and dismisses a thousand remote possibilities' before deciding where, when and how to act. 'Circumstances vary so enormously in war, and are so indefinable, that a vast array of factors has to be appreciated', Clausewitz writes. 'The man responsible for evaluating the whole must bring to his task the quality of intuition that perceives the truth at every point' (p. 112).

Such a holistic assessment, Clausewitz admits, is easier urged than executed. If war looks to policy for shape and intensity, then waging it must incorporate far more than military concerns. Likewise, aligning means and ends entails not just a knowledge of the wide-ranging factors at play – it also requires a sense of their relative significance, which may shift unexpectedly, not least because of the adversary's response to one's chosen strategy. Thus, in preparing for war, given its expansive context and interactive nature, Clausewitz reasons:

> We must first examine our own political aim and that of the enemy. We must gauge the strength and situation of the opposing state. We must gauge the character and abilities of its government and people and do the same in regard to our own. Finally, we must evaluate the political sympathies of other states and the effect the war may have on them. To assess these things in all their ramifications and diversity is plainly a colossal task. Rapid and correct appraisal of them clearly calls for the intuition of a genius; to master all this complex mass by sheer methodical examination is obviously impossible. (pp. 585–6)

To this daunting depiction of the intellectual challenge facing the commander, Clausewitz adds a dose of urgency: states have much to lose or gain in war. With 'the exact sciences of logic and mathematics' inadequate for such an uncertain yet high-stakes trial, Clausewitz puts a premium on art – an 'intellectual activity' reliant on 'using judgment to detect the most important and decisive elements in the vast array of facts and situations' (p. 585).

Yet intellect and creativity, while necessary, are not enough. 'Truth in itself is rarely sufficient to make men act', says Clausewitz. 'The step is always long from cognition to volition, from knowledge to ability.' To 'emerge unscathed from this relentless struggle with the unforeseen', a commander, he argues, must possess two qualities in combination: 'first, an *intellect* that, even in the darkest hour, retains some glimmerings of the inner light which leads to truth; and second, the *courage* to follow this faint light wherever it may lead' (p. 102; emphasis in original). Furthermore, the courage befitting a commander is of 'two kinds': 'courage in the face of personal danger, and courage to accept responsibility, either before the tribunal of some outside power or before the court of one's own conscience' (p. 101). Thus, he also posits a link between physical exertion and suffering, on the one hand, and uncertainty and chance, on the other. The wartime leader must master both challenges.

Drawing on the attributes of intellect and courage, commanders can overcome friction itself through 'iron will', which, according to Clausewitz, 'pulverizes every obstacle' (p. 119). But even willpower calls for prudent application, an awareness that the harder one pushes, the more one exposes the intricate parts of the military machine to ruthless grinding and wear. He goes on to capture the senior military leader's dilemma in another metaphor, shifting from the image of spinning metal gears to a ship's keel moving over water amid invisible threats:

> Every war is rich in unique episodes. Each is an uncharted sea, full of reefs. The commander may suspect the reefs' existence without ever having seen them; now he has to steer past them in the dark. If a contrary wind springs up, if some major mischance appears, he will need the greatest skill and personal exertion, and the utmost presence of mind, though from a distance everything may seem to be proceeding automatically. An understanding of friction is a large part of that much-admired sense of warfare which a good general is supposed to possess. (p. 120)

In the light of this portrayal of friction's ubiquity in war, the utility of harnessing it to acquire a position of advantage through deception, speed or initiative becomes clear.

As a prudential check on the military's traditional 'can-do' attitude, communicating to statesmen the concept of friction emerges as a critical skill. Friction, as Clausewitz describes it, may well be unfamiliar to some civilians.[53] Demands for no-fly zones in the early years of Syria's civil war and, more recently, over Ukraine discounted the difficulty and risk of such operations and belied a clinically precise view of modern war.[54] Scholars in the field of civil–military relations argue that military leaders ought to take more seriously their responsibility for engaging in sustained, iterative dialogue and providing best military advice to civilian superiors.[55] As a corrective measure, Jim Golby recommends empowering mid-level officers to contribute freely and early in inter-agency policy discussions; anticipating contingencies in which civilian decision-makers might contemplate the use of military force; and outlining in clear, candid terms the risks of employing the military in a particular contingency.[56] Implementing any of these recommendations relies on comprehending friction and its subtle yet formidable implications, and then articulating with clarity its potential to influence military operations.

Clausewitz's ideal commander embodies a 'blend of brains and temperament', with the latter embodying 'the qualities of determination, firmness, staunchness, and strength of character' (p. 112). This combination provides the basis of 'military genius', which enables the general to cut through the tangled knot of danger, uncertainty and friction inherent in war. For civilian defence officials, advisers and planners, familiarisation with the challenges of exercising military leadership in the politically driven context of war helps establish the mutual understanding necessary to engage in productive dialogue during strategy formulation.[57]

\*    \*    \*

Clausewitz's commentary on theory and routine sheds light on the qualitative distinction between thinking at the strategic and tactical levels. His description of war's nature offers excellent guidance for leaders to examine continuity and change in warfare over time, encouraging clear-eyed assessments of similarities and differences when comparing current or impending national-security issues with those from the past. And through its frequent plumbing of war's relationship to policy, *On War* delineates civil and military responsibilities in the development and implementation of strategy – two processes that crucially rely on dialogue between the two spheres.

In *War and Politics,* Bernard Brodie's penetrating examination of civil–military relations and the use of force during the first nuclear age, the author insisted that Clausewitz still had a great deal to teach us. Writing in the early 1970s, when the issue of US military involvement in Vietnam pervaded American strategic thinking, Brodie described the 'twinge of delight' Clausewitz triggered among readers who recognised passages in *On War* that continued to resonate. Acknowledging that drawing 'connections between events or insights remote in time and circumstances' marks the study of any classic work, Brodie stressed that reading *On War* conferred a real 'advantage' to readers who approached Clausewitz's work not as a how-to manual but as an exploration of the 'deepening of sensibility or insight' necessary for strategic thinking. Clausewitz 'does offer us rules', wrote Brodie, but 'he is at once avid to show us all the qualifications and historical exceptions to them'.[58]

What Brodie said 50 years ago holds true today. As much as anything else, *On War* traces and endorses an intellectual journey. Amid the qualifications and exceptions that course through analyses of contemporary events, Clausewitz's theory provides an invaluable springboard for military and civilian readers who grasp that they must look beyond it for prescriptions and develop their own.

## Notes

[1] Michael Howard, *Clausewitz* (Oxford: Oxford University Press, 1983), p. 1. Emphasis in original.

[2] *Ibid.*

[3] *Ibid.*

[4] See Hew Strachan, *The Direction of War: Contemporary Strategy in Historical Perspective* (Cambridge: Cambridge University Press, 2013), pp. 53–4.

[5] *Ibid.*, p. 63.

6   *Ibid.*, p. 46.

7   *Ibid.*, p. 63.

8   See Peter Paret, *The Cognitive Challenge of War: Prussia, 1806* (Princeton, NJ: Princeton University Press, 2009), pp. 73–5.

9   For an introduction to Clausewitz and *On War*, see Peter Paret, 'Clausewitz', in Peter Paret (ed.), *Makers of Modern Strategy: From Machiavelli to the Nuclear Age* (Princeton, NJ: Princeton University Press, 1986), pp. 186–213. Michael Howard's *Clausewitz* emphasises the military transformation that energised Clausewitz as a student of war and describes the implications for logistics, operations, tactics and soldier morale resulting from this transformation. On the writing of *On War*, see Hew Strachan, *Clausewitz's On War: A Biography* (New York: Grove Press, 2007). For an explanation of how the French Revolution changed the character of warfare in the late eighteenth century and the intellectual context that informed Clausewitz as he sought to demystify war's observed reality through the lens of theoretical discourse, see John A. Lynn, *Battle: A History of Combat and Culture* (Boulder, CO: Westview Press, 2003), pp. 179–216.

10  Jay Luvaas (ed. and trans.), *Frederick the Great on the Art of War* (New York: Da Capo Press, 1999), p. 47.

11  Professor G. Stephen Lauer introduced me to this consideration of theory in 2016 at the US Army School of Advanced Military Studies in Fort Leavenworth, KS.

12  See Norman Maclean, *Young Men and Fire* (Chicago, IL: University of Chicago Press, 2017).

13  An alternate formulation is that war is 'a true political instrument, a continuation of political intercourse, carried on with other means' (p. 87).

14  For this distinction between Clausewitz's definitions of war, I am indebted to William T. Johnsen, with whom I served on the faculty at the US Army War College in Carlisle, PA.

15  Strachan, *Clausewitz's* On War, p. 178; and Lynn, *Battle*, p. 207.

16  See, for example, Strachan, *Clausewitz's* On War, pp. 2–3, 178.

17  Thomas Bruscino makes the same point in 'Start with Book Three: Finding Utility in Clausewitz's *On War*', War Room, 21 April 2020, https://warroom.armywarcollege.edu/articles/start-with-book-three/.

18  Alan Beyerchen, 'Clausewitz, Nonlinearity, and the Unpredictability of War', *International Security*, vol. 17, no. 3, Winter 1992–93, pp. 70–1.

19  Michael I. Handel, *Masters of War: Classical Strategic Thought*, 3rd ed. (London: Frank Cass, 2004), p. 104.

20  *Ibid.*, pp. 104–5.

21  See Strachan, *Clausewitz's* On War, pp. 99–102.

22  See *ibid.*, pp. 193–4; and Lynn, *Battle*, pp. 204–5. For an extended discussion of Clausewitz's attempt to reconcile the tensions between war in theory and war in reality, see Azar Gat, *The Origins of Military Thought: From the Enlightenment to Clausewitz* (Oxford: Oxford University Press, 1989), pp. 199–226, 251–3.

23  Though written out of concern for contemporary US civil–military relations, an open letter endorsed by several former US secretaries of defense and chairmen of the US

Joint Chiefs of Staff exhibits solid consensus on the core principles of civilian control of the military. See 'To Support and Defend: Principles of Civilian Control and Best Practices of Civil–Military Relations', *War on the Rocks*, 6 September 2022, https://warontherocks.com/2022/09/to-support-and-defend-principles-of-civilian-control-and-best-practices-of-civil-military-relations/.

24 Strachan explains the problem with interpreting Clausewitz exclusively through an anachronistic 'liberal' lens coloured by the democratic norms of civil–military relations. See Strachan, *The Direction of War,* pp. 51–5.

25 See Edward J. Drea, *Japan's Imperial Army: Its Rise and Fall, 1853–1945* (Lawrence, KS: University of Kansas Press, 2009), pp. 190–4, 209–10, 256; Akira Iriye, *Power and Culture: The Japanese–American War, 1941–1945* (Cambridge, MA: Harvard University Press, 1981), pp. 39–41; and Annika Mombauer, 'German War Plans', in Richard F. Hamilton and Holger H. Herwig (eds), *War Planning 1914* (Cambridge: Cambridge University Press, 2010), pp. 48, 56–60.

26 H.R. McMaster, *Dereliction of Duty: Lyndon Johnson, Robert McNamara, the Joint Chiefs of Staff, and the Lies that Led to Vietnam* (New York: HarperCollins, 1997), pp. 326–7.

27 *Ibid.*, p. 154.

28 See Colin L. Powell with Joseph E. Persico, *My American Journey* (New York: Random House, 1995), pp. 303, 558–9.

29 See Matthew Moten, *Presidents and Their Generals: An American History of Command in War* (Cambridge, MA:

Harvard University Press, 2014), pp. 338–9; Strachan, *The Direction of War*, p. 55; and Russell F. Weigley, 'The American Civil–Military Cultural Gap: A Historical Perspective, Colonial Times to the Present', in Peter D. Feaver and Richard H. Kohn (eds), *Soldiers and Civilians: The Civil–Military Gap and American National Security* (Cambridge, MA: MIT Press, 2001), pp. 241–3.

30 Strachan, *The Direction of War*, p. 62.

31 See Powell, *My American Journey*, pp. 576–7.

32 Colin L. Powell, 'U.S. Forces: Challenges Ahead', *Foreign Affairs*, vol. 71, no. 5, Winter 1992, pp. 38–9.

33 For critiques of Samuel Huntington's theory and its implications for civil–military relations, see James Burk, 'Responsible Obedience by Military Professionals: The Discretion to Do What Is Wrong', in Suzanne C. Nielsen and Don M. Snider (eds), *American Civil–Military Relations: The Soldier and the State in a New Era* (Baltimore, MD: Johns Hopkins University Press, 2009), pp. 150–4; Eliot Cohen, *Supreme Command: Soldiers, Statesmen, and Leadership in Wartime,* revised ed. (New York: Anchor Books, 2003), pp. 245–7, 257–8; and John M. Gates, 'The Alleged Isolation of US Army Officers in the Late 19th Century', *Parameters*, vol. 10, no. 1, September 1980, pp. 37–9, 43.

34 Powell, 'U.S. Forces', pp. 37–8.

35 *Ibid.*, p. 39.

36 *Ibid.*, p. 40.

37 Strachan, *The Direction of War*, p. 78.

38 See Janine Davison, 'Civil–Military Friction and Presidential Decision Making: Explaining the Broken Dialogue', *Presidential Studies Quarterly*, vol. 43, no. 1, March 2013, pp. 130–1.

39  Howard, *Clausewitz*, p. 48.

40  *Ibid.*, p. 49.

41  *Ibid.*, pp. 49–50.

42  *Ibid.*, p. 51.

43  *Ibid.*

44  See Strachan, *Clausewitz's* On War, pp. 73, 77–8.

45  Peter Paret and Daniel Moran (eds and trans), *Carl von Clausewitz: Two Letters on Strategy* (Fort Leavenworth, KS: Combat Studies Institute Press, 1992), p. 24. Emphasis in original.

46  *Ibid.*

47  Williamson Murray, *Military Adaptation in War: With Fear of Change* (Cambridge: Cambridge University Press, 2011), p. 15.

48  Howard, *Clausewitz*, p. 51.

49  Barry D. Watts, *The Foundations of US Air Doctrine: The Problem of Friction in War* (Maxwell Air Force Base, AL: Air University Press, 1984), p. 53.

50  H.R. McMaster, 'On War: Lessons to Be Learned', *Survival*, vol. 50, no. 1, February–March 2008, pp. 20–1.

51  David Barno and Nora Bensahel, *Adaptation Under Fire: How Militaries Change in Wartime* (Oxford: Oxford University Press, 2020), p. 14.

52  *Ibid.*, p. 14.

53  I am indebted to Tami Davis Biddle for this observation.

54  See John T. Kuehn, 'Our Options in Syria: The Trouble with No-fly Zones', *War on the Rocks*, 29 August 2013, https://warontherocks.com/2013/08/our-options-in-syria-the-trouble-with-no-fly-zones/; and Mike Pietrucha and Mike Benitez, 'The Dangerous Allure of the No-fly Zone', *War on the Rocks*, 4 March 2022, https://warontherocks.com/2022/03/the-dangerous-allure-of-the-no-fly-zone/.

55  See Jim Golby, 'Improving Advice and Earning Autonomy: Building Trust in the Strategic Dialogue', The Strategy Bridge, 3 October 2017, https://thestrategybridge.org/the-bridge/2017/10/3/improving-advice-and-earning-autonomy-building-trust-in-the-strategic-dialogue; Richard H. Kohn, 'Building Trust: Civil–Military Behaviors for Effective National Security', in Nielsen and Snider (eds), *American Civil–Military Relations*, p. 287; and William E. Rapp, 'Civil–Military Relations: The Role of Military Leaders in Strategy Making', *Parameters*, vol. 45, no. 3, Autumn 2015, p. 16, https://press.armywarcollege.edu/parameters/vol45/iss3/4/.

56  See Golby, 'Improving Advice and Earning Autonomy'.

57  See Rapp, 'Civil–Military Relations', p. 17.

58  Bernard Brodie, *War and Politics* (New York: Macmillan, 1973), pp. 1–2, 452.

# Book Reviews

## Middle East
Ray Takeyh

---

**The Contemporary Middle East in an Age of Upheaval**
James L. Gelvin, ed. Stanford, CA: Stanford University Press,
2021. $28.00. 368 pp.

In the past two decades, the Middle East has faced an external invasion, civil wars and populist uprisings. Thus, it is fitting that a collection of Middle East scholars have come together to assess the future of this turbulent region. As with most edited editions, there is an uneven quality to the essays that make up *The Contemporary Middle East in an Age of Upheaval*, with some offering a familiar treatment of a topic that concludes with an obligatory 'why this is new' paragraph. Still, there is enough wisdom in this book to merit a close reading.

Twenty years ago, the United States launched a disruptive invasion of Iraq whose consequences are still being felt. In his introductory essay, James Gelvin highlights how the errant US intervention not only failed to achieve its objectives, but also unleashed forces that were bound to destabilise the region. Iraq, once an Arab bulwark, was left devastated and riven by sectarianism. To be fair, Sunnis and Shi'ites have a long history of troubled relations, and the Middle East was hardly defined by ethnic and religious harmony prior to the American invasion. The US proved adept at destroying things, but less capable of leaving something better behind.

In the years that followed the American invasion, governments not just in Iraq but also in Lebanon, Libya, Syria and Yemen lost control over large portions of their territory, allowing transnational Islamist forces to gain the upper hand. Suddenly, the Middle East was home to many failed and failing states. Both Peter Mandaville and Nathan Brown do a commendable job

**Survival** | vol. 65 no. 2 | April–May 2023 | pp. 191–197    https://doi.org/10.1080/00396338.2023.2193107

of surveying the trajectory of Islamist movements in a region where state structures had broken down. In Egypt, the Muslim Brotherhood briefly commanded the government, while the Islamic State (ISIS) gained control over large chunks of Iraq. For decades, many Middle East scholars had supported the view that, once in power, Islamist parties would behave judiciously and with moderation. The evidence of the early twenty-first century does not fully support that contention.

The Middle East is the one region to have experienced populist revolutions so far this century. Thus, it is surprising that the book spends little time and sheds little light on this topic. Mainstream understandings of revolutions are still shaped by the twentieth-century examples of Russia, China, Cuba, Algeria and Iran. These were revolutions waged by utopians who managed to lead national protest movements. Yet in the Arab uprisings, there were no utopians or ideological platforms, only young people connected to each other by social media. These were revolutions without revolutionaries. Is this a new model for social-protest movements in the Middle East? What can we learn from the fact that they mostly failed, allowing authoritarian regimes to reclaim their power? It would have been useful if this issue had been probed more deeply in a volume whose title refers to an 'Age of Upheaval'.

### Revolutionary Life: The Everyday of the Arab Spring
Asef Bayat. Cambridge, MA: Harvard University Press, 2021.
£30.95/$35.00. 336 pp.

Sociologists seem to be the scholars best placed to study social-protest movements. Revolutions are impossible to predict and difficult to chronicle in retrospect, posing difficulties to onlookers who must come to terms with events whose inflection points are often apparent only in the aftermath. Asef Bayat, a professor of sociology at the University of Illinois, Urbana-Champaign, has been a sure-footed observer of revolutions for decades, starting with the Iranian revolt. In his latest book, he turns to the Arab uprisings. *Revolutionary Life* is the follow-on to an earlier book, *Life as Politics: How Ordinary People Change the Middle East*.

The Arab uprisings were the first revolutions of the twenty-first century, and in some ways were notably different from their twentieth-century predecessors. The revolts of the past century were often led by utopians – Marxists, Islamists and anti-colonialists – who sought root-and-branch change. Once triumphant, they eviscerated the old elite and dismantled existing institutions. The Bolsheviks took the place of the tsars, while the monarchical order in Iran yielded to the Islamists. Revolutionaries appear to have been critical to the revolutions' success.

The Arab revolts unfolded differently, and thus with less success. The movements were led by young people who were connected to each other via social-media platforms. This is not to suggest that members of other social classes did not participate. Indeed, the Arab revolts appear to have had a greater degree of popular participation than their iconic twentieth-century predecessors. But these revolts lacked the leadership of impractical, imprudent rebels such as Ruhollah Khomeini and Vladimir Lenin, who seem indispensable to revolutionary success. In Egypt, the old order soon resurfaced, while elsewhere, civil wars ended the dream of democratic change. Only in Tunisia did the uprisings produce anything like reform, and even there, recent political changes call into question the future of the reformers' gains.

Although the Arab revolts appear to have largely failed, Bayat argues that even revolutions that do not reach the pinnacle of power leave behind lasting change. People's attitudes and expectations are different than they were before. The poor demand their share of national wealth; women press for their emancipation; and the young assert their rights. Bayat coins the phrase 'middle-class poor' to describe a growing segment of the public who should belong to the middle class by virtue of their education, but whose financial insecurity denies them the opportunities of that class. The inability of regimes to satisfy citizens' new-found expectations is fuelling ongoing turbulence in the Middle East. Repression may be the order of the day across much of the region, but that does not mean there is any refuge to be found in the trite notion of autocratic stability.

As a man of the left, Bayat takes his share of swipes at neo-liberal economic reforms. But command economies with their central planning were hardly harbingers of prosperity. Corruption and incompetence can afflict both models of development, as they have in the Arab world. The stagnation of the postcolonial Middle East cannot be blamed on the World Bank and its prescriptions.

The best way of reading Bayat's current book is in tandem with his previous one – a tall order, but one that will yield the most satisfaction for readers.

## The Unfinished History of the Iran–Iraq War: Faith, Firepower, and Iran's Revolutionary Guards

Annie Tracy Samuel. Cambridge: Cambridge University Press, 2021. £75.00. 302 pp.

The war between Iran and Iraq is one of the most consequential and least studied events in the modern Middle East. It remains the region's longest and most devastating inter-state war. It has shaped the mentality of many Iranian officials, deepening their hostility toward an international community that largely stood by as Iraq used chemical weapons with appalling effect. In one of the strange paradoxes of the Middle East, Iran's clerical state achieved most of its objectives in Iraq not during its own war with the country in 1980–88 but in the aftermath of the American invasion in 2003. Iran today stands as the most consequential external actor in Iraq, manipulating its sectarian divides and ensuring its instability.

*The Unfinished History of the Iran–Iraq War* is itself an unfinished history. The author relies on the massive study of the war compiled by Iran's Revolutionary Guard Corps. This reviewer once asked a senior Iranian foreign-ministry official about that archive, only to have it dismissed as a work of propaganda. But Annie Tracy Samuel demonstrates that the study has value beyond mere propaganda by shedding light on the corps' strategic calculations and war tactics. In her own history, Samuel often simply reports, rather than interrogating or contesting, the guards' claims. This is a useful and important exercise, but it does suffer from its own analytical limitations. There is little in this book about the political context that conditioned Iran's decision-making. Factional rivalries and feuds that did much to retard Iran's war plans are largely ignored.

Among the decisions that continue to haunt Iran is the way in which it prolonged the war after Iraq was evicted from Iranian territory in 1982. Iran rejected an armistice and reparations, pressing ahead with its own invasion of Iraq. It appears that the calculations of the Revolutionary Guard Corps were eerily similar to those of American politicians two decades later. Saddam Hussein may have been rebuffed, but it was widely accepted that his appetite for aggression remained limitless, and that, once he had reconstituted his power, he would launch another act of aggression. This may have been a reasonable assumption, but Iran's war aims were still too expansive for its actual capabilities. The Islamic Republic and its praetorian guard could only end the war once they abandoned their quest for regime change in Iraq.

Chemical munitions are usually considered weapons of terror that rarely determine the outcome of wars. But as Samuel demonstrates, Iraq's chemical attacks on Iran, and particularly the fear that Saddam would soon target Iranian cities, played a crucial role in Iran's decision to terminate the war. Iraq's persistent and aggressive use of such weapons scarred a generation of Iranians. The debates surrounding the end of the war are barely touched on in this book, but there was a clear divide between Iran's civilian leaders, led by Hashemi Rafsanjani as speaker of the Iranian parliament, who were ready to end the war, and the Revolutionary Guard Corps, which wanted to prolong it. The end came when Iran's economy was too devastated and its armed forces too diminished to continue the fight.

Despite the Islamic Republic's ritualistic celebration of its martyrs, the war remains a deeply controversial topic. *The Unfinished History of the Iran–Iraq War* is a useful contribution to the literature but, given its limitations, is hardly the last word.

### Escaping the Conflict Trap: Toward Ending Civil War in the Middle East
Paul Salem and Ross Harrison, eds. London: I.B. Tauris, 2022.
2nd ed. £19.99. 288 pp.

Civil wars are not a new phenomenon in the Middle East. Lebanon and Yemen can lay claim to the dubious distinction of being persistently ravaged by such conflicts. In the twenty-first century, they have been joined by Afghanistan, Iraq, Libya and Syria. These countries may never have been models of good governance, but today the central authorities in each of them exercise only limited control over their territory. Other regional states, such as Iran, and great powers such as Russia and the US, have regularly become involved in these conflicts. Indeed, one of the criticisms of various US administrations is that they have not been sufficiently interventionist.

Edited books tend to be choppy and uneven, and *Escaping the Conflict Trap* is no exception. The mixture of analysts, scholars and practitioners represented does, however, lend much authority to this book. The introductory chapter lays out its principal arguments in a concise manner and offers an important set of recommendations. Borrowing freely from political-science literature, various chapters outline how civil wars end and the role of external actors in resolving them. Two outstanding chapters are those on Syria by Robert Ford and Iraq by Randa Slim. Each of them sets a different tone: no one should be optimistic about Syria, but Iraq is showing signs of self-improvement.

The Iraq War is often considered the original sin that undermined the teetering regional order. Slim does an outstanding job chronicling the various turning points that provoked a sectarian civil war and the rise of ISIS, which for a time had its own caliphate in Iraq. The paradox of Iraq is that it was most unstable when the Americans were most involved. The Obama administration's disengagement was not wholly beneficial, but it did eventually compel the Iraqis to reclaim their nation, modulate their sectarian squabbles and even limit Iran's reach. This is a work in progress and things may still unravel, but there is finally some good news coming out of that tragic nation.

Ford was America's envoy to Syria and had a front-row seat as the country came undone. The Arab Spring was thought to be contagious and expected to triumph. Syria proved that force can still be the arbiter of disputes. It also demonstrated that external intervention can succeed, as both Iran and Russia ensured the survival of the Assad dynasty at a time when its end was in sight. A hesitant Obama administration chose to remain on the sidelines and displayed too much faith in the mediation process led by the United Nations. The various Geneva agreements were useless as Bashar al-Assad and his allies were playing to win. Even so, Assad still does not control the entire country. It remains in the grip of a humanitarian crisis, with a ruined economy and millions displaced.

Any attempt to come to grips with the Middle East's civil wars mandates an examination of this important volume for its share of insights and lamentations.

### The Struggle for Iran: Oil, Autocracy, and the Cold War, 1951–1954
David Painter and Gregory Brew. Chapel Hill, NC: University of North Carolina Press, 2023. $32.95. 324 pp.

The oil-nationalisation crisis in Iran and the subsequent coup that overthrew Mohammad Mossadegh, the nationalist prime minister, has been the subject of enormous historical interest. The recent release of a treasure trove of American documents has sparked another slew of studies that add more detail but basically affirm the parameters of the existing historiography. *The Struggle for Iran* is a deeply researched book marred occasionally by an imbalanced perspective. That said, it is worth a careful read.

The crisis began in 1951, when Iran appropriated the assets of the Anglo-Iranian Oil Company. For decades, the company had exploited Iran's natural resources and deformed its politics. The act of nationalisation was correct and justified. The authors are meticulous and fair-minded in their assessment of the bewildering negotiations that tried to resolve the dispute. Britain is rightly censured for its dogmatic opposition to a negotiated settlement and for its insistence that the crisis could only be resolved by a change of regime. The British even contemplated foolish schemes for military intervention, but such gunboat diplomacy had no place in the post-colonial world.

Mossadegh was no less unreasonable in his approach to the negotiations, though authors David Painter and Gregory Brew seem less inclined to blame the premier for his missteps. Even more problematic is their glossing over of Mossadegh's despotic tendencies as he purged his critics, orchestrated a fraudulent plebiscite to rid himself of a cantankerous parliament and accumulated powers not accorded to his office by the constitution. In the authors' telling, most, if not all, of Mossadegh's detractors were agents of Britain. That means a large swathe of the Persian elite, including parliamentarians, clerics, generals, newspaper editors and the landed gentry, were beholden to foreign interests. This is an unfair indictment of Iranians who were nationalists in their own right and wished to save their country from its ruinous path.

The chapter on the coup that finally overthrew Mossadegh in August 1953 revisits a debate between traditionalist historians who blame foreign powers and a small band of revisionists who insist on Iranian agency. All the historians involved in this debate have read the same documents and arrived at different conclusions. Painter and Brew lean toward the orthodox version of this history. A consensus view is not necessary. The debate will go on, and it should go on.

Mossadegh should not be made in death what he was not in life. He was a patriot who wished to emancipate Iran from the clutches of foreign domination. He was progressive in his politics and wanted the government to deal with social ills. He was a secularist who abhorred religious reaction. As prime minister, however, he was a poor custodian of power. He never understood that diplomacy is the art of the possible and that maximalism is the prerogative of a parliamentarian. His ascent to power was not without its share of unscrupulous tactics. He knew in advance that his predecessor, Ali Razmara, was about to be assassinated but did nothing to stop it. This is a curious omission in a book that purports to set the record straight.

# United States
David C. Unger

---

**Silent Invasion: The Untold Story of the Trump Administration, Covid-19, and Preventing the Next Pandemic Before It's Too Late**
Deborah Birx. New York: Harper, 2022. $29.99. 506 pp.

Deborah Birx was response coordinator for the White House Coronavirus Task Force from March 2020 to January 2021. That meant she worked for Donald Trump, but her direct access to that president was very limited, and, as she tells it, her ability to influence his policies was even more so. While much of this book details the internal battles she fought, and mostly lost, within the Trump administration, her main concern is to warn Americans of the continuing dangers posed by the coronavirus pandemic. As she sees it – correctly, I think – that requires countering the misinformation and flawed messaging put out not only by the Trump administration, but also by the Biden administration and American public-health agencies such as the Centers for Disease Control and Prevention (CDC).

Birx begins by explaining the main transmission mechanism of SARS-CoV-2, the virus that causes COVID-19. Because infected people can transmit the virus for two days before showing any symptoms, and because many infected younger people never show any symptoms at all, the virus is being silently transmitted by healthier, more socially active young people to older, more vulnerable and less healthy people – hence the 'Silent Invasion' of the book's title. Much of this transmission takes place within families, especially in America's large number of intergenerational households.

Testing programmes that target only people already feeling ill cannot stop this silent invasion. Such programmes identify infectious spreaders of the virus too late and too inconsistently to slow their transmission of the virus to other people. Yet testing the already symptomatic is the only kind of testing generally recommended by American public-health authorities, under both the Trump and Biden administrations. Instead, Birx recommends the widest possible testing efforts, including of the non-symptomatic, so that those infected are able to isolate early enough to protect vulnerable family members and workmates. As Birx explains, this is not a 'lockdown' strategy, but its opposite, a strategy for keeping schools and businesses safely open.

Trump believed, correctly, that the more testing that was done, the higher the confirmed COVID case count would be. But he wrongly concluded from this that the less testing America did, the less of a COVID problem it would experience. Rather than follow Birx's unwelcome advice about wider testing, Trump preferred to listen to a Stanford University radiologist named Scott Atlas, who urged him to abandon public-health efforts to slow the spread of COVID on the grounds that a faster spread would create something called 'herd immunity' that could quickly bring the pandemic to a halt. The trouble with this herd-immunity hypothesis, Birx explains, is that as the SARS-CoV-2 virus continues to mutate, the immunity temporarily conferred by past infections, much like the temporary immunity conferred by vaccines, steadily fades. Meanwhile, some percentage of the extra millions likely to be infected as effective public-health practices are abandoned in the vain pursuit of herd immunity will die or experience severe illness. Birx credits Trump's aide and son-in-law Jared Kushner and vice president Mike Pence for her limited successes in containing the damage done by Atlas and Trump.

Birx advocates an all-out infection-prevention and -mitigation strategy, including greatly expanded testing, indoor mask-wearing, vaccination, installation of quality air-filtration systems and limitations on large indoor gatherings. She recognises that not everyone can follow every element of this strategy. Two-year-old children in daycare, for example, cannot be expected to keep masks on all day. Not everyone, especially in rural areas, has ready access to vaccines, and many others are hesitant to be injected, even where vaccines are available. Many households are too crowded for effective home isolation.

Birx doesn't wag her finger at the vaccine-hesitant or blame the victims. She advocates decentralising public-health efforts and seeking out and responding to people's concerns. As a White House official, she wasn't allowed to publicly call for many things she considers necessary to combat the virus and save lives. Though she no longer has a White House platform, this readable and passionate book deserves the widest possible audience.

**Democracy's Chief Executive: Interpreting the**
**Constitution and Defining the Future of the Presidency**
Peter M. Shane. Oakland, CA: University of California Press,
2022. £25.00/$29.95. 304 pp.

In this useful and timely book, the constitutional scholar Peter M. Shane argues that since the Reagan administration, presidents of both parties, enabled by favourable Supreme Court opinions, have reinterpreted the powers of the US presidency in an authoritarian direction, undermining the democratic potential of the US Constitution's architecture of checks and balances. Republicans, he writes, especially George W. Bush and Donald Trump, have pushed most aggressively, building their claims on an expansive doctrine of the unitary executive that Shane argues has no solid basis in American history or constitutional text.

Article II of the Constitution vests executive power in the president, then goes on to enumerate a few specific elements of that executive power. Some of these, such as commanding the armed forces, are granted exclusively to the president. Others, such as appointing ambassadors, Supreme Court justices and other principal officers of state, and making treaties with other nations, can be exercised only with the advice and consent of the Senate. The Constitution's text offers no explicit guidance on presidential authority over officials of the vast administrative state that Congress has since legislated into existence. How could it, when the Constitution was drafted and ratified in the 1780s and that administrative state mainly came into being in the twentieth and twenty-first centuries? Hence the fierce political battles over what can and cannot be inferred from the spare language of Article II's vesting clause.

How accountable should these appointed executive-branch officials be to, respectively, the elected president, the elected Congress and their own canons of professional conduct and constitutional governance? How far can these officials go in interpreting the statutes delegating power to their agencies? Do presidents have the right to dismiss at will the directors and commissioners of independent regulatory agencies, departmental inspectors general, independent prosecutors and so on – the people Trump referred to as the 'deep state'?

One set of answers has come from the Justice Department's Office of Legal Counsel (OLC). Traditionally, the OLC's role has been to advise the president and other executive-branch officials on the legality and constitutionality of actions they are considering undertaking. The credibility of these opinions depends on how the wider public perceives the OLC's independence. Shane recounts how that independence has been cast in doubt in recent years by decisions placing the OLC in a different role, one of confecting legal briefs in favour of any actions presidents wanted to take.

Recent OLC rulings have flowed from the extreme version of the unitary-executive theory favoured by recent Republican presidents and best summed up by Trump during the Mueller investigation into alleged abuses of presidential power in the firing of FBI director James Comey: 'I have an Article II, where I have the right to do whatever I want as president' (p. 105). On the accountability issue, Trump's OLC leaned toward favouring an almost unlimited right for the president to dismiss any executive-branch official who has fallen out of presidential favour.

It is the Supreme Court, not the OLC, that ultimately gets to rule on the constitutionality of presidential actions, as George W. Bush was reminded when that court ruled against him on several Guantanamo-related issues. Thus far, the Supreme Court has not embraced the extreme version of the unitary-executive theory. What the court has increasingly embraced is a theory of constitutional interpretation based on what it considers to be the original understanding of constitutional language. Shane persuasively demonstrates that applying language and understandings from 1787 to cases in 2023 can prove an impossible task. Nevertheless, a growing majority of today's Supreme Court justices seem determined to try.

Shane, a law professor emeritus at Ohio State University who served on the OLC during the Carter and Reagan administrations, sees great danger in this synergism of White House unitary-executive claims and Supreme Court originalism, a combination he refers to as 'presidentialism'. In its place, he calls for a democracy-driven approach to constitutional construction which he calls 'constitutional pluralism'. This approach would acknowledge the textual gaps and ambiguities in the Constitution and look to resolve these, where possible, with interpretations that revitalise the document's badly eroded institutional checks and balances. This too can be called a form of originalism, one based more on concepts and institutions than on textual literalism.

As Shane readily concedes, his desired shift away from presidentialism will not come about on its own. Presidentialism serves incumbent power too well, and its beneficiaries, from presidents on down, will likely fight hard to sustain it. Shane rests his hopes on the wider public, which is decidedly less well served by presidentialism, but may be too worn down by self-reinforcing cycles of disillusionment and disempowerment to rise to his challenge.

## Partisans: The Conservative Revolutionaries Who Remade American Politics in the 1990s
Nicole Hemmer. New York: Basic Books, 2022. $32.00. 368 pp.

In *Partisans*, Nicole Hemmer, who wrote an informative book on right-wing media (*Messengers of the Right*, reviewed in the December 2017–January 2018 issue of *Survival*), takes on a related but far broader topic: the remaking of Republican Party politics beginning in the 1990s. Hemmer challenges the widely held view that Donald Trump's challenge to Republican orthodoxies came out of nowhere. It's true that successive Republican presidential nominees in the post-Reagan era sought to broaden the party's base toward the political centre. But during those same years, a different set of Republicans, people Hemmer styles 'conservative revolutionaries', made their names through radical provocations and by stoking up a cluster of wedge issues – immigration restriction, protectionism, opposition to foreign military interventions – designed to stir up the party's rank-and-file base, and more specifically to help Tea Party-style challengers unseat moderate Republican office-holders.

The people Hemmer features in this book include media pundits such as Pat Buchanan, Rush Limbaugh, Dinesh D'Souza, Laura Ingraham, Ann Coulter, Lou Dobbs, Matt Drudge and Bill Maher, along with holders of elected office such as former Republican House speaker Newt Gingrich and former Republican member of Congress Helen Chenoweth-Hage. These individuals belonged to different generations, followed different career paths and displayed varying levels of ardour and consistency in propounding their conservative-revolutionary views. But Hemmer's citations of their pre-Trump rhetoric illustrates her point that there is more continuity than discontinuity in Trump's takeover of the Republican Party.

Looking back at Buchanan's mid-1990s campaign speeches calling for a double security fence along the Mexican border to stop an 'invasion of the country' by immigrants (p. 217), or at Dobbs's CNN telecasts during the following decade defending American workers from 'corporate America's lust for cheap labor' (p. 280), is like hearing early test runs for some of the key themes Trump later rode to the White House.

This isn't the whole story, however. The more mixed results of the 2018, 2020 and 2022 US elections suggest that other important things may be going on in Republican and right-wing politics. Hemmer tends to generalise too much from her knowledge of right-wing media, at the expense of other areas of grassroots and electoral politics. Most of the conservative revolutionaries she chooses to spotlight in this book developed their political personas in the US media. Limbaugh, Dobbs and Maher were talk-show hosts, while Buchanan was a regular on television's *Crossfire*. Coulter and Ingraham made frequent media appearances as guest opinion commentators. Trump himself hosted a reality TV show, *The Apprentice* (later *The Celebrity Apprentice*).

Hemmer uses categories such as 'conservative', 'conservative movement', 'Republicans' and the 'right' as if they were more or less interchangeable. They didn't use to be, and they still aren't.

**Diplomacy and Capitalism: The Political Economy of U.S. Foreign Relations**
Christopher R.W. Dietrich, ed. Philadelphia, PA: University of Pennsylvania Press, 2022. $29.95. 302 pp.

The theme of this edited volume is that while private corporate power and motives are standard factors in US foreign policy, they do not usually operate in a separate, purely economic sphere. More typically, they are integrated with other elements such as geopolitics, modernisation theory and cold-war ideology to produce an integrated whole. To understand US foreign policy, say the authors of *Diplomacy and Capitalism*, one needs to understand the political economy. But to understand the political economy, one needs to understand US foreign policy.

Different contributors focus on particular countries and regions, from Latin America and the Caribbean to Africa, South Asia, East Asia and Europe. The quality of the arguments and evidence varies from chapter to chapter. In some cases, as in Abou Bamba's chapter on the Ivory Coast, this may be a result of gaps in the availability of relevant data. Other chapters are marred by their authors' too simplistic preconceptions about how American corporate influence operates in the corridors of Washington and overseas. Such speculative excursions lose sight of the main theme and value of this collection: the finding that, as Christopher Dietrich puts it, 'the shared history of U.S. diplomacy and capitalism is about much more than a balance sheet' (p. 13).

Several particularly valuable chapters merit special mention. In one, Joseph Fronczak shows how the interventionist career of US Marine Corps General Smedley Butler in the decades after he was first commissioned in 1898 was tied together by the larger theme of creating a global transportation infrastructure for expanding trade. In another, Giulia Crisanti describes how American elites, convinced that Italy's fascist past and future susceptibility to communism stemmed from the conservative-traditionalist attitudes of Italian businesses and workers, sought to instil, through officially sponsored film showings, a new, Americanised mentality of productivity and mass consumption. In a third, Nicole Sackley relates how Washington worked with America's agricultural co-ops during the Cold War to humanise the international image of US capitalism. In a fourth, Jennifer Miller explains how Washington promoted the post-war Japanese economy as a regional model for post-war economic growth, expecting other Asian countries to forget Tokyo's wartime record in the region.

Because US foreign policy emphasises different considerations in different geographical areas, the volume as a whole sometimes seems to lack a clear focus. But that weakness is more than offset by the greater attention to nuance and variation permitted by its global, but also more granular, approach.

**Before the Religious Right: Liberal Protestants, Human Rights, and the Polarization of the United States**
Gene Zubovich. Philadelphia, PA: University of Pennsylvania Press, 2022. $45.00. 391 pp.

Mainline American Protestantism hasn't drawn as much attention from historical researchers as has the highly visible and politically powerful evangelical

Christian right. Gene Zubovich, who teaches history at the University of Buffalo, SUNY, usefully remedies this imbalance with an account of the considerable influence liberal Protestant leaders once wielded in America's most consequential mid-twentieth-century debates, including those over economic and social justice, civil rights, internationalism and foreign policy.

Zubovich focuses on church leaders rooted in the so-called ecumenical denominations: Baptist, Church of Christ Congregationalist, Episcopalian, Lutheran, Methodist and Presbyterian. Until recently, those denominations were the numerically and politically dominant face of American Protestantism. His account of the rise and fall of liberal Protestantism not only helps us better understand mid-twentieth-century social movements, but, Zubovich argues, also helps explain the subsequent rise of the religious right. That rise, he contends, gathered strength from a backlash against controversial positions taken by liberal Protestant leaders but not shared by many or most lay members of their own denominations.

It's a story that weaves through several decades. It moves from the Social Gospelers of the Progressive Era through the World Order Movement of the 1940s, then on through the church-sponsored civil-rights and anti-war activism of the 1960s, to the gay and feminist movements of the 1970s. The many characters Zubovich briefly profiles (too many to fully list even the main ones here) include foreign-missionary leaders during the decades of decolonisation, naively uncritical visitors to the Soviet Union during and after the term of its Second World War alliance with Washington, and crusaders for a United Nations that could transcend the limits of sovereign nationalism. The political leanings of Zubovich's subjects range from the Christian socialism of Norman Thomas and A.J. Muste to the anti-communism of John Foster Dulles and Reinhold Niebuhr. The common thread is that all were recognised leaders of influential church organisations, mostly those grouped around the Federal (later National) Council of Churches.

In a society as distinctively religious as the United States, scholars overlook such areas of church and religious history at their peril. Zubovich does historians a great service by rescuing this story from creeping oblivion.

# Environment and Resources
Jeffrey Mazo

### To Have and Have Not: Energy in World History
Brian C. Black. Lanham, MD: Rowman & Littlefield, 2022.
£26.00/$34.00. 310 pp.

Survival – of the human species, of civilisations, of nation-states, of individuals – ultimately rests on the ability to harvest, exchange and use energy. Historians, says Brian Black, need to bring the stories of distinct cultures, societies and eras together into a coherent picture of energy transitions to reveal broader patterns that can inform our understanding of and approach to current energy conundrums. *To Have and Have Not* is not a history of energy or energy use per se, but something more ambitious: a history of the world structured around energy and energy transitions. But it is first and foremost a history, albeit one that brings us up to the present day and the ongoing transition from fossil fuels to sustainable energy.

Black explores the chronology of energy transitions from reliance primarily on human and animal power (the 'biological old regime') to wind (the age of sail) to fossil fuels and beyond. Each of his eight chapters begins with a vignette related to the theme, such as the development of Amsterdam as a medieval trading hub, the invention of the phosphorus match, the invention of the Honda Civic or twenty-first-century Arctic politics. Further vignettes are used to bring out and amplify patterns and trends in each period.

While it is the broad sweep of history that gives *To Have and Have Not* its power, Black's treatment of the phase we are transitioning from (which began in 1900, 1914 or 1920, depending on perspective, and lasted until 2000) is of particular interest. 'At the root of the epoch that defined the twentieth century', he says, 'was a clarifying new aggressive fashion of viewing energy: flexible sources in the form of fossil fuels that might be gathered in one locale, assigned a value, and then used elsewhere' (p. 4). Although, for example, coal and coaling stations were strategic assets in the nineteenth century, with the transition to oil, energy became both an explicit tool and an organising principle of national security. Between 1903 and the outbreak of the First World War, Britain's Royal Navy (driven to a great extent by Winston Churchill) went from first experiments with petroleum to ending the procurement of coal-powered vessels, changing the strategic landscape and forcing other navies to react. The global use of petroleum (sea, land and air) increased by 50% during the First World War. In 1919, Dwight D. Eisenhower, then a US Army captain, took two months to lead a military convoy across the continental US, an experience that led to the first federal efforts to build a road grid and to Eisenhower, by then US

 https://doi.org/10.1080/00396338.2023.2193109

president, championing an interstate highway system in the 1950s. The Second World War can be viewed as a war for oil, strategically (although perhaps not in terms of grand strategy), operationally and tactically (pp. 150–62). The Cold War likewise pivoted on energy – oil and gas, but also atomic weapons and power. The rapid but far-from-universal development and increasing complexity of energy systems significantly widened the gap between the energy (and hence also economic) haves and have-nots.

This brief summation cannot do justice to the three chapters that cover this period, let alone the whole book. *To Have and Have Not* is a broad, sweeping history, but one informed by a level and variety of detail and close argument that makes it both fascinating and persuasive. Energy and energy flows may be seen, as Black argues, as the most fundamental element of human existence, but the book's value does not rest on this view. Even if energy is only on a par with other drivers of history, *To Have and Have Not* offers a fresh and at times surprising perspective on the past, and hence the future. We are in the midst of the sort of energy transition seen only a few times in history, and the more we understand about past instances, the better.

### Global Environmental Politics: The Transformative Role of Emerging Economies
Johannes Urpelainen. New York: Columbia University Press, 2022. £30.00/$35.00. 344 pp.

Perhaps the most successful international environmental agreement, by a clear margin, has been the 1987 Montreal Protocol to regulate production and use of chemicals that damage the ozone layer. As Johannes Urpelainen explains in *Global Environmental Politics*, however, it was only one of hundreds of successful multilateral agreements negotiated in the twentieth century to protect aspects of the natural world, culminating in a 'golden decade': 384 new agreements came into force between 1990 and 1999, including several major ones.

Why, then, has the problem of greenhouse-gas emissions proved so intractable? The United Nations Framework Convention on Climate Change was agreed in 1992, and its Kyoto Protocol in 1997, yet its capstone 2015 Paris Agreement still appears inadequate to the task. The latter is, moreover, only one of three major multilateral environmental treaties agreed in this century so far (the others are the 2013 Minamata Convention on Mercury and the 2023 High Seas Treaty, agreed after this book was published). What changed? Urpelainen's answer is that 'robust economic growth in emerging economies has changed the basic logic of global environmental politics' (p. 254). The number of governments that contribute significantly to a given environmental problem has risen dramatically, but their environmental goals and institutional capacity have tended not to converge with those of the major players of the past. In the twentieth century, a small number of industrialised countries could deal with issues of pollution among themselves. Now, negotiation and enforcement are both more difficult, and agreements imposing top-down commitments are no longer likely to work.

Urpelainen uses the interaction of four variables – the number of governments with the power to destroy the environment, their relative degree of such power, the strength of their environmental preferences and their institutional capacities – to derive theoretical predictions about the effect of changes to any or all of them. He then tests these predictions against the observed changes in the international political economy over the last 50 years, focusing on climate change, biodiversity loss and regulation of chemicals as particularly important but typical examples. He then looks at detailed case studies, including Brazil, China and India (three of the BRICs), a group of smaller emerging economies (Indonesia, Nigeria, Philippines and Vietnam), and a group of least-developed countries with economic potential (Bangladesh, Ethiopia, Myanmar and Tanzania). China and India share a trajectory for economic transformation, structural power and environmental preferences, albeit on different schedules. But China has shown a greater capacity to turn those preferences into practice at every stage of the process. Key emerging economies appear to be on the same trajectory as India.

'The balance of power in the world', he concludes, 'is shifting, with emerging economies now, and increasingly, holding most of the trump cards … The whole notion of global environmental politics as an exercise in multilateral treaty making is an anathema' (pp. 262–3). The only practical solution is to bring the emerging economies on board through a narrow focus on specific sectors and on 'brown' problems – that is, things that directly and immediately impact their citizens, such as soil erosion or air and water quality – while linking the solutions to progress on 'green issues' such as climate change and deforestation. Despite its apparent weaknesses, the Paris Agreement's focus on flexible and decentralised approaches to a common goal is the best way forward, both as a structure for solutions to these quotidian issues and as a model for other twenty-first-century environmental accords.

**Science for a Green New Deal: Connecting Climate, Economics, and Social Justice**
Eric A. Davidson. Baltimore, MD: Johns Hopkins University Press, 2022. £23.00/$27.95. 264 pp.

The title of *Science for a Green New Deal* is somewhat misleading. 'The' Green New Deal, as a formal US congressional resolution proposed in 2019, was as much about mitigating poverty, ill health and social injustice as it was about climate change. Or, rather, it was about drawing the links between them, to use the existential imperative of climate mitigation to advance those issues, just as the original New Deal used the crisis of the Great Depression. Eric Davidson's book does, like many recent publications, include a laundry list of potential technologies and solutions to climate change, but it stands out because of its broader themes. Like the Green New Deal itself, and as his subtitle suggests, Davidson's book is about the convergence of natural science, social science and economics. Although he is a natural scientist, he skilfully connects these disparate approaches. Ultimately, the book is not a proposal for specific scientific or technical solutions but rather a contemplation on the nature of science.

Although the book is structured around chapters on wealth disparity, population growth, regenerative agriculture, decarbonisation and 'circular' or sustainable economics, there are unifying themes. One is the importance of 'convergence thinking' (p. 15) and 'co-production of knowledge' (p. 29): expanding the diversity of backgrounds among researchers and forming novel frameworks by integrating knowledge, methods and expertise from different disciplines and from laypersons, in both research and everyday life. This requires concerted effort and planning by both civil society and government. Another is the vexed question of science versus disinformation in public discourse, which Davidson illustrates through a comparison of the reaction of non-scientists and the 'denialsphere' to climate change and COVID-19 treatments and vaccines.

Basic research by trained experts in narrow fields – that is, science with no immediate, practical goal in mind – has always driven new discoveries, and should continue. But, Davidson concludes, the greatest opportunities lie in promoting and encouraging more interdisciplinary work and engagement with people outside the academy, and greater diversity within both groups. This last is a means to an end – more innovative thought and ways of thinking – rather than an end in itself. Wider engagement outside the academy has benefits in both directions: it can also help reduce misinformation not just about the science but also about how scientists work. Trends towards interdisciplinary work and wider engagement and opportunity are already evident, driven by wider cultural trends, but would benefit from deliberate policy changes from funding criteria to grievance mechanisms.

One short anecdote (pp. 89–90) – almost a throwaway – elegantly sums things up. The early American women's-rights campaigner Eunice Foote (1819–88) was the first scientist to demonstrate the greenhouse effect from atmospheric carbon dioxide at a national conference in 1856, three years before John Tyndall, who is traditionally credited with the discovery. Yet she was not allowed to present her paper herself – a man did it for her – and it was left out of the official proceedings. It remained obscure for nearly a century and a half. While we've come a long way, cultures and policies that exclude large numbers of people with diverse viewpoints can only hold back the advance of knowledge. The bottom line, says Davidson, is that while natural resources may be limited, ideas and ingenuity are infinite. I hope he is correct; I worry that he is not. But he certainly makes the case that the existential threat of climate change is best addressed through a scientific culture and broader society that embraces the viewpoints and promotes the welfare of all.

**Rethinking Environmental Security**
Simon Dalby. Cheltenham: Edward Elgar, 2022.
£85.00/$120.00. 224 pp.

Half a century after the Club of Rome's 1972 *Limits to Growth* report, writes Simon Dalby in *Rethinking Environmental Security*, we find ourselves at the crisis point that report identified at which planetary trajectories would converge in a potential socio-environmental catastrophe. While perhaps wrong on the details, its warnings have proved prescient. We face an environmental disaster because they were, in practice, ignored. The impassioned arguments that report inspired, Dalby suggests, are precursors to our attempts to deal with the current crisis.

Dalby begins by exploring the concept and place of environmental security in traditional international-relations and security discourse, especially since the 1970s and 1980s. He then discusses the dynamic nature of Earth systems and humanity's growing ability to affect them directly. This leads to an assessment of how imperialism and capitalism have driven both rivalries and the security structures set up to contain or resolve them, and have framed discussion of resources, sustainability, security and conflict. He then covers the range of existential environmental threats created or aggravated by human activity, from climate change to pandemics and nuclear war, and the security implications of human attempts to ameliorate the risks and effects through yet further intervention, such as geo-engineering or new modes of food production.

The core of his argument is not so much that the relatively stable environmental context for humanity that has prevailed for 10,000 years is over, but that failure to recognise this fact – that humanity can now change the global ecosystem at all scales – can itself be dangerous, leading to further rapid and disruptive changes. Business as usual in how we think about what we do at the broadest level is as problematic as what we actually do to the environment: 'traditional notions of state rivalries, and the struggles for power as supposedly the source of insecurity, are now part of the problem' (p. 2). This is, in effect, a new kind of security dilemma, in which it is the reaction of physical systems rather than the reaction of a potential adversary that endangers what is supposedly being secured.

Rethinking environmental security, he concludes, requires shifting the primary formulation to the Earth itself, rather than territorially bounded states – not as an ideological position but as a recognition of the novel ecological context faced by all powers. Survival is no longer a matter of constraining the firepower of nuclear weapons but rather the firepower of fossil fuels. What needs to be secured is not specific elements of the economic or social order, but the ability to adapt in an environment where unpredictability and change is the default condition for planning.

Two small quibbles: the conceit of contrasting multiple figurative and literal meanings of 'firepower' pervades, even frames, the book, but is more distracting than enlightening; and Dalby only treats in passing the possibility that human-ity may be on the verge of expanding beyond the Earth system and breaking many environmental constraints. This last prospect is speculative, of course, but given that he is in effect offering a 'view from 100,000 feet', its neglect is disap-pointing. These minor points aside, Dalby admirably succeeds in rethinking, or getting us to rethink, the concept and practice of environmental security.

## The Geopolitics of Climate and Security in the Indo-Pacific
Robert Glasser, Cathy Johnstone and Anastasia Kapetas, eds.
Barton: Australian Strategic Policy Institute, 2022. Free PDF
download. 156 pp.

Like ships passing in the night, the Australian Strategic Policy Institute's (ASPI) *The Geopolitics of Climate and Security in the Indo-Pacific* was released only a week or so after I submitted my own short chapter on the subject to the International Institute for Strategic Studies' (IISS) 2022 Strategic Dossier, the *Asia-Pacific Regional Security Assessment*. My chapter was perforce a broad overview and based on general trends projected to mid-century, while the ASPI report contains in-depth analyses of 16 specific security challenges from more than 20 subject-area and regional specialists, based on a 2035 climate-change reference scenario. It is both encouraging (given the different approaches) and discouraging (given the enormity of the climate-security problem) that we came independently to similar conclusions.

The ASPI report groups its chapters into sections on human security (food, water, health, poverty and inequality), regional conflict (ethnic separatism, transnational crime, migration, military forces, great-power competition, digital disinformation), economics (energy transition and geopolitics, sovereign risk, regional trade systems) and regional institutions (the Pacific Islands Forum, ASEAN, the Asian Development Bank). Some of the topics have rarely been discussed elsewhere in the climate-security debate, for example the potential for bad actors to exploit the climate crisis for their own ends.

This is exactly the sort of fine-grained regional implementation of global themes of climate security that policymakers and planners have for the most part been waiting for (even if they haven't realised it). It stands as a model for further assessments covering other parts of the world. If there is a weakness in the report, it is that the concluding chapter focuses more on familiar policy recommendations than on drawing out common themes from the individual topic areas, although it does do both. It highlights the continuing need for better information, especially regional-level climate models and projections, the social impacts of climate change, and crucially the complex connections and feedbacks between and among various climate risks. This has been a constant drumbeat, but this report identifies the South China Sea (sea-level rise and territorial claims), the southern Philippines and the Papuan provinces of Indonesia (ethnic separatist movements), and the Mekong, Brahmaputra and Indus river basins (transnational water issues) as key areas for future research. Given China's geopolitical importance, role in the global energy transformation and particularly high climate risks, moreover, 'a comprehensive climate and security risk assessment of China's role in the Indo-Pacific should be produced as a matter of priority' (p. 143).

By focusing on 2035, the ASPI report excludes the long-term existential security threats of climate change, where the danger is clearer but the details more obscure. But this focus on a date only a few years away also highlights the immediacy of the risks and the rapid pace of developments – a pace that might outstrip the ability of analysts to keep up. In that respect this report could not be more timely.

**Closing Argument**

# Historical Imagination and the Unspoken Assumptions of Our Age

**Benjamin Rhode**

I

In March 1981, the historian Michael Howard – who had co-founded the International Institute for Strategic Studies (IISS) almost a quarter of a century earlier – delivered his inaugural lecture as Regius Professor of Modern History at the University of Oxford. 'The Lessons of History' is a work of startling lucidity which rewards reading in full.[1] In his lecture, Howard explored how the study of history could be useful – indeed indispensable – in the education of future leaders, although not in ways once thought typical.

The notion that history was a teacher of direct lessons for the present, a natural source of insight for the contemporary statesman, had been commonplace since the ancients. How else were leaders to succeed, without learning from their predecessors? 'There is this exceptionally beneficial and fruitful advantage to be derived from the study of the past, that you see, set in the clear light of historical truth, examples of every possible type', argued the Roman historian Livy. 'From these you may select for yourself and your country what to imitate, and also what, as being mischievous in its inception and disastrous in its issues, you are to avoid.'[2] Ancient history and historians, including Livy, were themselves later mined for supposed lessons. Perhaps the world's most famous adviser – or would-be adviser – to statesmen, the veteran of Florentine

**Benjamin Rhode** is Editor of the *Adelphi* book series and IISS Senior Fellow.

**Survival** | vol. 65 no. 2 | April–May 2023 | pp. 213–228    https://doi.org/10.1080/00396338.2023.2193110

Renaissance politics Niccolò Machiavelli, wrote in his examination of Livy that, since the character of human nature was unchanging, 'wise men say … that whoever wishes to foresee the future must consult the past; for human events ever resemble those of preceding times'.[3] In his lecture, Howard noted that the establishment of the chair of Modern History at Oxford in 1724 was justified by the need of future public officials to understand the past.[4] And it was not only historians and writers who espoused history's utility. Shortly before his death, Napoleon Bonaparte – the conqueror of Europe, the 'great man' whom the philosopher G.W.F. Hegel famously observed riding past his window, considering him 'history on horseback' and the embodiment and enactor of his age's supposed *Zeitgeist* – instructed the executors of his will to 'let my son often read and reflect on history. This is the only true philosophy.'[5]

Perhaps more nuanced variations of this outlook recognised that the discipline of history offered more than simply a catalogue of possible outcomes to inform present decisions, while holding that it was not just the study of the past for its own sake. 'Striv[ing] to bring back the past for the sake of the past' was the work of the simple antiquarian, argued the late-nineteenth-century American historian Frederick Jackson Turner, whereas 'the historian strives to show the present to itself by revealing its origin from the past. The goal of the antiquarian is the dead past: the goal of the historian is the living present.'[6]

By the later twentieth century, however, the use of history to provide 'lessons' or even to illuminate Turner's 'living present' had generally fallen into disfavour, certainly in the academy. This was due at least in part to that century's grim display of what Karl Popper decried as 'the poverty of historicism'. Popper dedicated his book of that name to 'the countless men, women and children of all creeds or nations or races who fell victims to the fascist and communist belief in Inexorable Laws of Human Destiny'.[7] Too many historians, writers or politicians of the nineteenth and twentieth centuries, often half-understanding followers or imitators of Hegel, had cherry-picked the historical record to produce overarching schemas that purportedly explained human events and, crucially, allowed one to predict the future. Once the apparent truths of 'History' and its inevitable future struggles and triumphs had been revealed, then – like other revealed religions that explain humankind's past, present and future – they often served as licence to accomplish History's destiny somewhat faster; and to justify any 'necessary' quantity of suffering and death. Racism, like Marxist determinism, is a theory of history; and a belief in supposed 'laws' of history was often correlated with genocide and concentration camps. When one considers the barbarism which such historicism inspired and justified, it is tempting to consider history less as an intelligible story of progress, purpose or development, as the expounders of teleology have claimed, and perhaps closer to being, in the phrase of Alexander Herzen, 'the autobiography of a madman'.[8]

Such perversions of the historical method prompted an understandable wariness about self-advertised 'lessons of history'. It does not follow, however, that history, or the intellectual skills its study fosters, is irremediably dangerous or unhelpful when trying to understand the present, provided one assumes sufficient caution about the directness or simplicity of its possible insights.[9]

In a 1966 book review in this journal, Howard had expressed just such a healthy suspicion of glib 'lessons' of history, writing that 'if "history" teaches us anything, it is that men fall into quite as many errors in trying to learn from the past as they do trying to ignore it'.[10] Indeed, he later argued in his 1981 lecture that the first 'lesson' historians were 'entitled to teach is the austere one: not to generalise from false premises based on inadequate evidence'.[11]

This did not mean, though, that Howard considered the study of history irrelevant to understanding the present. In fact, 'to know the way in which our society came to be formed, to have some understanding of the conflicting forces that created it and are still at work within it', was an 'indispensable' part of the education of anyone in public life.[12] While history 'provides few answers', as he acknowledged in 1966, 'it may shape our attitudes, engendering a scepticism, a humility, and an appreciation of the role of the contingent and the unforeseen in human affairs of a kind not always developed by a more positivist approach'.[13] As I have written elsewhere, Howard's 'deep and broad historical learning brought with it a historical sensibility' that shaped his understanding of the present.[14] This sensibility might be described as

> the ability to see the present through the eyes of a historian; to be aware both of history's contingencies and its recurrent patterns; to be suspicious of immutable 'laws' of international relations; to be alive to the power of ideas in human events; and to locate contemporary developments within the *longue durée* for, as [Howard] put it, 'there is little point in considering where we should be going if we do not first decide where we are starting from'.[15]

Such a sensibility, which recognises history's complexities and prizes epistemological caution, stands in direct opposition to the teleological, simplistic and destructive historicism that Popper had condemned. It understands that history is neither a science nor a religion, and provides no direct lessons or universal schema. Indeed, as Howard argued, 'there is no such thing as "history". History is what historians write, and historians are part of the process they are writing about.'[16]

Howard's second 'lesson' had also sounded somewhat stern: 'the past is a foreign country; there is very little we can say about it until we have learned its language and understood its assumptions; and in deriving conclusions about the processes which occurred in it and applying them to our own day we must be very careful indeed'.[17] There was perhaps a way, though, in which this aspect of the historical method, applied properly, could go some way towards educating those charged with contemporary challenges, and provide far more useful insight than superficial 'lessons'.

Howard amusingly described the layperson's infuriation with historians, who refused to provide such direct lessons but instead marinated themselves in the past and repeatedly reopened old historical questions. In turn, most historians disdained such demands for direct insight because their 'time is cut out trying to discover as best [they] can, not only what "really happened" in the past, but, increasingly, what the past was really *like*; in recreating the intellectual and social structures which will enable [them] to "explain" events; trying, for example, to understand the social and intellectual framework which made the war of 1914 or the Revolution of 1789 *possible*'.[18] Howard argued that 'the most rewarding, as it is the most difficult, of the historian's tasks', is 'the *understanding* of the past, particularly of the beliefs and assumptions that held societies together and determined those activities on the level of high politics that are normally regarded as "history"'. This understanding required 'the quality of imagination'.[19]

Many thinkers have employed the term 'historical imagination', typically in somewhat differing ways.[20] Here, Howard used 'imagination' to mean 'a quality that is best used, not in creating alternative "scenarios" of the past, but in recreating the structure of beliefs that determined action and perhaps made some actions more likely than others'. This historical 'imagination' in turn entailed an understanding of its objects' historical consciousness. 'All societies have some view of the past; one that shapes and is shaped by their collective consciousness, that both reflects and reinforces the value-systems which guide their actions and judgement', explained Howard. 'Far more than poets can historians claim to be unacknowledged legislators of mankind; for all we believe about the present depends on what we believe about the past.' He warned that 'the value of history as a training of the judgement and of the imagination' depended not just on 'recreating our own past' but also 'the often very divergent structures of other societies'. He described post-1945 leaders as 'people often of masterful intelligence, trained usually in law or economics or perhaps in political science, who have led their governments into disastrous decisions and miscalculations because they have no awareness whatever of the historical background, the cultural universe of the foreign societies with which they have to deal'.[21]

Howard believed that studying history and cultivating 'imagination' (along with learning foreign languages) could teach us an empathy essential to navigating our contemporary world. He argued that historians should teach laypeople 'how to step outside their own cultural skins and enter the minds of others; the minds not only of their forefathers, enormously valuable though this is, but of those of our contemporaries who have inherited a different experience of the past'.[22]

Howard's historical sensibility eschewed the grandiose, all-encompassing narratives of the historicists that supposedly dictated humanity's path, and instead – along with many other attributes – entailed a more humane understanding of how humans' ideas and their own historical consciousness affected their beliefs, decisions and therefore their history. Insights for the present could not be derived directly from 'History', but perhaps indirectly from the methodology of historians.

## II

Of course, Howard was not the first historian to underscore the importance of understanding the mindsets and mental structures that underpin historical decisions. 'The course of national policy is based upon a series of assumptions, with which statesmen have lived since their earliest years and which they regard as so axiomatic as hardly to be worth stating', wrote the diplomatic historian A.J.P. Taylor in the 1930s. 'It is the duty of the historian to clarify these assumptions and to trace their influence upon the course of everyday policy.'[23]

One of the more famous expositions of this view was made by James Joll in his 1968 inaugural lecture as Stevenson Professor of International History at the London School of Economics and Political Science. In '1914: The Unspoken Assumptions', Joll referred to those 'beliefs, rules or objectives' that are rarely articulated within a documentary record because they 'go without saying', but knowledge of which is crucial to a full understanding of that record. He argued that such 'unspoken assumptions' are particularly powerful in shaping people's behaviours during a crisis. He suspected that politicians and bureaucrats, more than revolutionaries and students, tended to be affected more by 'the ideas of a generation earlier, as filtered through vulgarisers and popularisers'. He placed particular emphasis on the pernicious influence of social Darwinism on the thinking of political and military leaders leading up to the First World War, and of sub-Nietzschean ideas on that of revolutionary actors. While Joll acknowledged how difficult it was to connect a general intellectual atmosphere to specific political decisions, he concluded that 'it is only by understanding the minds of men that we shall understand the causes of anything'.[24]

'Much labour would have been saved', noted Howard rather drily in Joll's obituary some decades later, 'if the American political scientists who made so much work for themselves studying the "crisis management" of 1914 had read the 5,000 wise words of that lecture'.[25]

The interaction between general intellectual currents and specific events or decisions may remind us of many historical thinkers, including Alexis de Tocqueville, who, when explaining great events such as a revolution, described the blend of 'antecedent facts' and 'the nature of institutions' with 'the cast of minds and the nature of morals', along with a complex 'tangle of secondary causes'.[26] The historians Ernest May and Philip Zelikow studied the relationship, within the process of historical decision-making, between what they termed the historical actors' 'reality judgments' (what they thought was happening), 'action judgments' (what they thought could be done) and 'value judgments' (what they cared about), arguing that 'each of these kinds of judgments constantly informs and interacts with the others'.[27]

Mindsets and implicit assumptions are like many other largely intangible factors in human affairs, such as 'morale' in wartime: difficult to measure, but crucial to any meaningful understanding of why things occurred as they did. Indeed, an interest in a period's intellectual environment, its *Weltanschauung*, world view, mentality or *mentalité* (as the French Annales school of historians described it), is very common among historians, although not always directly articulated. The historian Keith Thomas, writing about his working methods, repeated the late G.M. Young's goal of 'reading until I can hear the people talking'. 'Because I am as interested in the attitudes and assumptions which are implicit in the evidence as in those which were explicitly articulated at the time', Thomas explained, 'I have got into the habit of reading against the grain.' Whatever the text itself is, 'I read it not so much for what the author meant to say as for what the text incidentally or unintentionally reveals'.[28] Perhaps rather ironically, Howard suggested in his inaugural lecture that self-aware historians 'know that our work, if it survives at all, will be read as evidence about our own *mentalité* and the thought processes of our own time rather than for anything we say about the times about which we write, however careful our scholarship and cautious our conclusions'.[29]

One must acknowledge, though, that while it is vital to account for the *mentalité* of a given time, it is unwise to take too totalising a view. Generalisations about *mentalités* must acknowledge that world views may differ significantly between social classes, genders, nations or other categories of humans existing at the same time. Anyone with siblings or children knows that not everyone raised in the same family at the same time shares the same outlook, and sometimes not even the same basic assumptions. Indeed, most individuals contain within themselves various cognitive dissonances or countervailing opinions. As Joll put it, 'people acted on a number of contra-dictory assumptions or half-formulated philosophies of life'.[30] And discerning purely 'unspoken' or unconscious assumptions is much harder than those assumptions which were in fact articulated, even if only rarely or indirectly.

All that being said, one can frequently feel stunned by the alien world views of our ancestors, especially given the irrefutable reality that these beliefs often determined their judgements and decisions. Without travel-ling too far back in time, we quickly reach a point at which most people believed profoundly in the reality of the afterlife; or considered slavery a natural institution; or felt it wise to beat one's wife and children suppos-edly for their own good; or thought it reasonable to burn others alive in the town square to save their souls.

One does not need to travel back centuries to feel oneself in a profoundly foreign place. Howard noted that the 'quality of historical imagination is needed as much in dealing with the recent as it is with the more remote past'.[31] Some examples may help illustrate this. Many in the late nineteenth century (and later) perceived international relations through the prism of semi-understood 'scientific' concepts, encompassing factors such as 'energy', racial willpower, or gendered national or racial 'characters'. It is not always clear to what extent these beliefs dictated behaviours. While it would be incorrect to label simply as 'social Darwinism' the declaration of the British prime minister and statesman Lord Salisbury in 1898 that the world's nations could be divided into categories of 'living' and 'dying', with the former inevitably preying upon and 'cutting up' the lands of the latter, one can judge that he subscribed to a fatalistic world view in which inter-national relations was largely dictated by the law of the jungle.[32] When one learns that Otto von Bismarck, that colossus of nineteenth-century history, a near-contemporary of Salisbury and the personification of hard-headed realpolitik, supposedly believed in the categories of (Northern European) 'male' and (Celtic or Slavic) 'female' races, it may be difficult to prove that such a belief had any determinative effect on his actions, but it may also be rash to declare too quickly, perhaps because it seems to jar with his more 'rational' views which may still appeal to contemporary 'realists', that it had no effect.[33] What is startling for me personally is to recall that by the time Salisbury was pronouncing about 'living' and 'dying' nations, in the same year that Bismarck died, one of my grandfathers was already alive. Only two generations separate a 40-year-old man today from the Victorian age.

It is easy enough to observe how our predecessors of a century or so ago may have conflated semi-understood simplifications of contemporary natural science with their models of human affairs. It is salutary, though, to recall more recent possible examples. Donald Trump's use of golf carts to transport him a few hundred metres – stemming from his curious belief that human energy is a finite resource like a depletable battery, and that exercise is a zero-sum activity which only accelerates that battery's expenditure – prompted much mirth when he was president.[34] It is less amusing when one realises that Trump's conceptions of energy, exercise and the human bodily economy mirrors his understanding of the global economy: a mercantilist view that a fixed amount of wealth in the world means that trade is a zero-sum activity.

## III

Howard argued that the historical 'imagination', honed by attempts to grasp the foreignness of our ancestors' minds and the minds of foreigners' ancestors, could help us to understand our chronological contemporaries in foreign lands. But if it is important to understand the assumptions, mental structures and historical consciousness of past periods or foreign cultures in order truly to understand them, then might it also be worthwhile to understand those same factors in our own culture?

While the *mentalités* and unspoken assumptions of our ancestors may require an element of historical 'imagination' for us to grasp, somewhat paradoxically the 'unspoken assumptions' of our *own* culture may be even harder for us to identify with real clarity, precisely because they are unspoken and, like we ourselves, are products of our own time and our own culture. We would need to leave our 'own cultural skins and enter the minds of others', in Howard's phrase – but then look back at 'ourselves' in our present time, as foreigners or our descendants might do. Yet as Howard noted, there is nothing like what Jacob Burckhardt called an 'Archimedean point outside events' from which historians can objectively observe their own time.[35]

Examining the present through the eyes of a historian, however imperfectly, entails understanding that we are living inside the historical process; that many values or institutions we take for granted and believe are universal or eternal are actually contingent, intersubjective human creations and likely to change; and that future historians a century hence are likely to be as puzzled by us as we are puzzled by our ancestors a century ago.[36]

Joll was correct to suggest examining educational systems as a way of discerning implicit social assumptions in a historical period.[37] I suspect that a culture or historical period's humour and advertising also provide useful clues, because they function through appealing to the preoccupations and assumptions that their audience takes for granted. This is why both often seem so strange and alienating to observers from outside the intended culture. Even humour and advertising from one's own culture in relatively recent memory can feel jarring, a reminder of how quickly shared assumptions may shift.

One can easily speculate about how future generations could be shocked at our moral practices: perhaps that we ate sentient beings because we enjoyed their taste; owned possessions we knew were likely to have been made in authoritarian prison camps or sweatshops; or did our best to ignore the implications of climate change. (It is also possible, of course, that our descendants may be struck more by the quaintness or naivety of our moral beliefs, as Europeans waging total war in 1945 may have felt about their ancestors' limited wars two centuries earlier.[38]) It may be somewhat harder, but still possible, to detect traces of more atavistic behaviours in beliefs mostly considered modern, such as politicians' desire to appease 'the market' through various policy offerings, as their ancestors did with offerings to the gods in the hope that they would bring good fortune; or the willingness of some firearms fundamentalists to accept a number of school massacres each year as the price of 'liberty', much as certain societies sacrificed children on the altar to ensure the Sun continued to rise.[39]

It may be very difficult for us, though, without sufficient chronological or sociological distance, to perceive clearly the unspoken assumptions of today, no matter how attuned our historical imagination may be. But attempting to do so may still be a worthwhile exercise, if done with suitable caution. Questioning our assumptions helps us to see which of these may or may not be shared not only with our ancestors or descendants, but also with our chronological contemporaries in foreign cultures.

Many policymakers in certain European capitals prided themselves on their supposed understanding of Vladimir Putin and his outlook. They believed that he might bluff for further concessions by amassing his military forces on Ukraine's border, but that a full invasion and attempted annexation of his neighbour was highly improbable: territorial conquest in Europe was an anachronism, and the costs to Moscow would outweigh any benefits. This judgement overlooked several crucial assumptions in the mind of Putin and his advisers, some more explicit than others, and most infused with Putin's distorted and resentful reading of history. These included the convictions that Russia's security depended on its freedom to invade neighbouring countries when it feared ideological contagion from liberal developments there, as it had done successfully in 1830, 1848, 1956 and 1968; that the 'special military operation' would be a brief affair like these historical predecessors (many Russian troops brought their parade uniforms to Ukraine in preparation for their triumphal march through Kyiv); and that most Ukrainians would not resist Russian invaders because, in essence, an authentic, separate Ukrainian state, a civic Ukrainian nationalism or a Ukrainian attachment to democracy did not really exist.[40] While many of Putin's beliefs about the world may jar with us as anachronistic, we must acknowledge that they are just as much 'of our time' as our own beliefs, and have very material consequences.

It is also helpful to consider how our own policymakers' unspoken assumptions and mental structures might function during a crisis.

Like Putin with Ukraine, many in the West believed that the invasion of Iraq would be a straightforward business. An exercise as simple as making one's unspoken assumptions 'spoken' could have been clarifying in Western capitals some 20 years ago, before the invasion of Iraq.[41] Sociologists, psychologists, anthropologists and constructivists might object that such an exercise, or more generally the examination of contemporary mental structures, would hardly be novel for their disciplines. And they might well be correct. History, as Howard acknowledged, can benefit greatly by drawing on the work of other disciplines. The historical discipline, though, works on the axis of time; and Howard maintained that, despite useful contributions from other disciplines, only 'the study of history' (combined with the study of modern languages) could teach one how 'to enter into the minds of others'.[42]

There are risks, of course, in an excessively idealist or constructivist understanding of human events, just as there are in an excessively materialist understanding of the world. As Peter Jackson has noted, however, one of the benefits historians enjoy is that they are not required to choose one camp or the other, but can draw from both.[43]

Unspoken assumptions in the individual, as in larger groups, can be a thorny topic: often difficult or impossible for the entity itself to identify, but often determinative of its actions. For those external to the individual, however, whose profession it is to psychologically observe and treat them, the effect of such tacit assumptions, internal narratives or 'unconscious phantasies' is often powerfully evident. Whole lives can be shaped, in large part, by what has been described as the 'unthought known'.[44] Consciously examining one's beliefs can be useful in many ways, for 'unconscious beliefs are treated as facts', argues the psychiatrist and psychoanalyst Ronald Britton. 'They can only be evaluated once it is realised that they are not facts but assumptions.'[45]

Translating matters of individual psychology to the societal level is dangerous intellectual territory and should never be done incautiously, but can perhaps be suggestive. We should consider the stories we construct about the world, in the hope not only that we do not unthinkingly allow these stories to determine our own individual lives, but also the lives of our societies or states. This is not least because our leaders are themselves individuals and 'in the end, military and diplomatic policymakers operate against a vision of the world at least in part of their own making', as the historian Jonathan Steinberg put it. 'The nightmare is always real to the dreamer.'[46]

## Acknowledgements

This article is derived from lectures I delivered at the Applied History teaching sessions at the Engelsberg Ironworks, hosted by the Ax:son Johnson Foundation in conjunction with the Center for Statecraft and Strategic Communication at the Stockholm School of Economics (SSE). I am grateful to Mattias Hessérus, Carl Ritter, Rikard Westerberg, Charlie Laderman, Francis J. Gavin, Andrew Ehrhardt, Henrik Borelius and many thoughtful SSE students for the stimulating discussions which have helped refine my thinking. I am also grateful to Graham Allison and Calder Walton for all I have learned from them about the topic of Applied History, and for much else.

## Notes

1    Michael Howard, *The Lessons of History* (New Haven, CT: Yale University Press, 1991), pp. 6–20.

2    Livy, trans. William Masfen Roberts, *The History of Rome*, vol. 1 (London: Dent, 1912), p. 2.

3    Maurizio Viroli (ed.), *The Quotable Machiavelli* (Princeton, NJ: Princeton University Press, 2017), p. 97.

4    Howard, *The Lessons of History*, pp. 6–7. There were obviously also those, such as Edmund Burke, who warned against drawing concrete lessons from history. See Philip Zelikow, 'The Nature of History's Lessons', in Hal Brands and Jeremi Suri (eds), *The Power of the Past: History and Statecraft* (Washington DC: Brookings Institution Press, 2015), pp. 281–2.

5    John S.C. Abbott, *Confidential Correspondence of the Emperor Napoleon and the Empress Josephine* (New York: Mason Brothers, 1856), p. 370. For a brief discussion of Hegel's view of Napoleon, see Ishaan Tharoor, 'We're Still Living in the Age of Napoleon', *Washington Post*, 7 May 2021, https://www.washingtonpost.com/world/2021/05/07/napoleon-legacy-france/.

6    Stephen Vaughn (ed.), *The Vital Past: Writings on the Uses of History* (Athens, GA: University of Georgia Press, 1985), p. 180.

7    Karl Popper, *The Poverty of Historicism* (London: Routledge & Paul, 1957).

8    Isaiah Berlin, *Russian Thinkers*, vol. 1 (London: Hogarth Press, 1978), p. 90.

9    There have been various efforts over recent decades to amend the academic over-correction against historicism – manifested in the rejection of any supposed applicability of historical insight to the present – notably by Ernest May and Richard Neustadt, and more recently by Graham Allison

and Niall Ferguson, who in 2016 co-launched the 'Applied History Project' at Harvard University. This more recent 'Applied History' movement is an intentionally broad church and has inspired or encouraged many similar projects or centres which have flourished at various universities in Europe and North America in recent years.

10 Michael Howard et al., 'Book Reviews', *Survival*, vol. 8, no. 10, October 1966, p. 334.

11 Howard, *The Lessons of History*, p. 13.

12 *Ibid.*, p. 9.

13 Howard et al., 'Book Reviews', p. 334.

14 'Editor's Introduction' in Benjamin Rhode (ed.), *A Historical Sensibility: Sir Michael Howard and The International Institute for Strategic Studies, 1958–2019* (Abingdon: Routledge for the IISS, 2020), p. 8. Many others have used the term 'historical sensibility', or variants of it: see, for example, Graham Allison and Niall Ferguson, 'The Applied History Manifesto', October 2016, https://www.belfercenter.org/publication/applied-history-manifesto; and especially Francis J. Gavin, 'Thinking Historically: A Guide for Policy', in Andreas Wenger, Ursula Jasper and Myriam Dunn Cavelty (eds), *The Politics and Science of Prevision: Governing and Probing the Future* (Abingdon: Routledge, 2020), pp. 73–87.

15 'Editor's Introduction' in Rhode (ed.), *A Historical Sensibility*, p. 8. The quotation is taken from Michael Howard, 'Deterrence, Consensus and Reassurance in the Defence of Europe', in IISS, 'Defence and Consensus: The Domestic Aspects of Western Security', Part III (Papers from the IISS 24th Annual Conference), *Adelphi Paper*, vol. 23, no. 184, 1983, p. 17.

16 Howard, *The Lessons of History*, p. 11.

17 *Ibid.*, p. 13

18 *Ibid.*, p. 12. Emphases in the original.

19 *Ibid.*, pp. 13–14. Emphasis in the original.

20 Perhaps the most famous example was by the philosopher R.G. Collingwood: *The Historical Imagination: An Inaugural Lecture Delivered Before the University of Oxford on 28 October 1935* (Oxford: Clarendon Press, 1935).

21 Howard, *The Lessons of History*, pp. 13–19.

22 *Ibid.*, p. 18. See also Philip Zelikow's remark that 'to revisit these strange other worlds in the past, breaking down how some puzzling choices actually happened, does require some imagination. Our senses now sharpened to the "changing, multicoloured, evanescent" beliefs that once held sway, we are that much better equipped for the amalgam we encounter every day.' Zelikow, 'The Nature of History's Lessons', p. 302.

23 A.J.P. Taylor, *The Italian Problem in European Diplomacy, 1847–1849* (Manchester: Manchester University Press, 1934), p. 1.

24 The lecture was published the year it was delivered: James Joll, *1914: The Unspoken Assumptions – An Inaugural Lecture Delivered 25 April 1968* (London: Weidenfeld & Nicolson, 1968). It also appears as a chapter in a more accessible volume: H.W. Koch (ed.), *The Origins of the First World War: Great Power Rivalry and German War Aims* (London: Macmillan, 1984), pp. 307–28.

25 Michael Howard, 'Obituary: Professor James Joll', *Independent*, 17 July 1994,

https://www.independent.co.uk/news/people/obituary-professor-james-joll-1414619.html.

26 See Zelikow, 'The Nature of History's Lessons', pp. 287–91.

27 *Ibid*.

28 Keith Thomas, 'Diary: Working Methods', *London Review of Books*, vol. 32, no. 11, 10 June 2010, https://www.lrb.co.uk/the-paper/v32/n11/keith-thomas/diary.

29 Howard, *The Lessons of History*, p. 11.

30 Joll, '1914: The Unspoken Assumptions', in Koch, *The Origins of the First World War*, p. 316.

31 Howard, *The Lessons of History*, p. 14.

32 See Benjamin Rhode, 'Living and Dying Nations and the Age of COVID-19', *Survival*, vol. 62, no. 5, October–November 2020, pp. 223–4.

33 See Lord Frederic Hamilton, *The Vanished Pomps of Yesterday: Being Some Random Reminiscences of a British Diplomat* (New York: George H. Doran Company, 1921), pp. 28-9; and Hajo Holborn, 'Bismarck's Realpolitik', *Journal of the History of Ideas*, vol. 21, no. 1, January–March 1960, p. 98.

34 See Chris Cillizza, 'Donald Trump Has a Very Strange Theory About Exercise', CNN, 15 May 2017, https://edition.cnn.com/2017/05/15/politics/donald-trump-exercise/index.html.

35 Howard, *The Lessons of History*, p. 11. Of course, historical study itself can help one to perceive what is distinctive about one's own time. In the words of the historian John Arnold, 'visiting the past is something like visiting a foreign country: they do some things the same and some things differently, but above all else they make us more aware of what we call "home"'. John Arnold, *History: A Very Short Introduction* (Oxford: Oxford University Press, 2000), p. 122.

36 Intersubjective reality is that created by shared human understandings or beliefs. The historian Yuval Harari, originally trained as a scholar of medieval warfare, has enjoyed immense popular success with his book *Sapiens* (London: Harvill Secker, 2014), which highlighted the (well-established) significance of intersubjective reality and the facts that history has not ended, and that the contemporary belief systems and institutions we take for granted were not predetermined and may be quite transient. Harari has admitted that 'the more banal [his conclusions] are, the more impressed people are … All these things about the fictional stories [and intersubjectivity], this was one of the most basic things I learned in my first year doing a bachelor's degree in history … It turned out that for lots of people, it was a big discovery: that you had these social constructs and intersubjective reality. I thought it was the most banal thing in the world.' David Marchese, 'Yuval Noah Harari Believes This Simple Story Can Save the Planet', *New York Times*, 7 November 2021, https://www.nytimes.com/interactive/2021/11/08/magazine/yuval-noah-harari-interview.html.

37 Joll, '1914: The Unspoken Assumptions', in Koch, *The Origins of the First World War*, p. 316.

38 I am grateful to my colleague John Raine for this observation.

39 See Harvey Cox, 'The Market as God: Living in the New Dispensation', *Atlantic*, March 1999; and Rachel Sharp,

'Rep Jamie Raskin Compares US to Ancient Civilisations that "Practiced Human Sacrifice" in Gun Violence Hearings', *Independent*, 8 June 2022, https://www.independent.co.uk/news/world/americas/us-politics/jamie-raskin-gun-violence-hearing-b2096863.html.

40 See Paul Berman, 'The Intellectual Catastrophe of Vladimir Putin', *Foreign Policy*, 13 March 2022, https://foreignpolicy.com/2022/03/13/putin-russia-war-ukraine-rhetoric-history/; and Timothy Snyder, 'Putin's Case for Invading Ukraine Rests on Phony Grievances and Ancient Myths', *Washington Post*, 28 January 2022, https://www.washingtonpost.com/outlook/2022/01/28/putin-russia-ukraine-myths/.

41 I am grateful to Francis J. Gavin for this insight. For a more empathetic view on what US policymakers in 2001–03 might have reasonably assumed, see Zelikow, 'The Nature of History's Lessons', pp. 289–90.

42 Howard, *The Lessons of History*, p. 18. Joll, on the other hand, suggested that 'the help [psychologists, sociologists or economists] can give us is limited'. Joll, '1914: The Unspoken Assumptions', in Koch, *The Origins of the First World War*, pp. 311–13.

43 Peter Jackson, *Beyond the Balance of Power: France and the Politics of National Security in the Era of the First World War* (Cambridge: Cambridge University Press, 2013), pp. 12, 521. See also the work of Lawrence Freedman, who has been described as a 'constructivist realist'. See 'Celebrating Professor Sir Lawrence Freedman', King's College London, https://www.kcl.ac.uk/sspp/politics/newsevents/news/freed-manceleb; Benedict Wilkinson and James Gow (eds), *The Art of Creating Power: Freedman on Strategy* (Oxford: Oxford University Press, 2017); and Lawrence Freedman, 'Confessions of a Premature Constructivist', *Review of International Studies*, vol. 32, no. 4, October 2006, pp. 689–702.

44 See Christopher Bollas, *The Shadow of the Object: Psychoanalysis of the Unthought Known* (London: Routledge, 2017). In 1914, Sigmund Freud referred to patients who had unconsciously suppressed and then recovered 'forgotten' memories as remarking that 'as a matter of fact I've always known it; only I've never thought of it'. Sigmund Freud, 'Remembering, Repeating and Working-through (Further Recommendations on the Technique of Psycho-analysis II)', in *The Standard Edition of the Complete Psychological Works of Sigmund Freud*, vol. 12 (London: Hogarth Press and the Institute of Psycho-Analysis, 1958), pp. 145–56.

45 Ronald Britton, *Between Mind and Brain: Models of the Mind and Models in the Mind* (Abingdon: Routledge, 2018), p. 1. See also Ronald Britton, *Belief and Imagination: Explorations in Psychoanalysis* (London: Routledge, 1998).

46 Jonathan Steinberg, 'The Copenhagen Complex', *Journal of Contemporary History*, vol. 1, no. 3, July 1966, p. 24.